Brian Fleming Research & Learning Library
Ministry of Education
Ministry of Training, Colleges & Universities
900 Bay St. 13th Floor, Mowat Block
Toronto, ON M7A 1L2

PROPERTY OF
DEPARTMENT OF EDUCATION
REGION 3 LIBRARY

EDUCATION FOR PEACE

Focus on Mankind

PROPERTY OF
DEPARTMENT OF EDUCATION
REGION 3 LIBRARY

EDUCATION FOR PEACE

Focus on Mankind

Prepared by the ASCD
1973 Yearbook Committee

GEORGE HENDERSON
Chairman and Editor

Association for Supervision and Curriculum Development
1201 Sixteenth St., N.W., Washington, D.C. 20036

Copyright © 1973 by the
Association for Supervision and Curriculum Development

All rights reserved. No part of this publication may be reproduced or transmitted in any form or by any means, electronic or mechanical, including photocopy, recording, or any information storage and retrieval system, without permission in writing from the publisher.

Price: $7.50

Stock Number: 17946

The materials printed herein are the expressions of the writers and not necessarily a statement of policy of the Association.

Library of Congress Catalog Card Number: 72-90597

WE DEDICATE this Yearbook with deep respect to and in loving memory of our late colleague, Louis S. Levine, Professor of Psychology at San Francisco State College. Lou Levine was a chief initiator of this work, and it is therefore our hope that these efforts, which he did not live to see completed, somehow manifest what he saw as the purpose of this book:

> Little time lies ahead if we are to turn man toward man. And as painfully small as our efforts are, all who are concerned must pit their efforts against the forces that would destroy us. Each of us in our own way must avoid the paths that in the past have offered the seductive semblance of safety. Now the directions and the programs must be created to meet the challenge, for there is no alternative. We are, as Camus has said, "condemned to live together," or, as we all know, to die together.[1]

We, the authors and editors, choose to live together. These articles represent both our "painfully small efforts" in that direction and a tribute to Louis Levine, whose efforts and guidance we sorely miss.

[1] From a paper presented by Professor Levine at a meeting of the American Orthopsychiatric Association, March 22, 1968.

Acknowledgments

FINAL editing of the manuscript and production of this Yearbook were the responsibility of Robert R. Leeper, Associate Secretary and Editor, ASCD Publications. Technical production was handled by Nancy Olson and Teola T. Jones, with Mary Albert O'Neill as production manager. Cover and design of this volume are the work of Bob McMeans Graphics.

Contents

Preface	xi
1 Prologue	1
George Henderson	
2 Working for Peace: Implications for Education	9
Thornton B. Monez	
3 Antecedents of Violence	41
Aubrey Haan	
4 Let's Listen to Our Children and Youth	61
Part One: The Study	63
Juliette P. Burstermann	
Part Two: Some Implications	81
Gertrude Noar	
5 The Heart of the Matter	89
Theresa L. Held	
6 International and Cross-Cultural Experiences	101
James M. Becker	
7 Transformations into Peace and Survival: Programs for the 1970's	125
Betty Reardon	

8 Children and the Threat of Nuclear War   153
Sibylle K. Escalona

9 Peace: Today and Tomorrow   173
George Henderson

Appendices

    A. Data on the Human Crisis:
Teacher's Guide   **199**

        William A. Nesbitt

    B. Selected Bibliography on International
Education   **205**

    C. Additional Resources   **219**

    D. Consortium on Peace Research,
Education, and Development (COPRED)   **221**

Notes About the Authors   **223**

ASCD 1973 Yearbook Committee Members   **227**

ASCD Board of Directors   **229**

    Executive Council, 1972-73   **229**

    Board Members Elected at Large   **230**

    Unit Representatives to the Board   **230**

ASCD Review Council   **235**

ASCD Headquarters Staff   **237**

Preface

THIS 1973 Yearbook is the result of a dream. That dream was communicated to the Yearbook Committee in the following terms:

> We dream of a time when all the world will be at peace and when the needs of mankind will be met so that harmful deprivation will be unknown. In such an era the individual will be free to seek, both at home and abroad, that way of life that seems to offer enhancement both for him and for his fellow human beings.[1]

This noble dream, a vision of men and women who themselves have never known prolonged periods of national or international peace, centered on the theme "Education for Peace: Focus on Mankind." Ironically, the dream was passed on to a committee composed of men and women who were equally unfamiliar with peace.

From 1969 until the final editing of this volume, the 1973 Yearbook Committee was challenged—even taunted—by the grotesque nightmares of reality. Daily we read about and witnessed man's inhumanity to his fellow human beings. We were appalled by the cold statistical terms indicating millions of lives wasted in wars, disease, and neglect.

How, we asked each other, could we place the atrocities of Biafra, Bangladesh, Southeast Asia, and Northern Ireland within a framework of rationality? And how could we make our readers sensitively aware of the fact that most human beings live in a world where death and disease are commonplace, education and gainful employment are almost nonexistent, and squalor and stagnation are their environments?

[1] From the original charge to the Yearbook Committee.

Several times we came close to quitting. It seemed futile to dream of peace. Upon closer analysis we realized that life is futile if we do not dream. The future, we concluded, must not follow the precedents of violence set by the past and the present.

Thus from the depths of our despair came a renewed commitment to compile a yearbook that would inform, prod, and—we hope—encourage educators, parents, and others who read it. We want to inform our readers about the issues of war and peace, prod them to teach children about peace, and encourage all people to live peaceful lives.

Peace, we concluded, should be actively pursued instead of passively read about. In keeping with this concept, we have put together a brief statement about war and peace. Rather than presenting a large number of polemical minichapters, we decided to focus on literary references and statistical data that can form a foundation for individuals who are trying to improve their effectiveness as educators for peace. Finally, we want the 1973 Yearbook to be visually different to emphasize the newness and, we hope, refreshing format that world peace can have—if we dare try it.

Like the words in a familiar saying, the 1973 Yearbook is "something old, something new, something borrowed. . . ." While written by a few, this Yearbook represents the ideas and contributions of many people. We are especially grateful to Thomas Anderson, Rose Arnold, Sylvia Betts, Catherine Bruch, Carl Cherkis, Virginia Macagnoni, Mary Rogers, and David Philips for assisting us in securing our student questionnaire on war and peace. We are also indebted to the authors and publishers of the poems and articles reprinted in whole or in part in this Yearbook.

Betty Reardon summed up our feelings in two terse sentences: "God, we sure have enough data. When are we going to get some action?"

Norman, Oklahoma GEORGE HENDERSON
June 15, 1972 *Chairman and Editor*
  ASCD 1973 Yearbook Committee

Prologue
George Henderson

1

Words of war...

Enemy

We don't want their kind here.

Barbarians

We've got to stop
them before they
take over
another country.

KILL

Only the strong shall survive.

Words of peace...

Friend

Welcome to our...
neighborhood
community
school
country
world.

Brothers and sisters

Armed force shall not be used to promote the common interest.

Love

"...with liberty and justice for all."

From: *The People, Yes**
Carl Sandburg

(From Section 107)

    The people will live on.
The learning and blundering people will live on.
    They will be tricked and sold and again sold
And go back to the nourishing earth for rootholds,
    The people so peculiar in renewal and comeback,
    You can't laugh off their capacity to take it.
The mammoth rests between his cyclonic dramas....

This old anvil laughs at many broken hammers.
    There are men who can't be bought.
    The fireborn are at home in fire.
    The stars make no noise.
    You can't hinder the wind from blowing.
    Time is a great teacher.
    Who can live without hope?

In the darkness with a great bundle of grief the people march.
In the night, and overhead a shovel of stars for keeps, the people march:
                      "*Where to? what next?*"

---

* From: Carl Sandburg. *The People, Yes.* New York: Harcourt Brace Jovanovich, Inc., 1936. © 1936 by Harcourt Brace Jovanovich, Inc.; renewed, 1964, by Carl Sandburg. Reprinted by permission of the publishers.

Annual Amounts of International War, 1816–1965 [†]

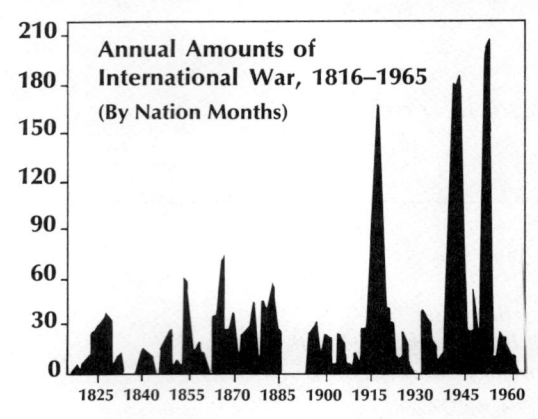

FIGURE 1. *Source:* J. David Singer and Melvin Small, Mental Health Research Institute, The University of Michigan; graph and data from the *New York Times,* May 6, 1971; p. 45. *Note:* A nation month is one month spent at war by one nation. War is defined as including both conflicts between states (interstate) and those between states and colonial or underdeveloped areas and involving at least 1,000 battle deaths.

During the 150-year period, there were 93 wars, of which 50 were interstate.

Wars were in progress during 126 of the 150 years.

A war between states began every 3 years on the average. There were 6.2 wars in the average decade.

Between 1816 and 1965, 144 nations spent 4,500 nation-months at war. Twenty-nine million battle deaths were reported. (If civilian deaths from war were included, the figure would be many times that.)

Periods of intensive warfare tended to occur every 20 years.

Europe has had more wars than any other area—68 as compared with 22 in the Middle East, the second most warlike area.

Countries fighting the most wars are England and France (18 wars each), Turkey (16), Russia (15), Italy (11), and Spain (9).

The win-loss record for some of the major powers in interstate wars is shown below.

	Won	Lost
Great Britain	6	0
United States	4	0
Russia	8	2
France	9	2
Japan	5	2
Germany (Prussia)	4	2
China	2	4

[†] William A. Nesbitt. *Data on the Human Crisis: A Handbook for Inquiry.* New York: Center for International Programs and Comparative Studies of the New York State Education Department, 1972. p .1. Reprinted by permission.

Working for Peace: Implications for Education
Thornton B. Monez

2

WITH increasing seriousness, thoughtful inhabitants of our contemporary world are asking ultimate questions: Can man as a species survive on this planet? How does it happen that an age capable of producing unprecedented advances in scientific and technical knowledge, offering a prospect of life-sustaining and life-enhancing resources for all, produces instead a quite different outlook? Why is there a widening gap between the promise of human fulfillment and the reality of human suffering arising from violence, destruction, and continuing war throughout the modern world?

Americans under the age of 35 cannot remember a time when war or threat of war and its offspring manifestations of violence have not been a proximal and pervasive force, daily conditioning their lives, both private and public. Indeed, it is as if the world in which we live is held together by a series of continuing threats, each threat carrying within its core some expression of human violence. The posture of our contemporary world toward itself is revealed in a familiar litany: the threat of nuclear warfare and continuing international conflict, acts of aggression and threats of violence in the streets of our cities, and assorted insults and threats to the natural environment of planet earth. Although diverse expressions of violence can be variously characterized as social, economic, political, or military, none of these can be examined rationally apart from the others. The varied manifestations of violence are related, and it is in their relationship that they combine to reduce the possibilities for enhancement and celebration of life and to deprive each of us of part of our humanity.

Human violence is no new phenomenon; the alarming aspect today is its rapid escalation. Students of history may argue that violence in some form has accompanied man on his long journey from prehistoric origin and that there have been few, if any, societies that have not engaged in at least limited warfare during the course of their known history. Calculations on a war-violence index, based upon such factors as size of population, fighting force, numbers of wars, and casualties involved, reveal escalation, showing that even before World War II violence in warfare was 25 times greater in this century than in the last—and more than 150 times greater than in the 12th century.[1] It has been estimated that in the 125-year period from 1820 to 1945 there were at least 59 million deaths stemming from human violence, an average of 1,300 a day, while countless millions more persons were injured and maimed at the hands of their fellow human beings.[2]

In the wars of this century, civilians have made up an increasing proportion of the total casualties. The percentage of civilians killed has grown from about 13 percent of the total casualties in World War I to 70 percent in World War II, 84 percent in the Korean War, to a possible 90 percent in the Vietnam War. The reasons for this rise in civilian casualties are not difficult to understand. As warfare has become more mechanized, so have characteristic attitudes toward killing. New strategies of warmaking have replaced earlier controls based upon established codes of "honor" in wartime. Guerrilla warfare and distance killing from the air, particularly in the absence of an opposing air force, have changed the scenarios of war. Once men and armies facing one another on battlefields could sense the nearness of death on both sides, and there was little room for indifference or casualness in the act of killing. The confrontation of soldier to soldier fostered a sense of the essential equality of man.

But the machines of modern warfare have made possible killing from a distance, so that massive, indiscriminate bombing campaigns can be carried out with no one knowing precisely on whom the bombs are falling or with what degree of violence. We have become accustomed to think of the arithmetic of killing in terms of low-keyed phrases like "protective-reaction strike," "air interdiction," and other euphemisms for mass casualties which help us avoid coming to terms with the reality and the image of the parent and child who perish as bombs are dropped from the sky. And

---

[1] Pitirim Sorokin. *Social and Cultural Dynamics.* Totowa, New Jersey: Bedminster Press, 1941; reprinted, 1962.

[2] L. Richardson. *Statistics of Deadly Quarrels.* Pittsburgh: Boxwood Press, 1960.

even when the nature of the ultimate devastation is ascertained, an account of the event is made in the dialect of contradiction best exemplified by the unnamed American major who said of the village of Bentre: "It became necessary to destroy the town to save it."

When we look at war for what it is and what it has done as it has both conditioned and intervened in the process of man's making of himself over long periods of time, we see that war also carries many side effects which extend well beyond the arithmetic of battles won or lost or the body count of those killed or wounded. From the children's toy market to television programming, a daily impact is created, and by-products of the war system thus generate life-destroying ways of thinking and behaving which can be absorbed subtly and unconsciously into the pores of all who are touched by it. In this way the waging of war becomes a casual and even acceptable means of solving conflict. Such impairments work against man's self-realization wherever and whenever he lives. Harold Taylor states it well when he views the war system to be a well-constituted system of education:

Considered as a system for teaching the debasement of human values, war is the most powerful of all educational institutions. Its curriculum lies in the art and science of deceiving, killing, and destroying. Its most successful students learn to ruin whatever they touch. Its highest honors go to those who have produced the most dead most advantageously.

Although its most effective educational work is done in the course of massacres, bombings, and similar demonstrations, war also has its own colleges and military academies across the world where the theory and practice of rational and strategic killing can be studied and taught. During 1970 in the United States alone, nearly 16,000 foreign officers and enlisted men from forty-four countries were trained for war, some from countries that intended to fight one another, some from countries that use their armies for repressing social change and frustrating democracy. It is as if the Borgia family ran a school for poisoning with an open admissions policy.[3]

It is obvious that a warfare curriculum for human beings has been developed and refined over the entire course of man's history. Its teachings have been part of man's education in almost all societies in each succeeding generation. The subject matter of this curriculum has now reached the point where it has its own vocabulary, its own patterns of thinking, its own means of perpetuating itself as a system comprising a formidable repertoire of knowledge in the science of killing. It is unlikely that this knowledge repertoire could be suppressed on an unbroken front

---

[3] Harold Taylor. "A Curriculum for Peace." *Saturday Review* 54 (36): 22; September 4, 1971.

over the world even if a suitable replacement for the function it serves could be introduced to all human groups. The knowledge of warfare, from stone ax to nuclear warhead, will still remain available even in a world totally at peace.

It is easy to be pessimistic about the possibilities for world peace in the last quarter of the 20th century. The specter of violence, conflict, continued warfare, and ignorance seems everywhere to loom. The complex interplay of forces which nourish this specter exhibits few signs of retreat in the present decade. The question to be raised is: Can the American educational system put its hand to the task of helping young people improve their understanding and ability to deal with those forces which constitute barriers to peace in our modern world?

If we are serious about what we are doing in education, it is difficult to understand why we cannot take a hard-nosed and reasoned approach to the problem of helping students raise to a conscious level the intellectual and behavioral skills required to understand and deal with the phenomena of violence. It is obvious, of course, that reasoned approaches might very well call into question prevailing institutional thinking and teaching concerning American foreign policy, or even criticism of the nation-state system itself. But if the power of intellectual analysis is to prevail as a central force in education, then this strength must be recognized as it is reflected in proposals and prescriptions for change in both policy and practices in the organizational and institutional life of our contemporary world.

If there is, as Harold Taylor observes, an international war system with its war colleges, he also asks: "Where is the peace system and its colleges? Where do politicians, scholars, diplomats, and citizens go to learn how to prevent wars and stop them once they have started?" [4]

Although the obvious answer is that we have few if any such places, this does not mean that we are not without visible proposals and programs arising out of a growing number of worldwide activities having to do with educational strategies for peacemaking and peacebuilding. Nor does it mean that there has been futility in the work of those teachers who have recognized the need and have tried to do something about it in their classrooms.

One can look at the future in terms of our present condition and be shaken by what it asks for survival. But ultimately the task of education is to help individuals learn what it takes to shape a society which is sustain-

[4] *Ibid.*

able, which creates the fullest possible condition for human growth. The task is now urgent, and when it is seen in this light, teachers and learners have unprecedented opportunities. One way to seize the opportunity is to deal directly, through education, with the social, political, and moral problems which the reality of change has produced throughout the world. This means that schools can and should become the centers for inquiry into social and political structures and processes, bringing to bear the power of moral and social intelligence so that clearer understanding and improved management of institutions, social change, and policy formation can be assured within the world society.

It is important to recognize that any solution to the problem of how schools as social institutions can respond effectively to the problems of society (and thus survive) will ultimately depend upon the students themselves. Design for education has entered a new era, and the meanings of an educational experience are now tested against the realities which students perceive as they engage in the process of making sense of the divisive environments surrounding their lives. The call for relevant social content and sense of purpose in education is coming from the learner himself, and the call is by no means limited to those who are moving through the upper years of our academic divisions, as the subsequent pages of this Yearbook will show.

TWO DIMENSIONS OF VIOLENCE

Violence has more than one dimension. It is expressed not only in terms of clashes among armed men on battlefields, the bombings of towns and villages, or the assassin's bullet, but also through circumstances which limit life and health through disease, nutritional deficiency, and other manifestations of exploitation in living and working conditions. Johann Galtung makes a clear distinction between two kinds of violence: direct and structural.[5] Structural violence occurs when the wealth of affluent societies and nations is based on essential resources and labor drawn from those who, as a consequence, are required to live diminished lives in conditions of poverty and deprivation. Superior instruments of warfare held by the developed nations are used to sustain a basic structure of economic and political inequality.

[5] Johann Galtung. "World Order Models Project: A Transnational Perspective." Paper prepared for the symposium on "Value and Knowledge Requirements for Peace," 138th annual meeting, American Association for the Advancement of Science, Philadelphia, December 1971.

Direct violence is easily recognized because it is volatile, overt, and dramatic, as portrayed in our history books and on our television screens. Structural violence, in contrast, is slower and less readily visible as an agent of destruction. It is linked more subtly to the social structure because it is built into the system which ties men and nations to one another. This phenomenon, however, is no less damaging to life. Structural violence expressed in the form of lead-paint poisoning in a slum neighborhood or drastically lowered levels of life expectancy in Latin America is no less violent or life-negating than that which is more directly expressed with napalm or bullets in warfare.

Violence of the structural kind is based on exploitation and is not, of course, limited to the community of nations. It can be seen in families, local communities, organizations, and other social institutions. It is a function of a division of labor whereby one person or group benefits much more than, and frequently at the expense of, others in the struggle to get what is best to have. What is best to have is not always perceived in terms of monetary or economic gain, although these are fundamental goals. Sometimes it involves social justice or a need to escape boredom or to realize a potential for growth and further development through challenging work and personality-expanding activity.

We live in a stratified world society in which the rewards for human labor are not distributed equally in terms of money, power, or social justice. Such stratification condemns by far the larger part of the world's total population to live impoverished and shortened lives, with most of the prospects for human fulfillment monopolized by the few. The alienation between the few who can count on challenging, rewarding pursuits and the many who can count on despair, personality-constricting labor, and early death is exacerbated as those who are deprived recognize increasingly that their acute condition is a structural characteristic of the system and could be mitigated if the modern tools and technologies held by those in power were put to life-sustaining rather than life-destroying uses.

Current worldwide economic and political structures define and prescribe the roles of nations and states in the world community. The characteristic pattern developed and refined during the 19th century is a familiar one. First, there is a center nation, which seeks to control smaller nations through military, economic, and political force based upon technological superiority. The center nation, then, possessing the machinery, requires the nations along its economic and political periphery to deliver the raw materials which it can then process and market. As long as the smaller nations are unable to form strong alliances with one another, the network can be held together by a vertical division of labor in which the elite of the smaller nations join with the elite of the center nation and are, indeed, trained by the latter, not only in the uses of technology but also in the skills of maneuvering their own governments and people into a position of subordination to the country that has trained them.[6]

Thus the world network of nation-states cannot be viewed solely in terms of horizontal or territorial perspectives deriving their principal characteristics from geographic and political boundary lines. A more penetrating approach to understanding the complex nature of the war system is to be found in a vertical perspective which ties the elite of one nation with that of another, along with a variety of interacting organizations and institutions transcending national boundaries and forming a network of mutually rewarding enterprise.

Thus smaller nation-states have been prevented by a vertical world structure, based upon transnational alliances, from placing their own national interests in world affairs and having a voice in determining their own destinies. Until very recently the uneducated, the poor, and the deprived have been unable to challenge these forces of imperialism and to demand an opportunity to place their own identities in the prevailing world economic and political structure. As long as they have been unable to raise to a conscious level the fact of their exploitation, only structural violence prevailed.

But the levels of consciousness are now being raised, and the third world is beginning to constitute a force of its own, demanding that political and economic power be shared with all whose lives are affected and that outmoded patterns of imperialism be abandoned. The challenge is frequently accompanied by direct violence, which then produces a response from the established structure in the form of counterviolence, also direct. In such a way structural violence ultimately produces direct violence. Problems of poverty, famine, racial conflict, and environmental abuse, along with economic, military, and political imperialism, are structural problems transcending national boundaries and, as such, provide the fuel for outbreaks of direct violence, which in turn call forth a counterresponse expressed in further direct violence.

Education for peace is concerned with both the direct and the structural dimensions of violence. One dimension cannot be treated apart from the other without risking a biased perspective. When viewed from a posi-

[6] *Ibid.*

tion of affluence and privilege, one is tempted to look at direct violence, deplore its consequences, and see it mainly as a threat to the maintenance of prevailing economic and political power patterns favoring the status quo. Viewed from the perspective of those living in conditions of unalleviated poverty, however, direct violence offers a prospect of emancipation from exploitation and the consequences of structural violence which appear to be built into the economic and political system. From such a perspective, direct violence and warfare are seen as useful tools for bringing about change. Therefore it is futile to speak of the cultivation of "inner peace" in individuals as a requisite for world peace in the presence of structural violence. Direct, personal violence and structural violence are two sides of one coin. Authentic peace in our world depends upon an absence of both.

THE NATURE OF PEACE EDUCATION

Peace education centers on the phenomenon of violence with a view toward understanding how it functions, what its causes and consequences are, and how such knowledge can be translated into enlightened attitudes and behavior which might help to control or eliminate anything that works against man's self-realization, wherever he lives. Its basic purpose is to help students design strategies of action which can contribute to the shaping of a world order characterized by social justice and absence of exploitation. The subject matter of peace education includes a wide range of inter-related issues and subjects like social justice, social change, ecological balance, and economic welfare, all viewed from global perspectives. It includes also the study of conflict management and of processes of organizations and institutions which cut across national boundaries to affect foreign policy; it includes a study of the effect of science and technology on worldwide social and political development. But peace education is not merely knowledge-oriented in terms of these key subjects; it is also concerned with clarification of value perspectives within these fields, particularly as these relate to global, transnational, and time-dimension variables. Peace education obviously has a knowledge orientation, but it has a value perspective and an action orientation as well.

Peace education is anchored in a relatively new field of study: peace research. Stated simply, peace research is a search for effective ways to study the conditions of peace and the causes of war. It is planted firmly in the belief that reason and scientific method can produce important clues for improved conflict resolution. Although it employs an objective methodology, it is not value-neutral, nor can it be as it seeks to find controllable links between direct and structural violence and lowered realizations of human potential among the inhabitants of the world.

Peace researchers assume that a stable world peace is a problem of social systems and not a problem of armaments and tactical warfare. They are motivated by a need to search for new methods for inquiring into complex and rapidly changing parameters of social systems as these create conditions for conflict, violence, and war. Peace researchers recognize the inconstancy of political and social systems; they are aware that world peace will remain elusive until reliable procedures can be found for identifying and altering the complex, interconnecting forces which combine to keep violence and the war machine functional.

Peace education and peace research involve a comprehensive and systematic study of relationships between man and total environment. There is a need to bridge the growing gap between the essential unity of what we know to be fact and the fragmentation of authority and power among nations and states which prevents us from designing strategies for action based upon our knowledge. Modern technical advances have long since spilled over almost all conventional political boundaries. Environmental pollution, radioactive fallout, transnational and multinational corporate enterprise, and satellite broadcasting are now operational on a global scale. We can no longer deal with these matters as if they were the exclusive and normal functioning of discrete territorial states. However, as the notion of national sovereign prerogative continues to prevail, these competitive patterns and fragmentations of responsibility frustrate efforts aimed toward finding and establishing programs for peace. As a consequence, huge amounts of resources are assigned to national defense, with structural violence generating direct violence and both prevailing as a way of life, spawning persistent forms of waste, conflict, and distrust.

THE SCHOOLS AND THE ESTABLISHED ORDER

Since 1945 the first priority on any agenda in education should have included, in addition to an examination of the balances and consequences of nuclear threat among the power-elite nations, an intense and well-supported search for those values and ways of thinking which might, through education, help us to eliminate both conventional warfare and the threat of nuclear war as a political tool. Unhappily, this did not occur.

Only recently have students made a clear call for education which would deal forthrightly and directly with the major social and ethical problems of our time. Student concerns, expressed in a variety of ways, have served to force many schools into unaccustomed paths of thinking about their purposes and programs. In the process many sharply conflicting points of view can usually be found. They range from those determiners of educational policy who tend to resist all but the most inconsequential proposals for change to those who readily advocate radical and sweeping reforms, with some even insisting that schools as social institutions be dismantled. Somewhere in between are those who view both schools and society as a mixture of change and stability, with timely but carefully planned change providing a natural and necessary way for a society to achieve the stability required for making essential change possible.

If we examine the characteristic response of the schools over the past two decades, we find that in the main they have followed a course laid down by policy makers in certain aspects of government, the military, and industry. It becomes difficult not to conclude that through this period education was viewed by some as a major instrument of national policy which included support of the war system. Although always avowing "academic objectivity" on controversial issues, historically the schools have tended to endorse the prevailing economic, political, and military policies of the established order. With the advent of the curriculum reform movement, however, they moved closer to forming a real partnership. Without asking too many questions concerning ultimate goals, the schools tended to accept proposals for widespread reform which were heavily subsidized by powerful groups and offered in the interest of national defense.

This is not to say that significant gains were not made. The nature and organization of content in the subject fields of science, mathematics, and modern languages during this period were given an intensive scrutiny, and the number of technically trained personnel in these fields was impressively increased. But if the possible consequences of the tasks the schools were asked to carry out had been examined with equal intensity, it might have been noted that at least one basic aim of the total effort was to buttress an established order intent upon preserving traditional patterns of nationalism in a world undergoing convulsive social change. The war machine created during World War II advanced its weapons system and refined its schemes for dominating the course of nationalism throughout the world. The power of the Pentagon was extended over a period of three decades, successfully resisting attempts from the outside community either to inspect or to control it.

Speaking of the coalition of scientific and military agencies which have fortified themselves with inordinate power within an "inner citadel —the Pentagon," Lewis Mumford has written:

> Thus the area of this self-enclosed citadel has widened steadily, while the walls around it have grown thicker and more impenetrable. By the simple expedient of creating new emergencies, fomenting new fears, singling out new enemies, or magnifying by free use of fantasy the evil intentions of "the enemy," the megamachines of the United States and Soviet Russia, instead of being dismantled as a regrettable temporary wartime necessity, were elevated into permanent institutions in what has now become a permanent war: the so-called Cold War. As it has turned out, this form of war, with its ever-expanding demands for scientific ingenuity and technological innovations, is by far the most effective device invented for keeping this over-productive technology in full operation.[7]

But beyond this, the reform effort, braced by generous financial inducement and aimed primarily at increasing technical competence in the sciences, had the further effect of giving excessive authority to the processes of mechanization, objectivity, and measurement, which eventually became reflected not only in the total school environment but throughout almost every aspect of formal education. There was little or no comparable effort to include or recognize in the reform movement humanizing experiences that might resist the application of depersonalized methodologies. The arts and humanities, for example, tended to be viewed as peripheral in the programs of many schools.

In the meantime, the social turbulence of the 1960's caught the schools off balance. The schools were largely unprepared to meet the challenges posed by rising expectations of economically oppressed populations throughout the world, by nonwhite minorities at home, and by student unrest related to these problems and the moral issue of the Vietnam War.

Educators tended to be caught up in a reform effort dealing mostly with the mechanics of education: structure of the disciplines, ability grouping, advanced placement, etc. In this effort many American policy makers who controlled various grants and subsidized programs in education failed to take into account overriding questions posed by the tensions produced between our national defense effort and the problems of the

---

[7] Lewis Mumford. *The Myth of the Machine: The Pentagon of Power.* New York: Harcourt Brace Jovanovich, Inc., 1970. p. 266.

third world. It can be said that little thought was given to what was learned and for what purpose, at least in terms of world peace.

The students themselves began to challenge the meaning of their education as they tried to put the facts together and began to ask basic questions about national and educational priorities. Beginning in 1967, it was the students who refused to accept passively a continuing war in Vietnam, the purpose of which they had difficulty understanding. They could no longer suppress their questions about the moral posture of a society that was spending 70 percent of its tax dollars on wars and their aftermath, along with the preparation for future wars. (A committee report to Congress estimated that the cost of the Vietnam War, if it had ended in 1970, would have been about $350 billion.) Students began to connect these and other facts with their growing knowledge of conditions in the third world and the deprivation of at least two-thirds of the world's total population, living in conditions of poverty and oppression. Largely as a consequence of student effort, school programs have just now begun to recognize the nature of the sweeping changes taking place on a worldwide basis which call for emphasis in any educational program that can be called meaningful.

One wonders whether the configuration and expression of these problems could have been altered if education since the 1950's had directed its reform effort toward full understanding of man and society based upon an integration of the total spectrum of human experience as embodied in the arts and humanities, as well as in the sciences. Our school programs have yet to find ways to integrate science or the humanities with life, to allow a commensurate regard for the many expressions of human imagination, subjective responses, and creative undertakings. There is now a need to get to the nerve center of the man-in-society issue in education, and to make the necessary revisions in our total conception of what students need for full understanding and how best the schools can be organized to meet this need and the needs of the wider community around them.

Peace education involves a comprehensive and systematic study of relationships between man and his total environment. Recent interpretations of interdependent phenomena seen from an ecological viewpoint have developed as a way of approaching scientific and social problems which are regarded as legitimate concerns in many disciplines. There is a need for the development of an "ecology" for peace education which takes into account all the issues and studies involved in building an adequate conception of a peaceful world order, as opposed to the war system. Such an approach would involve the humanities, as well as the physical and social sciences. It would examine war-peace ideologies as they have been glorified and represented in the myths and histories of every nation; it would examine also the literature, art, dance forms, and music of diverse cultures in an attempt to understand the cultural bases for the celebration of war and counter yearnings for peace among social, political, and national groups.

Issues related to war and peace can be identified and debated across the entire spectrum of the academic disciplines. Each discipline has its own important perspective, its own way of generating and dealing with knowledge related to peace. There is a need for synthesis, however; without some framework for integrating idea and attitude development, the many-faceted aspects of peace education remain dispersed and fragmented within separate disciplines. Some means must be found to bring together perspectives native to the various subject fields, enabling each student ultimately to build his own conceptual framework for understanding and dealing with the phenomena of violence and the search for peace.

BIOLOGICAL PERSPECTIVES FOR PEACE

We are told by some investigators that there is a biological basis for human warfare and that violence-proneness is but an expression of man's genetic equipment. Others have asserted that violence and warmaking are social inventions and are products of frustrations arising from environmental stress. Still others assert that violence is a learned behavior, a result of cultural and social conditions. For example, we are aware of the extensive amount of conditioning it takes to train a soldier to kill in ground combat. We are also aware of the effort required to prepare a nation psychologically for war.[8]

While it may be true that a disposition to violence is facilitated by certain biological characteristics and that various kinds of environmental stress may reinforce a learned response, none of these speculations—taken alone or together—is sufficient to account for so widespread and diversified a phenomenon. Investigations in the biological and behavioral sciences bring us to the realization that there are no simple explanations of causes and no simple solutions to the problems of human violence.

---

[8] René Dubos. "The Despairing Optimist." *American Scholar* 40 (4): 565–72; Autumn 1971. Copyright © 1971 by the United Chapters of Phi Beta Kappa. By permission of the publisher.

Peter Corning has recognized the need for a more comprehensive theoretical umbrella in the following terms:

> In the first place, aggression is not a unitary phenomenon. There may in fact be as many as eight different kinds of aggression (predatory, inter-male, fear-induced, irritable, territorial, maternal, instrumental, and sex-related). . . . As products of evolution, aggressive behaviors—like other behavioral traits—are subject to natural selection and could not be so widespread, either in *Homo sapiens* or other animal species, unless they were on balance adaptive. Of course, this is not to say that aggression is always adaptive, or that it will continue to be adaptive in the future. There are many instances in nature of behaviors that have become maladaptive as conditions have changed, and mass violence in human societies today may well be a case in point. . . . We must as behavioral scientists confront the fact that collective violence in human societies cannot be explained in terms of simple extrapolations from individual motivation states. Organized violence involves several elements of group dynamics—causal variables that transcend either the individual or any sort of summation of numerous individual behaviors.[9]

The various views of the origin of human aggression and warfare probably represent a false polarization of the issue. According to the biologist René Dubos:

> . . . This polarization of views constitutes in reality a pseudo problem, analogous in all respects to the now worn-out nurture *versus* nature controversy. The potentiality for aggressiveness is indeed part of man's genetic constitution, just as it is part of the genetic constitution of all animal species. But the manifestations of all genetic potentialities are shaped by past experiences and present circumstances. There is no genetic coding that inevitably results in aggressiveness, only a set of genetic attributes for self-defense that can become expressed as aggressiveness under particular sets of conditions.[10]

The argument, however, continues to persist, and there are claims that a built-in biological aggression factor may eventually be substantiated. At the same time we must recognize that there is still inadequate knowledge of the social and cultural determinants of human aggression. Some investigators believe that the present state of the evidence suggests that certain types of aggression may be "built into" some individuals and that, conversely, there may be some individuals who are endowed with built-in controls against lethal aggression. Within the total population of most

---

[9] Peter A. Corning. "Human Violence: Some Causes and Implications." Paper prepared for the symposium on "Value and Knowledge Requirements for Peace," 138th annual meeting, American Association for the Advancement of Science, Philadelphia, December 1971.

[10] Dubos, *op. cit.,* p. 566.

societies it would not be difficult to find large numbers of normal human beings who would find it next to impossible to kill another human being or even to exhibit aggressive behavior.

Further, widespread revulsion against violence is revealed in almost every era of recorded history. In our own time, revolt against war and the repudiation of violence have become increasingly popular causes as individuals and groups have examined the meaning of the tragic events of recent years, in terms of both themselves and the total human condition.[11]

AN ETHNOLOGICAL PERSPECTIVE

The notion that man by nature is a killer is based upon an almost universally accepted premise that much of what man is today is an expression of attributes he has retained from before and during the Stone Age as the Miocene precursors of *Homo sapiens* moved from the forest to become hunters and gatherers in the savannahlike country of East Africa. It has been estimated that the human species acquired its biological identity more than 100,000 years ago and has not changed in significant ways—anatomically, physiologically, or mentally—since that time.

Many investigators agree that biological evolution, which produced in man his original traits, has essentially ceased and that it has been replaced by cultural evolution, which is not inherited through the genes but is acquired through learning. This does not necessarily mean that the human species has now become unable to accommodate further biological evolution. Recent studies indicate that some significant genetic change can take place within about ten generations.[12]

It is probably correct to assume, however, that the deep influence of the past has survived in man and that modern man still functions with essentially the same genetic constitution as that of the Paleolithic hunters of the Old Stone Age and the more recent Neolithic farmers of the Agricultural Age. These retained traits become operative in modern man, for example, as he makes a "fight or flight" response when threat and danger are encountered.

But in stating this assumption, we are not simultaneously suggesting that the killing propensity in man is part of his genetic constitution. To do so would condemn us to submit to a gloomy future based on a fatalistic

---

[11] *Ibid.*
[12] See: E. O. Wilson, in: J. F. Eisenberg and W. S. Dillon, editors. *Man and Beast.* Washington, D.C.: Smithsonian Institution, 1969. p. 206.

outlook toward man and his destiny. There may be reason for optimism. There is mounting evidence that, if there ever was a "killer instinct" in prehistoric man, sufficient time has elapsed since the emergence of agricultural societies for "the evolution of some behavioral traits to have reversed themselves many times over." [13] In other words, if innate violence had been woven into the fabric of man's genetic code, there has been ample time for it to have become diluted during the 10,000-year stretch of the Agricultural Age, through which some 70 billion people lived as farmers in isolated farming communities. There is little archaeological evidence that great violence occurred during this period, and it is reasonable to assume that attributes of cooperation, social discipline, and absence of aggression—requisites of farm life even today—could have established the social conditions necessary for the progressive dilution of a killer instinct in man.

Thus we cannot safely assume that there is a built-in aggressive tendency to kill. There is increasing evidence that man's violence is largely determined by social factors. If there is a genetic basis for aggressive behavior in modern man, it is because it continues to be adaptive. It cannot be said that we have managed to organize our modern social institutions in ways that do not make it almost advantageous to possess a killer instinct. This is to say that when social life creates conditions which tend to distort instinctive responses (such as self-defense), certain men may become killers. Man's biological adaptation has not prepared him for the highly competitive environments which prevail in and around contemporary urban population centers. It is known that war and violence are far more common in highly competitive societies, especially during periods of rapid change and social turbulence. Man brings to his new environment a biological wisdom which has been built over a long period of time. This wisdom has had little or no experience with many of the artificial and constrictive environments of modern society. René Dubos suggests that violence, rather than possessing a genetic base, is a reflection of man's failure to create a social wisdom capable of matching a biological wisdom evolved under natural conditions.[14]

Thus, as man affirmed his identity in village and then in city life and began to shape it to his purposes, he found himself in environments marked by new forms of competition which differed radically from those under which he had evolved. His way of life, including his thought processes,

[13] *Ibid.*
[14] Dubos, *op. cit.*, p. 570.

was subjected to enormous stress. Instinctive self-defense mechanisms not only required an extension from self, family, or tribe to an entire village or city-state, but also tended to become aberrant as man found that his loyalties and identity could be reinforced and defined through offensive mechanisms, through waging destructive warfare on other villages, on outsiders, or on other city-states and nations. In this way the instinct for self-defense may have deviated from customary patterns of expression as man confronted conditions which differed profoundly from those under which he had evolved.

But networks of organization, loyalties, and power identifications became operative in another way, as these were strengthened and extended from village to village, from village to city, from city to nation-state and empire. Along with the emergence of empire, the institution of kingship arose, and, with it, the simplest tools and weapons in the hands of subjects were suddenly converted into a collective instrument of human energy—the human machine. Thus war as an extension of the human machine was born. Lewis Mumford has forcefully described the characteristics of the new machine as it began to replace simple tools and artifacts:

> By royal command, the necessary machine was created: a machine that concentrated energy in great assemblages of men, each unit shaped, graded, trained, regimented, articulated, to perform its particular function in a unified working whole. . . . The assemblage and the direction of these labor machines were the prerogative of kings and an evidence of their supreme power; for it was only by exacting unflagging effort and mechanical obedience from each of the operative parts of the machine that the whole mechanism could so efficiently function.[15]

The social constraints and biological adaptations achieved in earlier phases of man's life as a farmer did not bend readily to the new demands of a machine environment. Competitive attitudes and rapid technological change requiring social adjustment placed a severe strain on biological wisdom acquired under natural conditions over some 10,000 years. Although the machine culture fostered the shaping of much of man's abstract knowledge, as reflected in trading, writing, political organization, religion, the arts, and warfare, it also permitted him to begin to construct artificial and synthetic environments separated from the natural conditions in which he had evolved. History has shown that it is in such environments that violence and conflict are most frequent, especially during periods of

---

[15] Lewis Mumford. "Utopia, The City and the Machine." *Dædalus* 94 (2): 284; Spring 1965.

rapid change which upset the social order. Although the specialization in abstract knowledge which undergirds a technological culture can finally produce an extraordinary state of adaptedness between human life and the environment it creates, its very efficiency imposes severe limitations on the freedom to change.

SYMBOLIZATION IN MAN: A FACTOR IN WAR

If it is true that warfare is a social invention without a specific biological base, we need to examine the social and cultural factors which must be taken into account as we study its nature. Anthropological literature on aggression and warfare suggests that the factor of symbolization in man permits identification of an enemy suitable for killing.[16] Certainly one of the most important of man's characteristics is his capacity to use symbolic means to define those who are, and those who are not, members of his group. Man's ability to use symbols makes it possible for him to categorize and identify through his categories those who are inside his group—that is, members of his family, tribe, territory, state, or nation—and are thus inappropriate objects for killing. This ability also enables him to identify those who are outside as rivals or enemies and who are thus suitable objects for killing. Man even has the capacity, through his symbols, to read other humans out of his species and, through his ability to symbolize, make of his enemy a nonhuman being.

For example, our society has recently been forced to face, with a shock of guilt, the dichotomy between its stated ideals and the consequences of symbol training as a part of the war machine. To read the news accounts of Lieutenant William Calley's testimony on his part in the My Lai massacre becomes a numbing experience:

> I was ordered to go in there and destroy the enemy. That was my job that day. . . . I did not sit down and think in terms of men, women, and children. They were all classified the same, and that was the classification that we dealt with—just as enemy soldiers.
>
> I felt then, and I still do, that I acted as I was directed and I carried out the orders.
>
> Our job was to destroy everyone and everything in the villages. . . .

[16] Reprinted from "Alternatives to War," by Margaret Mead, page 67 of *War: The Anthropology of Armed Conflict and Aggression.* Special *Natural History* supplement based on a historic plenary session held on November 30, 1967, at the 66th Annual Meeting of the American Anthropological Association; *Natural History,* December 1967. Copyright © The American Museum of Natural History, 1967.

I never sat down to analyze it; men, women, and children. They were enemy and just people. . . .[17]

Similarly, in a statement of Captain Eddie Rickenbacker, made on October 27, 1967, we can readily recognize the effective use of symbol training for war to cancel out the humanness of the enemy:

. . . peace demonstrators are a bunch of bums. The U.S. should bomb the ports, dams, and population of North Vietnam. That's what airplanes are for. You're not fighting human beings over there—you're fighting two-legged animals. The people are just slaves. That's all war is for is to kill and win, to destroy, to defeat the population of your enemy.[18]

One is led to speculate whether this symbol of enemy as nonhuman could be learned so effectively if countervailing attitudes toward humanness had been nourished earlier, through education. But a society using warfare as a tool cannot afford to have its warriors accommodate notions alien to the war machine; the machine by its very nature requires the abstraction of masses of men and the symbol of the enemy as nonhuman. Both abstraction and symbol are social inventions, not to be eliminated until the war machine itself is dismantled.

If war can be regarded as a social invention or a cultural tool rather than as a phenomenon of specific biological origin, we can then examine it as we do other cultural artifacts, such as social organizations and other tools, in order to ascertain the functions it has served in the past. This is a necessary first step, because any discussion of alternatives to war must ultimately hinge on the question of whether the functions "fulfilled by warfare in the past are functions necessary today in modern society, and, if so, what other functions can fulfill them better."[19] It is reasonable to assume that any device invented by human beings will be employed by human beings until its usefulness is brought to an end, either through the appearance of another more functional invention or through the disappearance of the need or purpose it serves. In other words, if war is to be eliminated—in terms of the function it now serves—what is to replace it? If the replacement, whatever it is, is not grounded in a realistic appraisal of function, we can anticipate a continued use of the older invention as long as it fulfills some socially recognized purpose.

---

[17] Quoted in: "George Regas' Views on Vietnam, an Extension of the Remarks of Representative Jerome R. Waldie, House of Representatives." *Congressional Record,* May 5, 1971. p. 4001.
[18] *Ibid.*
[19] Mead, *op. cit.*

NUCLEAR THREAT NOT A DETERRENT TO CONVENTIONAL WARFARE

The functions of war have been made explicit by almost every historian since antiquity. Anthropologists have treated them with greater refinement. Depending upon the nature of the particular set of conditions which induce a call to arms, Margaret Mead lists the following functions:

> ... to repel attack; to add territory, subjects, or fellow citizens to one's own territory; to establish autonomy or freedom from subordination; to provide targets outside the country when the maintenance of power is threatened from within; to provide sources of food or minerals; and even in some cases to provide a market for munition makers or an excuse for the maintenance of a heated up economy that serves a group in power.[20]

If, as Mead asserts, these are the general conditions in which war is found to be functional, what then are the necessary conditions within which war will not be functional? Certainly the primary deterrent to war in our time is the realization that nuclear warfare would result in the annihilation of the perpetrator as well as the victim. The values held by members of the society which first launches a nuclear warhead against another society are just as vulnerable to extinction as the values of the society which is destined to receive it. It is difficult to explain the willingness of any power to resort to war of any kind under the conditions of nuclear threat which now exist. Such willingness carries within it the suggestion that a society would be willing to submit itself to destruction knowing that its own basic beliefs would perish with it.

However, the threat of nuclear warfare has not served to reduce the function of conventional warfare; it has not been a deterrent to the eruption of other forms of warfare in recent years, nor has it inhibited those outbreaks of violence which approximate civil war within national boundaries. In other words, although the invention of nuclear warfare has rendered immobile potential acts of provocation among the powers having access to its capability, over the past three decades this has not been a sufficient condition for achieving and ensuring the establishment of international order.

Indeed, the threat of nuclear warfare may have fostered acceptance of conventional warfare as a more acceptable means of dealing with conflict in recent years, thereby serving to heighten recourse to its use.

[20] *Ibid.*

All major revolutions involving changes in man's tools have been accompanied by basic changes in ideas, ways of thinking, and relationships with one another. The revolution which began with the advent of nuclear warfare as a tool is no different in this respect from the agricultural and industrial revolutions, which in turn brought about changes in ways of thinking, in human relationships, and in social institutions. What is different in the current revolution is the abruptness of the change. Almost overnight man has been required to shift his economic, political, and moral outlooks from national or regional bases to an international and whole-world perspective. But traditional ways of thinking are not easily relinquished, and the hold of custom, particularly around the power moorings of our economic and political institutions, is especially resistant to the requirements for change even through education.

WORLD CITIZENSHIP: A FIRST PRIORITY

If education is to be an important ingredient in any process designed to realize the possibility of an extended future for man, it must face the staggering task of helping members of a new generation give up outworn national and territorial perspectives and replace them with ways of thinking that will help them deal directly with the worldwide social problems which pervade their lives. The dilemmas posed by modern technologies, changing social institutions, and related moral and ethical considerations, all within a global context, need to be sorted out, their complex interrelationships examined, and conditions created for young people to make authentic connections between available knowledge concerning these matters and possibilities offered in terms of human fulfillment.

Until recently man could make relatively easy decisions about the direction his efforts might take as he attempted to alter some aspect of the particular environment which surrounded him, because he could safely view the consequences mainly in terms of his local relationships to it. Since World War II, however, he has confronted a world which requires radical adaptive changes in his behavior. The planet has now become accessible to virtually all its inhabitants, and local cultures and societies living in every part of the globe have simultaneous access to knowledge of events and information concerning everyone living in every other part.

In addition, the social and natural environments of man have become as one. The pollutants which are cast into the atmosphere tonight by fuming industrial furnaces of a city in England may envelop scores of

Scandinavian villages in smog by tomorrow morning. The fallout from nuclear tests conducted in Nevada may affect the quality of milk produced in Switzerland. Underground nuclear tests carried out in the Aleutians threaten sea life in the Pacific Ocean and set off currents of anxiety throughout the world. The political problems inherent in the recently acquired realization of one global environment supporting one human family in a technological age are only now beginning to be recognized.

This means that a new generation must find ways to reduce, control, and redirect drives for power, aggrandizement, and exploitation based upon former patterns of national interest. It means that it must quickly learn to replace these patterns with countervailing drives toward cooperation and community not only with local neighborhoods, regions, and nations but also with people unlike themselves, living in dissimilar cultures, with differing ways of perceiving and contrasting systems of behavior throughout the world.

There is no longer doubt that we are living in an era which is witnessing the breakdown of a dissociative world order based on racial and ethnic homogeneity, rooted in a no longer tenable notion that human beings living in discrete territorial units shall be of the same kind. Throughout the world there is increasing evidence that people will soon find that their neighbors look and act differently from themselves and that they will be decreasingly protected by traditional shields of homogeneity.

Man is now compelled to raise to a conscious level the fact and meaning of his citizenship in a worldwide culture. His survival may well depend upon how rapidly he can shed preeminent postures of exclusive, militant, and highly personal identifications with a particular society, local culture, or nation-state and establish dominant identifications and loyalty to humanity as a whole.

"BEYOND THE STABLE STATE"

One problem for education is how to reduce complexity without making conflict appear a simpler phenomenon than it is. We must guard against simplistic and clear-cut models for lowering complexity, because interactive forces leading to conflict are characterized by disorder, tangle, and unpredictability. Donald Schon notes, for example, that the ideal of a peaceful society often bears a resemblance to some mythical, calm, "stable state" which is to be achieved after a time of trouble. Such an ideal, he suggests, is based upon a belief in the ultimate power of man's constancy, the potential of his unchangeability.

Although we affirm the need for change and accept its inevitability in a cognitive sense, in an affective sense we tend to institutionalize the notion of the "final stable state," which can be viewed as an antidote to the threat of uncertainty and instability. The vision of the ultimate constancy of man and society is easily interjected, and during periods of stress man takes sanctuary in his stable institutions. However, these same institutions tend to identify whatever stability they offer with a concomitant capacity to preserve the status quo and its order. Schon believes there is a need to develop institutional structures and new frameworks for handling knowledge for the process of change itself which will offer alternative unthreatening response mechanisms "beyond the stable state." [21]

EDUCATION FOR PEACE: AN ECOLOGICAL POINT OF VIEW

It is possible that education for peace can best be approached from an ecological point of view.[22] Seen from an ecological perspective, building strategies for peace becomes primarily a problem of harmonizing the interrelationships in society between the developing individual and his evolving environment. Such a view would involve the study of complex interrelationships among diverse human groups living amid evolving technologies and environments ranging from the most primitive to the most sophisticated. But wherever individuals or societies are located along this continuum, an ecological approach would preclude their separation into convenient static categories; it would assume that the destinies of all are intertwined and that everything each does affects everything else.

Viewed from the standpoint of ecology, peace education becomes the study of the mutual interdependence of systems of man. As noted earlier, the problems of war, poverty, racial tension, and environmental deterioration are related, as are the systems of nationalism, imperialism, and other self-serving forces. Common factors are intertwined at the roots of both problems and systems, which means that viable proposals for

---

[21] Donald A. Schon. *Beyond the Stable State: Public and Private Learning in a Changing Society.* London: Temple Smith, 1971.

[22] See: Anthony J. N. Judge. "Peace as an Evolving Balance of Conceptual and Organizational Relationships." Paper for the symposium on "Value and Knowledge Requirements for Peace," 138th annual meeting, American Association for the Advancement of Science, Philadelphia, December 1971.

peace education must include techniques for understanding and handling a multitude of changing interactive forces of extraordinary complexity.

The point to be made is that peace is not a static state, and an ecological conception encourages a focus on the revolving set of relationships among a number of forces and systems. Further, many of these forces have harmonious relationships in common, and many more carry a potential for developing such relationships. It must be conceded that we do not as yet have sufficient understanding of the relationships between man and society to deal definitively with such questions as: Evolving to what? or, What is harmonious? But a conceptual framework based upon an ecological approach would enable us to do some hard thinking about the nature of the problems involved.

For example, Anthony Judge has posited four different kinds of ecology which carry identifiable "harmonious evolving interrelationships" upon which to build:

Organizational ecology, i.e., the harmonious evolving interrelationships between organizational units

Conceptual ecology, i.e., the harmonious evolving interrelationships between theoretical formulations, value and belief systems

Problem ecology, i.e., the harmonious evolving interrelationships between problems

Psycho-ecology or psycho-dynamics, i.e., the harmonious evolving interrelationships within a person's psyche.[23]

Such an approach would require a far more sophisticated appreciation of the variety and complexity of elements in the man-society system and their interrelationships than is currently provided in most approaches to peace education.

Viewed in these terms, world peace is not simply a matter of rearranging external or objective features of the man-society system as related to organizations, concepts, or problems. An ecology of evolving harmonious interrelationships calls for an individual internalization of these relationships based upon inner stability and integration of values, role, and conflict management. The constitution of UNESCO recognizes this when it states: "Since wars begin in the minds of men, it is in the minds of men that the defenses of peace must be constructed. . . . A peace based exclusively upon

[23] *Ibid.*

the political and economic arrangements of governments would not be a peace which could secure the unanimous, lasting, and sincere support of the peoples of the world."

At the root of political and economic systems are the subsystems in which individuals participate as they pursue specific goals related to specific roles. It is through the subsystems that defenses for peace must be built, for it is within and between them that the conditions for interspecific conflict are most likely to be extended, even if improved external arrangements of governments could be achieved. An ecology of evolving harmonious relationships inevitably calls for the destruction of some roles and relationships in order to protect and further its own process. As Anthony Judge notes, the problem becomes even more acute as we recognize individual identity for the powerful and subjective force it is, requiring some means of resolving tensions and giving help especially to those who are currently obliged to secure their identity in what is ultimately scheduled for destruction—that is, imperialism, colonialism, and territoriality.[24]

There is a need to find ways to generate new modes of thinking about peace which will permit us to integrate the enormous production of unintegrated knowledge currently producing complexity and overload. Integration in this sense means something beyond the integration of knowledge across conventional boundaries of separate disciplines, research, policy making, and so on. It means integration across boundaries of individual and personal identification systems and subsystems with their characteristic values, modes of thought, and action. The processes of interpretation and comprehension of interrelationships, however, will not alone suffice. Integration must extend from systems of interpretation to systems of communication which will enable human beings to influence one another and help people and organizations knit together the conflicting elements of organizational, conceptual, and value networks in which they participate. The need is for a society of individuals who can respond creatively to problems with increasing sensitivity to crucial interrelationships in the man-society system.

If education is to be a force in shaping perceptive and responsive individuals, it is essential that it view man-society as dependent on a global and multidisciplinary set of interdependent networks whose interaction calls for improved processes of interpretative integration and comprehension.

[24] *Ibid.*

FOCUS ON MANKIND

Finally, we need to look at education itself as an organized subsystem which is deeply rooted in the past. Schools of today have been shaped to accord with patterns and principles inherited from institutional forms and presuppositions concerning man and society prevalent in an earlier era. It can be said that more and more new images of man are being developed outside the schools and, along with them, different ideas of how to develop and nurture humanness through education. The student movement is certainly one expression of response to older institutional patterns which tend to resist the new image of man. Behind student unrest and general social turbulence are questions which teachers and administrators must ultimately face: What manner of man and society are we assuming in our organizational structures? What alternatives to this image are emerging? What changes in education do these alternatives involve?

As noted earlier, our contemporary educational environments hold more than merely residual traces of the quantifying and objectifying tendencies made operative in our schools during an earlier pragmatic age. The image of man reflected in this emphasis certainly does not exhaust current understanding of human potentialities. It is no longer feasible for programs of education to be dominated by an image of man wielding technological power over a threatening environment, accompanied by skeptical or even cynical questions about who man is or what direction his path is taking in the whole endeavor. There is a need to capture a positive vision of authentic human potentiality and build into our educational practices a wide range of humanizing experiences. Those who man the war machine have been able to exploit the absence of positive viewpoints and humanizing programs in education precisely because they have held a more fixed objective and determined perspective. Their goals have been clear, but the goals of education have been fuzzy as they have orbited uncertainly around the requirements of the business-industrial-military establishment.

Authentic humanness requires belief in and commitment to human values which go far beyond a mere self-sufficient ideal fostered by the competitive environments which characterize much of our current practices in education. Learning how to make a decent living is not necessarily synonymous with learning how to make a decent life. Education has a clear responsibility to help students mediate values at the root of this problem. Failure in this task can only result in further proliferations of exclusiveness at the expense of a human community of world citizens seeking to share meaningful human experience. Heterogeneous school populations, characteristic of increasing numbers of schools today, provide unique opportunities to help students appreciate the extraordinary values in life styles of ethnic and racial diversity. Operational and administrative conveniences in school must be viewed as intrusions if they impinge upon, or fail to make central, the larger question of human identity. The effort in education should be one of synthesis, bringing together the totality of elements which might serve to clarify man's experience in whatever culture and give needed direction toward realizing new continuities based upon authentic understanding.

Finally, schools need to become increasingly concerned with issues relating to the ethical aspects of their practices and endeavors. Among young people there is a growing awareness that society comes into crisis when ethical and moral substance is lost. These dimensions are seen as eminently utilitarian and are as essential a part of man's life as his biological and cultural needs. The only way to give an emphasis to ethical considerations in the curriculum is to begin dealing with the vital concerns of those affected by it. Ethical and humanistic learnings proceed out of felt experience. It is unlikely that such experience can be prescribed or followed chapter by chapter in a text. It is likely that serious thought about man, resulting in improved ways to cope with his contemporary problems, will emerge if alienation and even the phenomenon of conflict itself are made the basis for designing learning experience.

Such a basis might well propel learners to intensify their search for meaning and allow them to stretch out and manifest in their behavior those changes required for world peace.

While we do not now know all that is required to build permanent structures for peaceful change, we are aware that such knowledge can be achieved by sustained effort. Included in the task is the need to gather together the specialized and disparate fragments of knowledge which are now scattered over many subject fields. What is needed is an integrative framework of essential knowledge and value orientations which will enable us to do some hard thinking about what we need to know for constructive action to secure peace. Such a framework will not emerge from, or remain within, the exclusive domain of one subject field, one nation, or one group of nations. But such a conceptual framework will enable us to focus on man as he is and might become, help us deal with the processes of social institutions and technology in worldwide collective action, and assist us in designing educational environments in which modes of cooperation, competition, and conflict can be made consistent with education for peaceful change.

If we draw on every conceivable field of current human knowledge, a configuration of man which illuminates the multiple patterns of his experience in diverse cultures can become the focus of study and a basis for collective action for peace. Through education the probing of man's condition need no longer be speculative or impressionistic, and it need not be confined to the findings of biology and the behavioral sciences. Literature, philosophy, and religion, along with all of man's creative arts, reveal what man can become in the process of enhancing his humanness in diverse cultures throughout the world. It is through this diversity that basic human values are expressed and reinforced, allowing the extraordinary values of each culture to be preserved and made available to all others. It is through this diversity that real strength lies and that a workable educational framework for peace can be built.

In the pages that follow, thoughtful variations on the general theme of education for peace are presented. Each chapter focuses on the schools and on those who administer and teach in them; but, more important, each reflects a special concern for students and the impact their school experiences may have upon the ultimate realization of a peaceful world order. In the final analysis, it is the individual student who is struggling to see himself as a self-motivated person. If, as a result of his school experience, he seems to think of himself in relation to assumed manpower and military needs linked to an increasing effort to extend the gross national product to provide a larger base for imperialism, that will be one consequence of his educational experience. If, on the other hand, he is helped to think about what he wants to do with his life and its relation to the kind of world society he wishes to create and live in, that will be a different consequence of his experience in education. Each of the authors of the following chapters has some important things to say about this problem, each in his own way and each from his particular point of view.

Chapter 3 focuses on the factors that "build for violence in individuals and in institutions, particularly in schools." The author explains how our failure to achieve social justice is a major cause of violence. He examines racial tension and closed societies in relation to violence, and he extends his inquiry into the cultures of institutions, organizations, and environments of the school. He calls attention to the problem of moral judgment and the responsibility of schools in this domain of human development.

Chapter 4 turns attention to children and young students as they respond to some questions about ways in which they tend to conceptualize peace. Viewed from their perspective, meaning tends to center on "inner peace" and the absence of violence and war. The authors of this chapter, through an extensive survey of children's attitudes about peace, illuminate the need for improved education programs which can help the young make better distinctions between negative peace—controlling or eliminating violence or war—and positive peace—creating conditions of social justice.

Chapter 5 reveals the deep frustration experienced by a veteran educator and professional leader as she faces the constellation of forces operative in relation to peace and education for peace. The writer views the problem in terms of a need for political education and political action. Her statement reflects a growing recognition by many that "the problem of achieving and maintaining peace, like the problem of maintaining civil liberties or extending social justice, is a problem of power relationships."

Chapter 6 emphasizes the central role of international and cross-cultural experiences in peace education. The author describes recent developments of materials and approaches for dealing with conflict resolution, world law, deterrence, and international order. In addition, he examines several social studies curriculum projects related to the problems of war, violence, and peace research and presents some guidelines for program development. In a final section he deals with the impact of the media in teaching about world affairs.

Chapter 7 brings into synthesis the rationale and goal definition for developing curriculum trends in peace education. The writer establishes a base for current program design and points to the formulations of several current spokesmen, both within and outside the ranks of teaching, whose views are increasingly reflected in various program proposals. In addition to examining important links between alienation and violence, and between social injustice and the war system, the writer places a major emphasis on the need for a "survival curriculum" for the 1970's. She describes the essential elements of such a curriculum and makes a strong plea for creating conditions for continuing dialogue at the school and community levels regarding peace and survival.

Chapter 8 focuses on parents' roles in peace education. We readily acknowledge that schools alone cannot do the job of educating children for peace. The writer offers practical guides for parents and teachers.

In Chapter 9, attention is given to the man-in-society theme as it relates to our contemporary world and projects beyond it into the future. The writer makes central a human relations posture concerning social justice and world peace; he discusses the problems of the ethical imperatives as they relate to "the human side of education." His statement will serve to enliven and elevate the thinking of those who are seriously concerned about peace education and who understand the need for the range of perspectives on the human conditions which is required to make it a force in our schools and society.

Finally, the Appendices offer additional sources of reference for readers who we hope will have been inspired either to begin or to continue their efforts toward teaching students about world peace.

Selected References

Hannah Arendt. *On Violence*. New York: Harcourt, Brace & World, 1970.

Kenneth Boulding. *The Image*. Ann Arbor: University of Michigan Press, 1961.

Theodosius Dobzhansky. *Mankind Evolving*. New Haven, Connecticut: Yale University Press, 1962.

René Dubos. *Man Adapting*. New Haven, Connecticut: Yale University Press, 1965.

René Dubos. *So Human an Animal*. New York: Charles Scribner's Sons, 1968.

Richard Falk. *Our Endangered Planet*. New York: Random House, Inc., 1971.

M. F. Ashley Montague, editor. *Man and Aggression*. New York: Oxford University Press, 1968.

Lewis Mumford. *The Myth of the Machine: The Pentagon of Power*. New York: Harcourt Brace Jovanovich, Inc., 1970.

Gardner Murphy. *Human Potentialities*. New York: Basic Books, Inc., 1958.

Theodore Roszak. *The Making of a Counter Culture*. New York: Doubleday & Company, Inc., 1969.

From: *Hugh Selwyn Mauberley**
Ezra Pound   3

E. P. Ode Pour L'Election de Son Sépulchre

IV

These fought in any case
and some believing,
pro domo, in any case . . .

   Some quick to arm,
   some for adventure,
   some from fear of weakness,
   some from fear of censure,
   some for love of slaughter, in imagination,
   learning later . . .
some in fear, learning love of slaughter;

Died some, pro patria,
non 'dulce' non 'et decor' . . .
   walked eye-deep in hell
   believing in old men's lies, then unbelieving
   came home, home to a lie,
   home to many deceits,
   home to old lies and new infamy;
   usury age-old and age-thick
   and liars in public places.

   Daring as never before, wastage as never before.
   Young blood and high blood,
   fair cheeks, and fine bodies;
   fortitude as never before

   frankness as never before,
   disillusions as never told in the old days,
   hysterias, trench confessions,
   laughter out of dead bellies.

* Ezra Pound. *Personae*. New York: New Directions Publishing Corporation, 1926. Copyright 1926 by Ezra Pound. Reprinted by permission of New Directions Publishing Corporation.

U.S. Combat Deaths in Interstate Wars[†]

War	Deaths*	Battle Deaths per Million of Population
Mexican War (1846–1848)	11,000	480
Spanish American War (1898)	5,000	66
World War I (1917–1918)	126,000	1,300
World War II (1941–1945)	292,000	2,200
Korean War (1950–1953)	54,000	360
Vietnam War (1961–)	54,000+	270

* Includes deaths from disease and wounds.

FIGURE 2. *Source:* J. David Singer and Melvin Small, *The Wages of War.* New York: John Wiley & Sons, Inc., 1972.

Figures on battle deaths in war vary greatly, depending upon whether service-incurred disease and wounds are included, whether servicemen missing in action are included in death tolls, etc.

The battle death toll for all U.S. wars has been estimated at 600,000.

It has also been estimated that U.S. forces have been in active military operations somewhere in all but 20 years of American history.

Economic Cost of American Interstate Wars[†] (in Millions of Dollars)

War	Original War Costs	Veterans' Benefits	Estimated Interest on War Loans
Mexican War	73	64	10
Spanish American War	400	6,000	60
World War I	26,000	75,000	11,000
World War II	228,000	290,000	86,000
Korean War	54,000	99,000	11,000
Vietnam War *	110,000	220,000	22,000

* Estimate based on war ending by June 30, 1970.

FIGURE 3. *Source: Statistical Abstract of the United States, 1970.* Washington, D. C.: Department of Commerce, Bureau of Census, U.S. Government Printing Office, 1971. p. 248.

[†] William A. Nesbitt. *Data on the Human Crisis: A Handbook for Inquiry.* New York: Center for International Programs and Comparative Studies of the New York State Education Department, 1972. p. 12. Reprinted by permission.

Antecedents of Violence
Aubrey Haan

3

THE attempt in this chapter is to describe and analyze the factors that build for violence in individuals and in institutions, particularly in schools. Many kinds of relations and situations contribute to the outbreak of violence; a simplistic approach to the problems of violence will only help many people deny their participation in the complex end result. The solution is not the assignment of culpability but the development of acute awareness of what is going on in others and in the often inadequate creations of our community life—the institutions and organizations which do their own special kinds of damage.

VIOLENCE AS A PHENOMENON OF OUR CULTURE

The factors we are concerned with here—and their presence or absence in the situations that people experience—include the following:

1. The group of factors that involves choices: arriving at rational solutions, participating, decision making, problem solving, coping, handling conflict, facilitating environments, developing moral judgment

2. The group including the angers, hates, and manifest and hidden violence of its members: the angry, threatening teacher; the brutalization of children at home and at school; angry, upset homes; racial and ethnic hate groups; religious hate groups

3. Damaging educational practices and concepts: daily failures of children, dramatic year-end failures, track systems, "yell and tell" teachers, inappropriate demands for performance, ignorance or overlooking of the stages of cognitive and logical development, the impact of the IQ

4. Social injustices: poverty, inequitable sharing of income, inequitable distribution of public services, inequitable administration of legal justice

5. The teachers of violence: wars, television programs, motion pictures, angry homes, brutalization of children in school, hate groups

6. Institutions: bureaucracies as little, closed societies; organizations that ignore member welfare; organizations working only for their own survival; institutions that ignore humane values in their operations; institutions that prevent growth and fulfillment of their members.

The problem of violence in our society is not, of course, exclusively or always primarily a school problem, although the school's general failure to contribute to a just society; its participation in the denial of equality; its not-infrequent blindness to the stages by which children become adults able to cope with frustrations, novelty, ambiguity, and logical difficulty; its failure to develop higher levels of moral judgment; and its tendency to "yell and tell" instead of educate around cognitive development, individual choice, and decision making end too often with individuals incapable of using ways other than violence as solutions to problems.

Whether we as a nation are today more violent than we were in the past is not the most important question. Violence to human beings, unnecessary hurt, hidden violence that degrades and denigrates, institutions so set up and managed that they do violence to persons and precipitate violence are both current and historical. It is clear that the United States is much more violent than other Western nations. This violence is carried on by the Establishment (through corporations, institutions, and services); by students moved, however unwisely, to make the schools "relevant"; by labor unions struggling, however unjustly, to advance their particular bread-and-butter gains; by racial and ethnic groups battling each other out of economic competitiveness and psychotic fantasies; by government through dogmatic bureaucratic dictums and self-protectiveness; by ultra-leftists and ultrarightists, whose limited view of the consequences to human beings leads them to advocate war and violent revolution.

The schools can do a great deal to counter these influences. We educators have virtually all the children and youth of the land, and we have them for as long as two decades. If our understanding of child development were clearer, we could make a giant step in but one generation. At the outset, however, we must accept the premise that

> violence is strictly brutish in that it comes about through a falling away from what men have it in them to become, free and rational agents. Agreement in rationality and fraternity mark out the distinctively human com-

munity; insofar as social relations are determined by habit, passion, and force, they are in that degree less than human.[1]

It must be recognized that violence is one solution; it is a means decided upon consciously, unconsciously, or psychotically. It is a solution of a sort to a situation, a frustration, a threat, a frightening possibility. It is a defense against feelings of impotence, a defense against logical truths, a psychotic function arising from a sense of rejection.

The school can take part of its lead from these truths. Recognizing that violence is an inadequate solution to a problem by an individual or by groups, the school can become much more deeply involved with choices, decision making, cognitive processes, and values—all leading to solutions other than violence.

Unfortunately, violence as a solution to problems is fostered in our society, as exemplified by the average citizen's access to guns—now manufactured and sold at the rate of five million a year. It is also taught as a solution by many motion pictures and television programs and by the Vietnam War. Monroe Lefkowitz, who has to date made the only longitudinal study of TV, found that boys who watched the most violent programs at age nine were most aggressive at age nineteen. A study of 192 hours of television on seven stations in Los Angeles, monitored by the National Association for Better Radio and Television, showed that the programs included 501 killings, 61 robberies, 394 attempted robberies, 40 kidnappings, 5 suicides, and uncounted murder conspiracies and acts of arson.[2]

Violence is also taught in homes where physical assault is the method of handling conflict, disobedience, error, anger, and frustration. In the schools, even if violence is proscribed as a method of control, the *quality* of violence is often communicated in what teachers say and is implicit in the environment, which degrades and denigrates the child. Implicit violence in schools, as in society in general, may in ultimate destructiveness equal manifest violence. Preoccupation with power and hurt—as is exemplified in some sports—rather than with skill, strategy, fair play, and avoidance of hurt, is participation in still another kind of violence.

The ultimate force for violence is the hate group. Such organizations

---

[1] J. M. Cameron. "On Violence." *New York Review of Books,* special supplement, July 2, 1970. p. 30. Reprinted with permission from *The New York Review of Books.* Copyright © 1970 by The New York Review, Inc.

[2] "Reporting from the World of Television and Radio." *New York Herald Tribune,* August 1964.

peddle hatred of individuals or racial groups, capitalizing on the members' emotional immaturity and on their need to hate someone—anyone identifiable.

INNER CONFLICT AND VIOLENCE

We all recognize that conflict is an inevitable part of human experience and that inner conflict is also the fate of each human being. Conflict is not merely going to disappear either interpersonally or within the individual. Conflicts can be handled in many ways:

1. The person resolves the conflict at a higher level of thinking.
2. The person learns other solutions to conflict than direct aggression or withdrawal, for example, by logical analysis, tolerance of ambiguity, or scientific method.
3. The person is helped to develop self-awareness about his own feelings and how they are involved in conflict.
4. The person is helped to understand other people and to empathize with them, their problems, their pain, their inertia, and their fears.
5. The person comes to understand how others develop and learn as a part of his ability to achieve historical perspective and tolerance of ambiguity.

Clearly, the schools tend to be too busy with other approaches to learning to achieve these goals, but we know how to bring them about, if we would.

INEQUITY AND JUSTICE

The failure of our society to bring about justice at all levels is a major cause of violence. Classes, races, and occupational groups suffer feelings of deprivation and injustice rising out of inequitable compensation and lack of reward. The United States ranks among the highest of Western nations in inequality of income. Not only are incomes inequitable but social and economic insecurity is general, arising from our failure to work out a just society and to give individuals the assurance that they can trust their personal security to the arrangements and institutions of the society.

In many instances economic injustice is so extreme that individuals and groups engage in violence against property and persons out of need and out of anger. We are in a position to assure economic justice, but we do not do so. The belief that justice is withheld out of greed, out of rivalry, or out of self-interest is destructive to persons and leads to personal hate and social alienation. Violence seems to some an inevitable and justified response. The competitiveness of groups and classes, the guilt and fear of those who are overcompensated, and the general insecurity in the society work against efforts to find solutions to which society will commit itself. For example, the Full Employment Act of 1946 is still, more than 25 years later, not really implemented, the policy provisions continuing to be matters of controversy between and within the major political parties. The rights that employed men and women must have to end their anxieties about justice in institutions include:

    1. Full employment that challenges their abilities

    2. The right to have their ideas and proposals reviewed and assessed publicly, not dismissed by a supervisor, officials, or manager

    3. Genuine participation in policy making

    4. The right to compensation equitably related to responsibility.[3]

When these rights are not in fact secured, the result is psychopathology and, ultimately, violence. It is difficult to predict how long we have to bring these rights about. Some suggest that without such reforms our society will end in social chaos by the end of the 20th century.

WAR AND VIOLENCE

Facing these possibilities is the strong belief in some sectors of our society that poverty and its attendant problems of ill health, degradation, and despair are basically volitional and characterological. This kind of thinking is used to justify ethnic and racial inequities in compensation and well-being.

War is the ultimate violence. Wars are supported by the systematic cultivation of hatreds and blackouts of response to human suffering, and they have a residue of psychopathology and irrationality that sustains long periods of hidden and manifest violence. At the language level the terminology of war permeates the description and strategy of many sports, carrying with it for players, spectators, and coaches some of the same emotions. The Vietnam War outraged the moral values of a large sector of society of this country, as well as those of other nations. In other persons the American government's defense of the war brought on moral confusion. Justification of a war (whose brutality everyone witnessed on television) lowered the capacity of countless viewers for growth toward adequate moral judgment. The murder and mutilation attendant upon

---

[3] Elliott Jaques. *Work, Creativity, and Social Justice.* New York: International Universities Press, 1970. pp. 11–17.

aerial bombing was often justified in terms of "winning or losing," an appeal to a debased order of moral judgment.

A Harvard University survey of public attitudes toward Lieutenant William Calley showed 67 percent of respondents agreeing that most people who were ordered to shoot all the inhabitants of My Lai, including old men, women, and children, would have followed the orders. One-half of the respondents said that they too would have shot the villagers. Only 19 percent said that they would have refused to shoot. Those who disapproved bringing Calley to trial perceived no personal choice in obedience or refusal of authoritative orders. The public outcry in Calley's defense reflects the confusion arising from the fact that the people had supported the war as the authorities had asked them to do, and now the authorities were holding them personally responsible for the consequences of the war. There is no question that some of the violence of this century has proceeded from the hatreds and irrationalities attendant upon war and its justification.

RACE AND VIOLENCE

Injustice—social, racial, economic, psychological, and educational—is the real basis of violence. The historical pattern of discrimination and exploitation has woven an intricate web of family disorganization, poverty, educational handicaps, poor health, self-hatred, and frustration that enmeshes the child growing up in it. How to extricate him is a complex educational and psychological problem. Proposals to resolve it by a massive child care program may overlook alternative solutions, among them adequate support and help for persons struggling to keep their families intact and learning together.

RACE AS A THEME OF HATE GROUPS

Violence, hidden and manifest, is promoted by hate groups. Members of such organizations, whose activities and habits arise from unconscious fears, typically find groups, organizations, classes, and races they can identify as the "enemy." They imbue the enemy with all the monstrous qualities their unconscious fears conjure up. Minority races thus become some of the principal victims of these complex fears, which at a frequently unacknowledged level may also include economic competitiveness and sexual fantasies.

The hate groups do hidden violence to their hate objects, and they often do physical violence. Their irrationality weakens and sickens the political processes needed to secure justice in the society. In turn, the activities of such groups arouse responses among the targets of their hate—responses which may be violent and further impair chances for rational order.

VIOLENCE AND THE OPEN SOCIETY

Societies and institutions (among them school districts, governmental units, businesses, and political parties) can be characterized on a scale of "closed to open." A closed society or institution is characterized by decision making at the top, and a set of beliefs or practices—that is, a dogma not to be questioned or deviated from by persons who "live" within the organization. Hence conformity is the safest course, and injustice tends to build up.

The closed society is, of course, a special form of hidden violence against the individuals within it. It contributes to their immaturity; it frustrates their search for equality; it rewards special privilege; it denigrates and degrades them. Many school districts continue to be small, closed societies. The effect upon those subject to such societies is nonparticipation, covert anger, hostility among members, and, most tragic of all, a special kind of anger toward the children who are at the bottom of the ladder. For mobility in a closed society tends to hinge on conformity and special privilege.

In contrast, the open society or organization is committed to the discovery of truth, to the process of continual questioning and inquiry, and to the protection of the inevitable and valuable pluralisms of a democratic culture. These commitments mean a multiplication of leaders; they mean a decision-making process shared by everyone who is going to be affected by them. In a school district, as in a larger social framework, they mean the end of central administration dogmas that must be subscribed to, and a search by teachers, functioning as professionals, for significant questions and evolving answers.

In this period of industrial conglomeration, complex organizations, bureaucracies, and societies tend to become closed. The result is that privilege becomes established, ideas tend to be accepted from some persons and not from others, and dissent is increasingly perceived as troublesome. Postindustrial organizations are inclined to put the problem to be solved as central and to assemble and disband groups of people on the basis of their ability to contribute to solutions, their right to participation, and the overriding need to move on to other problems.[4]

Consciously or unconsciously, "leaders" of closed societies or organizations avoid confronting ideas or research material contrary to their firmly held beliefs. In closed schools this resistance may take the form of bland, even kindly, manipulation of the situation so that the victim's first feeling is that he is being lulled gently into acceptance of things he knows are false or at least moot. His ultimate feeling is one of desperation.

Minority members of the closed school system may find their experience in it much like their experience in the larger society. The hidden violence is perpetrated on teachers and children. For example, teachers may display an unwillingness to confront minority children with truth, with real expectation, thus in a hidden way communicating their own indifference. Policies common in some school districts of diverting minority children into vocational programs, into easier curriculums—away from languages, away from humanities—exemplify the stereotyped response, a response which is itself almost the essence of a closed society.

INSTITUTIONS, ORGANIZATIONS, AND ENVIRONMENTS

Institutions and organizations have cultures of their own, made up of complex, interwoven practices, relationships, arrangements, attitudes, traditions, formulated goals, implicit philosophical viewpoints, values, and beliefs. These cultures, or environments, have a permeating effect on everyone who "lives" in the institutions—on employees, on administrators, on patients in hospitals, on children in schools, and on their parents.

It goes without saying that the culture constitutes a major element in the total environment (psychologically speaking, the institution). It is the tendency of all of us to "exist" in the institution without consciously analyzing what it is and what it is doing to us. In the case of schools, new teachers are at once caught up in it. Convictions held in previous positions, earlier ideas and ideals are modified to conform to the new environment. If the newcomer resists it, he may be rejected, bullied, threatened, isolated, and ultimately forced to leave. Generally, however, the process of adapting to the environment is a gentler, subtler one. The desire to "get along with others," to please authoritative figures, to fit in,

---

[4] See: Warren Bennis. *Changing Organizations.* New York: McGraw-Hill Book Company, Inc., 1966.

to be accepted by persons one works with is usually strong enough to induce conformity.

In the case of school children, the environment can smother them unawares. It may miseducate with scarcely anyone—teacher, administrator, or children—realizing that damage is being done to the children's feelings about learning, to their attitudes toward authority, to the teacher's feelings about working with children, to the children's awareness of being boys or girls, and to the administrator's concept of his role in the school.

Institutions have infinite capacity for both good and harm. Institutions are "moral" or "less moral," in the secular sense of the term. Business institutions are often criticized for failing to provide for open, helpful relations between employees but instead promoting extreme competitiveness, secretiveness, stress resulting in distortion of values, ill health, psychological breakdown, and even death. There, as in schools, the process is not a completely aware one. The environment of the business institution is subtle; it seems to be an inevitable response to the pressures from outside the institution; it shares its characteristics with similar institutions; it seems out of the control of employees; and, in short, it is "just the way things are." The environment of the institution may lead men and women to cheat, to steal, to take unfair advantage, to put emphasis on money rather than on humanistic values, on remote satisfactions rather than on the needs of people now.

Erik Erikson has pointed out the need to review all our institutions and to determine whether they are good for men to live in—encouraging cooperation, growth, satisfaction, creativity—or whether they are corrupting, demeaning, and depersonalizing and are sources of basic insecurities.[5] Recent programs designed to motivate employees to be better human beings in their relationships have shown astonishing benefits to corporations in terms of increased productivity. Hence the destructive climates we are suffered to endure may be artifacts of another era, not inevitable consequences of being "in business."

One study of schools shows enormous differences in environment from school to school, from parochial to public school, from neighborhood to neighborhood school, and from race-to-race balance.[6] The environment of the school, furthermore, does not have the same effect upon everyone

---

[5] Erik Erikson. "On the Sense of Inner Identity." In: R. Knight and C. Friedman, editors. *Psychoanalytic Psychiatry and Psychology.* New York: International Universities Press, 1954. pp. 351–64.

[6] Aubrey Haan. *School Environment—Development and Effects.* In preparation.

living in it. Students and teachers have different experiences within the environment, and they vary in their ability to cope with the problems it presents. In the study, black children's experiences are significantly different from those of white children in the same school.

The differing environments of low-income schools and upper-income ones are demonstrated by the following statements made by sixth grade children. In a typical low-income school, such statements as these have been recorded: "In my school kids are spanked; we do little art work because the school gets too messy; kids call each other names"; "I am afraid of many kids"; "Somebody is always saying they are going to 'get' someone after school." In contrast, children in a typical upper-income school express their experiences in such comments as these: "In my school teachers like the kids"; "We talk in class about why we should behave well"; "We always have things to do"; "The principal talks with us and listens to us in the yard"; "We make new kids feel welcome"; "The principal knows my name." The school environment is very complex, and its nature can only be suggested by these comments. The data also suggest how varied environments are and how they tend to be ignored as important factors in everyone's education, black or white, rich or poor.

A high degree of child participation in the school environment involves easy, warm exchange of all participants—children, teachers, parents, and principal. A suppressive atmosphere and anxiety about the children are minimal, and teachers' sense of satisfaction is high. A low degree of child participation generally indicates suppressive regulation of children and emphasis on teacher efficiency, at the expense of warmth and responsiveness.

In part of the study, the administrators of the schools involved showed primary concern for teacher convenience, authority, and control, in contrast to child-facilitating arrangements, which were seen as more troublesome for the teaching staff.[7]

In many schools significant numbers of children are never really "seen," in the psychological sense, as they pass through school. The environment may strike them as indifferent, irrelevant, and hostile. For others the environment is inimical, and the angers they develop are focused on the school. The deprecation that they sense becomes a paranoidal base directed at the school and ultimately at authority. In child-participant, child-facilitating schools the environment is pluralistic, accepting, warm, relevantly confronting, and involving child action in the pursuit of many

[7] *Ibid.*

self-chosen goals. In such schools children are eager to accept responsibility for what goes on.

School environments that are adult-oriented, child-suppressive, and indifferent encourage children's feelings of failure and incapacity. These schools are guilty of such practices as failing the student at year's end; testing and failing instead of diagnosing and teaching; employing recitation procedure, wherein the student always knows less than the teacher and fails often—and sometimes constantly—in front of his peers; ignoring opportunities to allow the student to choose goals; denying him the right to share in evaluation; imposing physical punishment and exclusion; constantly pressuring him to perform cognitive tasks far beyond his developmental stage; and treating him differently because of his color, economic level, or ethnic origin. "That's well done, for a Mexican boy," said a teacher in a school in which 40 percent of the children were Mexican American.

In the end, the school environment determines many important educational outcomes. It also affects in significant ways what children feel about others, about strangers, about distant peoples, and, above all, about themselves. It may sow seeds of violence, self-hatred, defeat. The school with a child-participant, child-facilitating environment can be a constructive force in aiding children to learn coping behavior. To accomplish this goal, the typical school environment must be studied and modified. It cannot be surveyed solely by its own members, for they are trapped in the environment, caught in convictions of the inevitability of existing conditions and of the reasonability of even irrational procedures. With help from outside, different criteria can be applied and the institution opened to change and the development of a better environment.

Many of those schools that have successfully altered the environment have employed the Q-Sort technique.[8] This method permits an analysis of the environment as described by all the co-tenants of the school. With outside help and analysis of the data, such schools have begun to make specific changes in their culture. The Q-Sort technique permits the repeated measurement of change in the school environment.

There is little doubt that the environment promotes many of the feelings and attitudes which result in violence as an attempt at a solution to individual and societal frustrations. For individuals, the solution can be reached through coping behavior; for institutions, through environmental—cultural—changes in the institution.

[8] *Ibid.*

STAGES OF COGNITIVE DEVELOPMENT: RELATION TO THE SENSE OF PERSONAL SUCCESS AND FAILURE

Nothing is more destructive to children's sense of "being all right"—to their identity—than the widespread ignorance of their cognitive development.

Schools have tended to ignore the fact that, until a child has developed mental structures at the appropriate levels of thinking, he may not be able to learn what the school demands. Thus it is common for schools to ask performance of which the child is incapable and then to expect him to learn by rote learning and drill. When this alternative fails, the teacher complains that the child forgets what he has been taught, not realizing that he will always forget if he has not reached the cognitive development stage where he can fit the principle into his schema. The child feels the teacher's disapproval, his companions' derision. He begins to develop fear and hatred of the subject, of the teacher, of the school. His out-of-school activities become his refuge, but he is nagged by the sense of failure, which may persist as a lifelong attitude toward school and toward himself.

Failure to focus on the child's cognitive development stage results in enormous waste of time for both child and teacher. When the school fails to assess where the child is cognitively and to work within that framework, it may do much more harm than good. In fact, for many a disadvantaged child, whose experiences have been meager when he enters school, there may be no eventual solution but to drop out—an act that may be accomplished by leaving school or by withdrawing while still occupying a seat in the classroom. The basic reason for the failure of nearly all compensatory education programs has been neglect of experiences at home and at school that are centered on progress in cognitive development. The tendency of many programs to intensify approaches that have already proved failures results in waste, boredom, and frustration.

Part of this failure is the result of the use of conventional normative tests—that is, reliance on achievement tests instead of assessments of individual children's stages of cognitive development. The U.S. Office of Education helps to perpetuate this situation by emphasizing and financing conventional testing as its method of evaluation. The Office of Education also puts pressure on schools to spend enormous amounts of time, federal money, and energy on the multiplication of behavioral objectives—a mistaken, cumbersome approach to curriculum development that leads the schools to narrow their goals and to maintain the teacher as the only really active person in the classroom.

It may seem at first examination that the connection between violence, hidden and manifest, and the stages of cognitive and logical development is forced. In reality there is no more pervasive anger and despair than that of children who have been defeated, bored, and angered by the failures that schools force upon them.

There are, however, alternatives. Because children vary greatly in their cognitive development, the schools can individualize instruction, employ child-facilitating processes, and maximize children's choices and participation in their educational experiences. A school organized and conducted in this way is a small, open society in which the children assume greater responsibility, not passively—or violently—leaving it in the hands of the Establishment—the adults, the teachers, the school.

PEACE, VIOLENCE, AND MORAL JUDGMENT

In 1932, Jean Piaget published *The Moral Judgment of the Child*.[9] In that work he established the stages of moral development and the significance of peer-peer exchange as the process whereby genuine logic and morality come to replace egocentric, logical, and moral realism. He perceived the development of moral judgment as proceeding in stages, as he had previously described them in relation to language, reasoning, reality, and causality.

Subsequently Lawrence Kohlberg identified six stages of development in moral judgment.[10] These, as with all developments, he saw as invariant; that is, they occur in a fixed order, each stage based on the previous stage, none of which can be skipped. His cross-cultural studies also established this invariance as common in all cultures.

The stages of moral judgment as Kohlberg described them are summarized here:

I. Pre-Conventional Level
    Stage 1: Orientation toward punishment, deference to superior power. Physical consequences of action regardless of human meaning or action.

[9] Jean Piaget. *The Moral Judgment of the Child*. Glencoe, Illinois: The Free Press, 1932.
[10] Lawrence Kohlberg and Carol Gilligan. "The Adolescent as Philosopher: The Discovery of the Self in a Post-Conventional World." *Dædalus* 100 (4): 1051–86; Fall 1971.

Stage 2: Right action is that which satisfies one's own needs, sometimes others' (instrumental hedonism).

II. Conventional Level

Stage 3: Good boy—good girl. Good behavior is that which pleases or helps others and is approved by them. Seeking approval by being "nice."

Stage 4: Orientation toward authority. Right is doing one's duty, showing respect for authority, maintaining the social order for its own sake.

III. Principled Level

Stage 5: Social Contract. Right is defined in terms of general rights and in terms of standards which have been critically examined and agreed on by the whole society.

Stage 6: Orientation toward decisions of conscience and self-chosen ethical principles appealing to logical comprehensiveness, universality, and consistency. The principles are abstract and ethical (the Golden Rule, the categorical imperative).[11]

Kohlberg devised a research instrument and scoring manual to determine the level of moral judgment achieved by individuals. He based his method on a series of stories involving moral dilemmas. Today there is increasing use of specially planned games for groups, role playing, and moral-dilemma stories as a means of assessing and furthering moral development.

Elliott Turiel has similarly experimented with developmental processes and educational procedures related to moral judgment.[12] It seems evident that we are rapidly developing the means of assessing and educating around moral development.

Most individuals in our complex society probably adhere to a conformist moral judgment. The danger of this in a society that is increasingly novel and pluralistic is apparent: individuals whose basic moral justification is conformity to authority or laws or is oriented to secure approval of important "others" cannot judge the real meaning of change; they tend to shift their views in accordance with those of authoritative leaders instead of making their own moral judgments based on principles

[11] Lawrence Kohlberg. "The Child as a Moral Philosopher." *Psychology Today* 2: 25–30; September 1968.

[12] Elliott Turiel. "Developmental Processes in the Child's Moral Thinking." In: P. H. Mussen, J. Langer, and M. Covington, editors. *Trends and Issues in Developmental Psychology*. New York: Holt, Rinehart and Winston, Inc., 1969.

of justice, individual and social. The issues of peace and war are complex and cannot be solved by followers of conformist thinkers.

Individuals at the level of principled moral judgment can make decisions that take into account a complex conceptualization of the world's problems. Persons at the conventional level of moral judgment have difficulty thinking through complex, highly differentiated problems of peace in the emerging world. They tend to wait for authoritative leaders. This tendency makes leaders particularly dangerous whose own level of conceptualization is inadequate or whose idea of leadership is that of playing a role rather than thinking through the moral issues.

Schools give little attention to moral development despite its centrality to everyone's life. As long as morality was seen as a clerical concern, the schools held back—or the community held them back. In a pluralistic world, morality is also a secular matter revolving around justice, the sacredness of life, and the prevention of hurting others. The school is the ideal place for the development of moral judgment. Its children can relate to each other in dealing with countless human problems. Some teachers, of course, organize their rooms so that few relationships occur and sweep aside the few moral dilemmas that manage to intrude. In the open classroom the group experience is an intense one in the development of values, attitudes, and moral judgment.

CONCEPTS OF INTELLIGENCE AND THEIR SOCIAL CONSEQUENCES

American education has been greatly influenced by a concept of intelligence as a kind of genetic "given." Teachers have been sold on IQ's, on normative testing, and now on behavior modification. None of these theories has acquired the imperative of the IQ, however; once a teacher knew the child's IQ, he felt that he had touched the immutable core of the person. It set up his expectations or his lack of expectations for the child and hence, in the subtle way this interrelationship works, the child's achievement. The traditional concept of intelligence also had immense social consequences. Children of the well-to-do tended to have higher IQ's, entered the upper tracks in tracked schools, were expected to do well, and generally did so. These successes supported theories of the basic superiority of the upper socioeconomic levels and were used to justify inequality in income and a disproportionate share of the society's production of goods and services in the general population. In effect the traditional concept of intelligence supported segregations of various kinds: economic, racial, ethnic, and social.

Piaget's concept of intelligence is a different one. It recognizes intelligence as an outcome of the interaction of the human mind with the reality outside itself. This concept puts the emphasis on many early experiences, upon the act, and upon a school curriculum in which the child is in charge, makes decisions, has choices, plans, evaluates, and interacts with peers. This is a school world of objects, textures, machines, books, colors, conversations, people—a universe to interact with. The Piagetian concept of the origin of intelligence gives hope that disadvantaged children can be helped to full participation in the world of the mind. If schools and parents were able to pay attention directly to the development of cognitive and logical stages, compensatory projects would show genuine progress.

THE COPING INDIVIDUAL IN A NOVEL WORLD

For some time researchers have been working with the idea of the "coping individual." "Coping" in this research has a specific meaning, referring to conscious, flexible, purposive, differentiating behavior. This behavior is in contrast to those proceeding from defense mechanisms, which are unconscious, inflexible, driven, culture-bound, and rigid. Research over a 25-year period has shown that there is a positive relation between coping behavior and the fulfillment of the person—his ultimate success.[13] The coping individual is one whose acts are characterized by empathy, logical analysis, objectivity, concentration, tolerance of ambiguity, and intellectuality. In contrast, one whose behavior is generally of a defensive kind is characterized by unconscious, rigid behavior, proceeding from projection, rationalization, denial, isolation, intellectualization, doubt, and indecision.[14]

The members of these contrasting pairs, such as empathy–projection, are to be distinguished from each other in that empathy involves choice, flexibility, and purpose; takes account of reality; and involves differentiated thinking. Projection, on the other hand, is rigid, distorting, compelled, involves less differentiated thinking, and embodies an expectancy that anxiety can be magically relieved.

[13] Norma Haan. "Proposed Model of Ego Functioning: Coping and Defense Mechanisms in Relationship to IQ." *Psychological Monographs* 77 (8): 1–23; 1963.
[14] Norma Haan. "A Tripartite Model of Ego Functioning: Values, Clinical and Research Applications." *Journal of Nervous and Mental Diseases* 148 (1): 14–30; 1969.

In the longitudinal research, coping people tended to accelerate in IQ over a 25-year period, while people whose behavior was defensive tended to show deceleration of IQ over the period. Upwardly mobile people were characterized by coping behavior.

The relation of coping to a world of peace and nonviolence lies in its emphasis on rationality—on the individual's ability to objectify his experience. The solution of the peace-or-violence problem of world society lies in reduction of irrational, unconscious approaches to problems and situations and the development of more persons whose functioning is empathic, rational, and logical.

The promise of the coping method for education is great indeed, albeit only at the beginning. Broadly speaking, the school that helps children become coping persons includes these characteristics:

1. The school encourages children to choose their experiences and to control their environment to a large extent; the children are helped to choose rational solutions to problems of the classroom and beyond. Basically the school must be an open school with open classrooms.

2. Instruction is individualized; assessment is made of where children are in their cognitive and logical development, and curricular experiences are planned to help children progress to the next stages. The teacher is a facilitator.

3. Peer discussions and peer projects are emphasized, in recognition of the importance of the peer relationship in logical and moral growth.

4. The school itself is an open, active, discussing, mildly confronting society.

Selected References

Hugo Boyko. *Science and the Future of Mankind*. Bloomington: Indiana University Press, 1965.

J. M. Cameron. "On Violence." *New York Review of Books,* special supplement, July 2, 1970. pp. 24–32.

David N. Daniels, Marshall F. Gilula, and Frank Ochberg. *Violence and the Struggle for Existence*. Boston: Little, Brown and Company, 1970.

John Dewey. *The Quest for Certainty*. New York: G. P. Putnam's Sons, 1960.

F. Fanon. *Wretched of the Earth*. New York: Grove Press, Inc., 1963.

Else Frenkl-Brunswik. "The Anti-Democratic Personality." In: D. J. Levinson and R. N. Sanford, editors. *Readings in Social Psychology*. New York: Holt, Rinehart and Winston, Inc., 1947.

A. Freud. *The Ego and the Mechanisms of Defense.* New York: International Universities Press, 1966.

J. Glidewell, M. Kantor, L. Smith, and L. Stringer. "Socialization of Social Structure in the Classroom." In: M. Hoffman and L. Hoffman, editors. *Review of Child Development Research.* New York: Russell Sage Foundation, 1966. Volume 2, pp. 221–56.

Aubrey Haan. *Education for the Open Society.* Boston: Allyn and Bacon, Inc., 1962.

Aubrey Haan. *School Environment—Development and Effects.* In preparation.

Norma Haan. "If Violence Were Banished, Would Civility Ensue?" *Contemporary Psychology,* Vol. 15, No. 12; 1970.

Norma Haan. "Moral Redefinition in Families as the Critical Aspect of the Generation Gap." *Youth and Society* 2 (3): 259–84; March 1971.

Norma Haan. "A Tripartite Model of Ego Functioning: Values, Clinical and Research Applications." *Journal of Nervous and Mental Diseases* 148 (1): 14–30; 1969.

Norma Haan, M. Brewster Smith, and Jean Block. "Moral Reasoning of Young Adults: Political-Social Behavior, Family Background, and Personality Correlates." *Journal of Personality and Social Psychology* 10 (3): 183–201; 1968.

Jerry Hirsch. "Behavior-Genetic Analysis and Its Biosocial Consequences." *Seminars in Psychiatry* 2 (1): 59–195; February 1970.

Elliott Jaques. *Work, Creativity, and Social Justice.* New York: International Universities Press, 1970.

Lawrence Kohlberg and Carol Gilligan. "The Adolescent as a Philosopher: The Discovery of the Self in a Post-Conventional World." *Dædalus* 100 (4): 1051–86; Fall 1971.

Daniel P. Moynihan. *The Problem of Violence.* Official Report of American Association of School Administrators. Washington, D.C.: the Association, 1968. pp. 5–18.

Jean Piaget. *Insights and Illusions of Philosophy.* New York: World Publishing Company, 1971.

Karl Popper. *The Open Society and Its Enemies.* Princeton, New Jersey: Princeton University Press, 1950.

M. Rokeach. *The Open and Closed Mind.* New York: Basic Books, Inc., 1960.

Teaching About War, Peace, Conflict, and Change: An Experimental Curriculum Development Project, Initiated and Carried Out in the Schools of Contra Costa County, California. Orinda, California: Diablo Valley Education Project.

Elliott Turiel. "Developmental Processes in the Child's Moral Thinking." In: P. H. Mussen, J. Langer, and M. Covington, editors. *Trends and Issues in Developmental Psychology.* New York: Holt, Rinehart and Winston, Inc., 1969.

Wilson Yandell. *Teaching About Conflict as It Relates to War.* Berkeley, California: Center for War/Peace Studies.

*Simple Song of Freedom**
Bobby Darin

4

Come and sing a simple song of freedom.
Sing it like you've never sung before.
Let it fill the air,
Tell the people ev'ry where
That we, the people here, don't want a war. . . .
No doubt some folks enjoy doing battle,
Like presidents, prime ministers, and kings.
So let us build them shelves
  where they can fight among themselves
  and leave the people be who like to sing.
Let it fill the air,
Tell the people ev'ry where
That we, the people here, don't want a war.

* Copyright © 1969 Hudson Bay Music Company, 1619 Broadway, New York, New York 10019.

25 Examples of Military Power 1970 †

Country	Military Budget Estimated (billions)	Population (millions)	Armed Forces Estimated (thousands)	GNP Estimated (billions)
United States	71.8	205.3	3,161	932.0
U.S.S.R	40.0	244.0	3,305	466.0
France	5.9	50.7	506	140.0
Britain	5.7	55.7	390	109.0
West Germany	5.6	59.0	466	150.0
China (People's Republic)	4.8	750.0	2,780	80.0
Italy	2.4	54.3	413	82.3
Poland	2.2	32.8	242	40.5
East Germany	1.9	17.1	129	32.0
Canada	1.7	21.4	93	67.4
Czechoslovakia	1.6	14.4	168	28.3
Japan	1.6	103.6	259	167.0
India	1.4	550.0	930	42.0
United Arab Republic	1.2	33.0	288	6.3
Australia	1.2	12.6	185	31.7
South Vietnam	1.1	18.0	481*	3.3
Israel	1.0	2.9	75**	4.5
Nigeria	.9	66.0	185	5.2
North Korea	.7	13.6	413	3.0
Brazil	.6	92.5	194	22.9
Pakistan	.6	128.4	324	15.5
North Vietnam	.5	21.9	433	2.3
Argentina	.5	24.3	137	16.5
South Africa	.3	20.0	44***	15.9
South Korea	.3	31.8	645	7.5

* Regular. ** Plus 300 reserves. *** Full time.

FIGURE 4. Source: *The Military Balance, 1970–1971*. London: Institute for Strategic Studies, 1970.

Much of the data can only be approximate. Even the population of China is not certain.

Countries are put in order according to the size of military budgets in dollars as an indicator of military strength. However, military budgets are often not made public, at least not entirely, and must be roughly estimated. Also, conversion into dollars may distort purchasing power in original currency. Finally, cost of supporting one soldier may be much cheaper in some countries than in others; for example, it has been estimated that the United States spends $23,000 per member of the military, whereas China spends $2,400.

† William A. Nesbitt. *Data on the Human Crisis: A Handbook for Inquiry.* New York: Center for International Programs and Comparative Studies of the New York State Education Department, 1972. p. 17. Reprinted by permission.

Let's Listen to Our Children and Youth

4

PART ONE: THE STUDY
Juliette P. Burstermann

CONFLICT and conflict resolution are relevant to every age. They affect the young child in his relations with his parents, his playmates, his school. As he grows older, he becomes conscious of the conflicts in his community, his city, his state, his country, and his world. An open, clear, and honest effort to deal with conflict in all its ramifications and ambiguities can help not only restore relevance to the school but also teach the child to use conflict creatively and constructively. If children and youth are to gain sufficient training to become constructive participants in the complex societies which they now face, then they must learn about conflict—how to analyze it, how to deal with it, how to solve it.

A real contribution to sufficient training can be made by the student if we give him an opportunity to express himself. Furthermore, we must be guided by the fact that research in the intellectual development of the child indicates that at each stage of development the child has a characteristic way of viewing the world and explaining it to himself. The task of teaching a subject or a concept to a child at any particular age is one of representing the structure of the subject or concept in terms of the child's way of viewing things. The work of Piaget and others suggests that one may distinguish several stages in the intellectual development of the child.[1] How then can a teacher develop a meaningful curriculum centering around the concept of peace and consider the most effective means of expanding the cognitive and affective domains? To ask questions which focus on the

---

[1] A clear description of these developmental stages as postulated by Piaget appears in: Barbel Inhelder and Jean Piaget. *The Growth of Logical Thinking from Childhood to Adolescence.* New York: Basic Books, Inc., 1958.

concept is one effective method of developing a concept. We start together, student and teacher, to build the curriculum or to develop a program on the information which the student demonstrates in his responses to the questions and from the information which the student seeks. Careful analysis of the youth's expressions can give us additional valuable material to add to our usual steps of examining research and good practices in the work of curriculum revision.

The Connecticut study, "Teach Us What We Want To Know About Health,"[2] and others have included the expressed wishes, as well as presupposed needs of the person to be taught. Similarly, we should listen to children and youth speaking, drawing, writing, and role playing about the subject of peace. We conducted a study in which we asked the children and young people the following questions:

1. What does the word "peace" mean to you (that is, what do you think about "war and peace")?

2. Who is a peaceful person (that is, what do you learn from your parents and others about peace)?

3. How can we have peace in our town, our state, our nation, and the world (that is, what do you learn directly and absorb indirectly in school about peace)?

Representative—and revealing—answers are quoted in the following pages.

Teachers in 21 towns in Connecticut and Eastern Connecticut State College and faculty members from the University of Georgia, the University of Oklahoma, the Bank Street School for Children in New York, the College Bound Program of the City of New York, a high school in Moretown, Vermont, and a school in Niagata, Japan, assisted in collecting the answers to these questions and supplying meaningful data. The ages of the children and youth questioned ranged from kindergarten through college level. Methods used were interviews, group discussions, written responses to questions, drawings of peaceful activities, tape recordings, and role playing. Two thousand children and youth and five hundred college students participated. The participants were white, black, Oriental, and Indian and came from all the social classes and the major religions.

These youth live in small and large towns and cities and come from rural and urban areas which are agricultural or industrial centers. Their

[2] A report of a survey on health interests, concerns, and problems of students in selected schools from kindergarten through grade 12. Children from inner city, rural, suburban, and high socioeconomic environments were asked these questions: (a) What is good health, or who is a healthy person? (b) What would you like to study in health? (c) What do you want to know about your bodies?

parents are mainly skilled and unskilled laborers; about one-fourth of them are engaged in the professions of law, medicine, and the ministry.

The schools range from traditional to modern. They include public and private elementary schools, comprehensive and technical high schools, and liberal arts and teacher-preparation colleges.

Each teacher included in his data a description of the town, the school, and its philosophy; the class group; and, in a few cases, information about the families of the youths questioned. The material was submitted in the form of expository writing, tables, graphs, and tapes. Written responses, with accompanying drawings, are presented here on the basis of frequency, beginning with the kindergarten level and proceeding through college. After each group of responses are comments on the implications for a "curriculum for peace."

KINDERGARTEN AND PRIMARY CHILDREN, AGES 5 TO 7

What Is Peace?

Peace means quiet in school, in church.
To be quiet, not to fight.
To be alone sitting under a tree reading a book.
No war.
Love.
Family eating supper at night.

Who Is Peaceful?

A peaceful person is someone who doesn't talk when others are talking.
God.
Mom and Dad.
Someone who doesn't fight.
One who helps people in trouble.
Someone who shares.

How Can We Have Peace?

We can have peace if we do not bother somebody when they are doing something.
Don't bother your father when he is listening to the news.
Being friends.
Making the peace sign.

my house when everyone is asleep at night

JAMie

Peace signs

Stop people from doing bad things.
Send people to court.

Primary children think of peace as synonymous with quiet. A nice person is peaceful, and those who "provide" (whether love, care, or food) are peaceful. The way to have peace is to be friendly. These children seem to express themselves more freely by drawing pictures of peaceful or quiet people and things. They relate the concept of peace to themselves or to their families, and they are somewhat aware of the physical happenings in the world around them (as exemplified in the use of the peace symbol).

The vague or erroneous concept of peace as "quiet" should be disturbing to educators. The repression to which the child has been subjected is evident—"peace and quiet." Quietness does not always mean peacefulness. It can mean subjection to authority—teacher, parent, or older peer group. Conflict is a part of life, and even young children can be taught to resolve conflicts peacefully by beginning in the early years to learn to resolve them.

The persons and the family relationships represented in the children's pictures are significant. We want to encourage them to have concern for others, to have some feeling for the roles of members of the family, and to recognize the fact that roles are different without necessarily being limiting. Since each youngster seems to feel a part of his world, it is wise for the adult to begin early to relate large issues to the daily life of the child. Do we know how to do this?

MIDDLE SCHOOL YOUTH, AGES 8 TO 11

What Is Peace?

> Peace means to stop the war and to like people.
> To share your toys, not be selfish.
> To be kind.
> To love.
> To respect others.
> To stop riots.
> Two fingers.
> To be free.
> To obey the law.

Who Is Peaceful?

> A peaceful person is God, Mary, and the whole Saint family.
> The Pope, teachers, parents, priests, nuns, babies.

Dead people.
One who loves people.
One who does not pollute our beautiful country.

How Can We Have Peace?

We can have peace if we stop killing.
Pray to God every day for people not to take drugs or steal.
Obey parents, teachers, older people.
Have peace talks.
Stop complaining and do something about peace.
Treat people equally.
Stop being prejudiced.
By being clean American citizens.
Try to stop wars and things like kidnapping and robberies and crime.

One teacher made a chart of her pupils' responses. Another teacher, reporting from a parochial school, made a graph plotting the jobs of the fathers of the children in her class. The graph supports the fact that the great majority of her students come from hard-working low-middle class families. Other teachers simply categorized responses by sex, male or female.

Some of the lists the eight- to nine-year-old children compiled follow. Note the emergence of the Judeo-Christian ethic in the lists.

What Is Peace?

1. ✌ (two fingers).
2. Quiet.
3. No fighting.
4. Being friendly.
5. Stop the wars.
6. Sharing and kindness.
7. ☮ (peace symbol).
8. Church.

Who Is Peaceful?

1. God.
2. Indians.
3. Peter, my friend.
4. President Nixon.
5. Policemen.
6. Priests and ministers.
7. Queen Elizabeth.

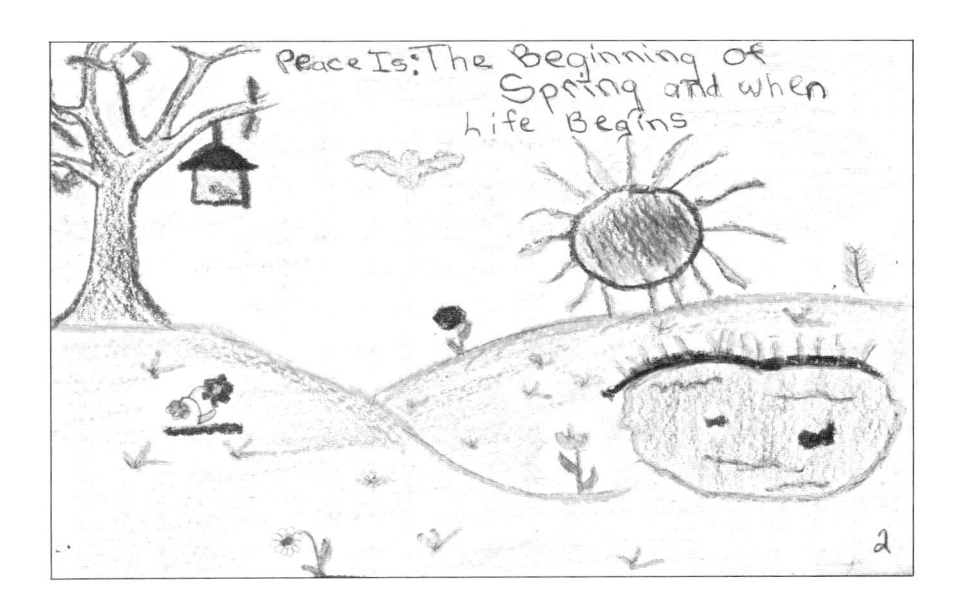

Peace Is: The Beginning of Spring and when Life Begins

How Can We Have Peace?

1. Vote for peaceful people.
2. Stop wars.
3. Arrest people who break the law.
4. Stop people from fighting.
5. Help people.
6. Stop killing.

Here again it can be seen that children of this age group tend to interpret peace as meaning "quiet." They are repeating cultural stereotypes. It seems to be the correct thing, the "in" behavior, to respond to questions posed by adults in such a way as to show respect for society's laws, whether they understand them or not. Curriculum designers must be concerned with acceptance or conformity without an understanding of the real meaning.

These children's responses are less personal than those of the younger group. It is "someone else's job" to stop the wars, arrest the criminal, vote for peaceful people. Teachers need to develop a concern for inner peace and self-involvement. The children's responses can be a place to start to develop personal concern. Rather than leaving the development of beliefs about war and peace to chance, conflict curriculums must be introduced in the schools to offset negative events reported by the news media.[3]

JUNIOR HIGH SCHOOL YOUTH, AGES 11 TO 13

What Is Peace?

Peace means all wars are about people who think they own things that they really don't.

Sharing and not being so greedy and selfish.

Peace is without war, demonstrations, violence.

Friendship and unity, freedom, respect, and cooperation with those in authority.

All races being able to live together.

Who Is Peaceful?

A peaceful person is the Pope, the President, your parents, your teachers.

Everyone is peaceful inside but they get in with the wrong type of people and they fight.

---

[3] Magnus Haavelsrud. "The Development of Views on Peace and War Among Berlin Public School Students." West Berlin: *Journal of Peace Research* 2: 99–120; 1970.

Peace is Brotherhood

William
going out in a boat

Peace of Mind!!

PEACE

LOVE NOT WAR

HELP THE PEACE BIRD

Missionaries, nuns, priests.
No one is peaceful really; only the dead are really at peace.
A kind person who has no enemies.
Political figures like Nixon, Kennedy, Gandhi, Martin L. King.
Religious figures like Jesus.

How Can We Have Peace?

Peace has to begin in the classroom and everyone who sees someone acting peacefully will copy it.
Peace starts in your own home.
Talk peace with groups of people in towns and countries.
Close the gap between generations, drop voting age to 18.
Less riots, live as Christians, stop all wars and come home.
I don't think we can have peace because if we did we wouldn't know what to do with it.

This age group has begun to realize how difficult it is to be peaceful and to have peace. One teacher recorded the number of seventh and eighth grade pupils who reacted the same way to a question. For example, 89 students out of 127 said that peace meant "to end wars"; 57 said that their parents and relatives were peaceful people.

These youths' replies show influence outside the school in the form of some sort of action to stop wars, such as demonstrations, peace movements, and peace talks. Because preadolescents have heroes, one could develop a curriculum around persons who helped, or tried to help, make the world a better place in which to live. These youths lead the way as they refer to political figures like Richard Nixon, John F. Kennedy, and Martin Luther King and to religious figures like Jesus, the Pope, and missionaries. Curriculum builders can supplement such responses by including scientists and inventors (Marie Curie, Thomas Edison), sportsmen, and entertainers, expanding the horizon of persons who have made or are making this world a better place in which to live.

One can begin to see some internalizing about the meaning of peace as these youth say: "Everyone is peaceful inside"; "Peace is sharing"; "Peace starts in your own home." As for questions dealing with peaceful behavior, no more exciting material can be found than the responses of children within the group. Preadolescents are in the process of being "socialized." Many of the boys will seek personal solutions by physical fighting. By now they have all become peer-oriented. If the teacher acts as a truly peaceloving and peacekeeping adult and helps the children find peaceful solutions, some of the children will internalize this behavior.

Although this goal is a very difficult one for any human being to realize and calls for constant self-evaluation of his behavior, the result can be far-reaching. Here, with the help of the adult, the youth can begin a process of evaluation that can transcend personal conflict solutions and can advance through the years to group and finally to international conflict solving. I do not think this is too farfetched or idealistic, for we live in an era when it is more imperative than ever to avoid large-scale wars. The nuclear capability of the great powers is too enormous to allow any other alternative.

SENIOR HIGH SCHOOL YOUTH, AGES 13 TO 16

These responses came from students of a regional technical high school, a Roman Catholic high school, a regional comprehensive high school, and several classes of college-bound youth.

What Is Peace?

Regional technical students replied:
Understanding between persons.
Worldwide friendship.
No wars.
No violence.
Absence of conflict.

Catholic high school students replied:
Tranquillity.
Harmony.
Love.
Cope with conflict.
Not at war.
Compromise.
Equality.

Regional comprehensive high school students replied:
Freedom and equality.
Internal peace.
Controls.
Understanding others and their beliefs.

College-bound students replied:
Having equality.
Not being prejudiced.
Togetherness.

No conflict between people or nations.
Calmness and love.
No crime, racism, bigotry, or fascism in the world.
Alone and free.
Peace of mind.

Who Is Peaceful?

Regional technical students replied:
Dead people are peaceful.
One who never lets himself get too excited.
Does not like war.
Loves the beauty of the land and values other peoples' things.

Catholic high school students replied:
No such thing as a peaceful person.
One who respects laws and is at peace with himself.
Gandhi, Martin Luther King, and one who attains fulfillment.

Regional comprehensive high school students replied:
A peaceful person is a dead person.
One who loves life and people.
One who is not selfish and believes in peace.

College-bound students replied:
One who can cope with life and can know himself.
One who is kind and orderly.
Persons who respect and understand others.
One who does not look for trouble.
No real peaceful people, sorry to say.
God, Martin Luther King, Robert and John Kennedy, Gandhi.
One who cares.

How Can We Have Peace?

Regional technical students replied:
Write to our Congressmen to get them to help stop the war in Vietnam.
By being kind to everyone.
By not being prejudiced.
Also by giving to funds that are fighting for peace.

Catholic high school students replied:
I feel that you can never have peace anywhere.
By total cooperation.
Treat people and all nations fairly.
By reducing the national aggressive characteristics.

Regional comprehensive high school students replied:
Strive for peace.
Unite for a common cause.
Spend money on education.
Develop peaceful leadership.

College-bound students replied:
Never, because there are not enough nonviolent people to overtake the violent ones.
Follow the Ten Commandments.
Give people an opportunity to improve before using strict discipline measures.
Too hard to obtain.
Eliminate racism, oppression, social and economic classes, slums, etc.
Peace must exist in the minds and hearts of men first.
Never, as long as we have selfish men.
Better government.
An idealistic fantasy.
No way to have peace but worth working together for peace.

These high school students seemed to be more pessimistic about the possibility of having peace; however, their meanings for the word "peace" included such words as "understanding," "harmony," "love," "freedom," and "internal peace"—good criteria for a peaceful society, are they not?

These high school youths place emphasis on the fact that people are peaceful when they concentrate on being calm and trying to find a better way than fighting to solve problems. They see some value in coping with conflict rather than concentrating on the negative side of conflict. They recognize the need for diversity of opinion in this pluralistic society; cooperation and compromise are paramount.

The pessimism reflected in the youths' statements must also be dealt with. They say, "No such thing as a peaceful person"; "We can never have peace as long as we have selfish men"; and peace is "an idealistic fantasy." A teacher has to be sensitive enough to learn how most of the students view the nature of man. People do not agree about the basic nature of human beings. Some say that man is basically good, that he can be trusted, that he is loving, kind, intelligent, helpful. Others think that man is basically evil, that he must not be trusted, that he is lazy, selfish, greedy.[4] These feelings shape a person's values. The teacher, the adult, must adjust his objectives for each student on the basis of what he knows about his students' views.

[4] M. E. Wirsing. *Teaching and Philosophy: A Synthesis.* New York: Houghton Mifflin Company, 1972. Chapter 4.

SENIOR HIGH SCHOOL, JAPANESE YOUTH, AGES 16 TO 18

What Is Peace?

Peace means to be living in Japan where we have no war.
A happy family.
Life without dispute, mutual respect, freedom of speech.
A mediocre life.
Freedom.
The word does not appeal to me at all.
No conscription law.
No sacrifices.

Who Is Peaceful?

A peaceful person: people living peacefully, including me.
None.
My parents.
Jesus Christ, Helen Keller, Florence Nightingale, John F. Kennedy, and Albert Schweitzer.
The men who have sway over the world today have strife consciousness and so they are not peaceful.

How Can We Have Peace?

We can have peace by remembering that the important thing is how to adjust the desire among nations, races, or individuals by mutual consideration using our reason.
Strengthening the United Nations.
Using nuclear arms for peace.
Giving up lust for world domination.
There must be no gulf between rich and poor.
No use of armed forces.
No racial discrimination.[5]

These questions were answered by Japanese youths for an American teacher who had lived in Japan and knew them. The questions were considered difficult for them because many of them had not had cause to think about them earlier. The teacher commented:

Most of the children in this class seemed to be in an ecstasy of happiness caused by peace in Japan today. However, others entertained apprehensions

[5] Statements translated by an American teacher in Niagata, Japan.

that peace in present Japan is going in the wrong direction. These few students think seriously about what peace is and they are struggling for peace.

Evidently most Japanese youths think of their future or the future of Japan, but seldom think of world peace. Responses from both American and Japanese youth seem to point out how difficult it is for them to gain an understanding of the world community of which they are a part.

According to Allen D. Glenn:

> Research on children's feelings toward various aspects of the international community speaks of the great intellectual distance that is traversed by children in the span of a few years. At approximately age six, children show almost complete ignorance of the wider international community. Some five years later the overall conceptualization of this community has changed a great deal, and most children have acquired a set of conceptual tools which enable them to organize their environment meaningfully and to make a distinction between their society and other societies.[6]

These comments have significant implications for curriculum development. The key factor in developmental growth may be the extent to which children succeed in differentiating and ordering their ever-widening geographic environment. Until children and youth can do this, it is difficult for them to understand the world community, world problems, and the importance of world peace. Should not the curriculum have an impact on how children and youth view the international community?

COLLEGE STUDENTS, AGES 18 TO 21
What Is Peace?

>Peace means no war.
>A living together with friendship, understanding, and hope.
>Peace is freedom.
>Freedom to think, work, and play without unfair restrictions.
>Inner tranquillity of the soul.
>People unite to make the world better.
>No young boys dying in Vietnam.
>No racial prejudices, no hang-ups on drugs or alcohol, no pain, no sickness, no hate, just a good life.
>Absence of conflict.

Who Is Peaceful?

>A peaceful person is anyone who treats his neighbor as he would expect his neighbor to treat him.

---

[6] Allen D. Glenn. "Elementary School Children's Trust in Nations and Acceptance of Foreign Children." Paper presented at the annual meeting of the National Council for the Social Studies, New York, November 24, 1970.

One willing to consider alternatives to his own viewpoints.
Nonviolent, using mind to solve problems, not fighting.
At rest himself and can communicate this *peace* to others.
A God-fearing person close to beauty and nature.
Gandhi, Martin Luther King, Jesus, Eugene McCarthy, Henry David Thoreau.
No one really.

How Can We Have Peace?

We can have peace through unselfishness as the key.
Tolerance.
A better standard of living for all.
Try to face up to problems and solve them.
The key lies in all of us; *only people* can make "peace" a reality!
Impossible, for man has inherited tendencies which divert his interests to his own pleasurable satisfaction and needs.
A better government that can guide us fairly.
Love is more powerful than hate.
Develop a sensitivity to differences.

These young college men and women, from various ethnic and religious backgrounds, appear to understand the problems involved in making a peaceful world and to be aware of the directions that solutions might take. They see the need for reduction of the many social problems, which in turn can reduce psychological concerns. These young adults see power in better government. Can we help them develop the necessary skills to participate significantly in our universal problem of survival?

As we reflect on these samples of the data collected from thousands of young people, we see relevance to the goal of "Education for Peace: Focus on Mankind." Youth from the North, South, East, and West have spoken. Youth from all races, creeds, and social and economic classes, heterogeneous in ages, abilities, and interests, have shared their ideas.

It is clear that the older youth have some understanding of peace and are able to express their viewpoints about it. They are definitely against violence, and they seem to be aware that to have peace we must have equality of opportunity for all to develop fully. If we define peace as a nonviolent system of conflict resolution, it seems clear that we must find means for increasing tolerance of differences, freedom from fear, and trust in mankind. Are these not some of the tenets of a truly democratic society? How do we help advance these goals? What directions do these conclusions give to a curriculum for peace?

In the process of developing such a curriculum, we need to ask further questions (keeping in mind the developmental and interest levels of the student):

1. What is peaceful behavior? How can one solve conflicts without physical violence?
2. What causes conflicts in today's world?
3. Have nations tried to resolve conflicts and wars? When have nations succeeded? When have nations failed?
4. What kinds of institutions could be created in the future to guarantee nonviolent solutions to conflicts?

And there remains a significant question for those of us engaged in the search for our goal: How can we plan for better use of television, newspapers, and magazines in "Education for Peace: A Focus on Mankind"?

In our time, peace is a vague concept in most people's minds. It will not be easy to develop a curriculum in which students can examine critical questions related to the concept of peace and create their own models of a peaceful world. But it can be done. Each model which can succeed will depend upon man's changing or controlling his own behavior. No one has learned how to do this completely. Can we ever have a peaceful world? We must start somewhere. Who knows what effect a peace curriculum could have on some students?

PART TWO: SOME IMPLICATIONS
Gertrude Noar

AT EVERY age level, children in and out of school are involved in one or another way with conflict. By the time they are four years old, they have begun to fight with siblings and playmates. They are also bystanders, and sometimes pawns, in more or less violent altercations between their parents. When they are adolescents, many of them "wage war" with parents and teachers as they try to emancipate themselves, to move toward independence and decision making with respect to their own lives. In later adolescence, with greater maturity, they participate—directly, indirectly, or vicariously through movies and television—in intergroup conflict and perhaps eventually in international war.

It becomes increasingly essential, therefore, for the young at all levels to have the help of responsible adults (who better than their teachers?) in gaining some understanding and insight into the causes of conflict and the techniques of conflict prevention, and in beginning to think about becoming involved in efforts to solve the human, institutional, and political problems that are responsible for nation-state wars.

In order to plan appropriate learning experiences, teachers need to find out what children and teen-agers (who have never experienced a time of international peace—or even a time in which their own country has not been engaged in war somewhere) already know. Are they ready to grasp and assimilate new relevant information? Are they able to deal with symbols (words and signs) and abstractions (concepts and ideas)? Can they translate particulars into generalizations, or vice versa, and implement their conclusions? What are their personal experiences with conflict as such? What have they been taught in school? What have they absorbed or failed to absorb because their teachers were silent or talked too softly to be heard?

From Part One of this chapter it is apparent that the best answers to such questions come from the young themselves. Young children, it appears, describe peace—and its opposite, conflict—mostly in reference to their own home, school, and neighborhood experiences. When they see peace in larger terms, they say: "Peace is stop war"; "Peace is stop killing." Adolescents move beyond their intimate environments: "Peace is without war, demonstrations, violence"; "It is worldwide friendship; no violence;

absence of conflict." Not all students can comprehend such a world. One writes: "Nothing comes to my mind. Political peace is impossible." Another contends that "peace is an idealistic fantasy." Still another maintains, "Never can attain peace because there aren't enough nonviolent people to overtake the violent ones." One teen-ager muses, "Peace is one of those things you are a lot in favor of, but never really feel within or see without." Another said: "Everyone is turned off by the word; it turns me off. Perhaps it wouldn't if I only knew what people mean by it." Many older adolescents seem to be waiting uneasily or impatiently for the command "Enlist," or, "Register for the draft," or, "Get ready to go to war."

What characteristics do the young think of when they are asked to describe peaceful people? They gave examples of people they evidently use as role models. Many of their ideas of people, as well as of ways of obtaining peace, are based in religion. This tendency was especially noticeable in the replies of parochial school students. For instance, they gave as examples of peaceful people God, Jesus, Mary, the saints, the Pope, ministers, priests, nuns, and missionaries. Nearly all the older children thought of the Reverend Martin Luther King and Mohandas Gandhi as peaceful persons. Some found examples among political leaders and government officials, among them Queen Elizabeth, John and Robert Kennedy, Eugene McCarthy, and Richard Nixon. Japanese youth included Helen Keller, Florence Nightingale, and Albert Schweitzer.

And so one asks: What criteria did these young people use to decide whether or not a particular hero was peaceful or could lead the world toward universal peace? The descriptive terms and phrases they used were "loving," "obedient," "unprejudiced," "unselfish," "quiet," "kind," "respectful of others' rights," "law-abiding," "free of hate," "friendly," "tranquil," "free," "orderly," and "nonviolent." An occasional older and more sophisticated student described the peaceful person as "one who can cope with life, can know himself, and does not look for trouble." Another said, "One who treats his neighbor as he would expect his neighbor to treat him." A third wrote, "One willing to consider alternatives to his own point of view." An older student said, "One who tries to face up to problems and solve them." "Sensitivity to differences" was mentioned by a few.

It became evident that those who found their answers to the questions in previous discussions of or instruction in religion had not learned that many of the bloodiest wars have been religious wars. They had forgotten (if they ever knew) that the Crusades, waged in the name of religion, were often expeditions of marauders who tortured and killed non-Christians. Perhaps even the older students have not seen the hatred of the two religious groups in Ireland or heard the children on either side say that they do not know what Catholics (or Protestants) are but that they hate and are determined to kill them. Have they read about World War II, one wonders, a war in which the Nazis visited upon the Jews the most hideous tortures ever witnessed by mankind?

But the young do have some ideas about conditions that may foster peace. They say that peace is "understanding between people" and is brought about through "compromise." Many replies seem to indicate that the children are thinking about their own personal lives rather than about war. They talk about "good family life," "friendliness," "sharing," "equality," "cooperation with those in authority," "absence of prejudice," "calmness," "inner tranquillity," "tolerance," "love of life and people," "unselfishness," "a better standard of living for all," "a better government," and "using the mind to solve problems."

One of the more mature students has some knowledge of the causes of war: "We must have no racism, bigotry, or fascism in the world." Another thoughtful reply: "Peace must exist in the hearts and minds of men, first." Another suggests that we must "adjust desires among races, nations, and individuals by mutual consultation using reason." Still another reply that indicates insight was: "Give up lust for world domination." Among the students' answers are terse comments about the conditions necessary for world peace: "Absence of fighting"; "No war"; "Treat all nations fairly." Many seem to be thinking mainly about peace within the nation: Eliminate "racism," "oppression," "social and economic classes," "slums," and the "gulf between the rich and the poor." Evidently some students are alluding to forms of government and life styles—and possibly political ideologies other than capitalism, competition, and democracy—about the validity of which they entertain some doubts.

Some of the school children and college students have ideas about what to do to achieve peace. They think that it is necessary to "have peace talks," "to use the two-finger sign," "to vote for peaceful people" (doves rather than hawks?), and "to stop killing and come home." At a little older age, a hopeful respondent suggests that "everyone who sees someone acting peacefully will copy it." And one reminds us that "it has to begin in the classroom."

Older students believe in the efficacy of communication. One says, "Talk peace with groups of people in towns and countries." One, at least, believes in the possibility of direct action: "Stop the war and come home!" Many use words and phrases like "compromise," "controls," "consultation," "reason," "respect for and understanding others and their beliefs." The more mature students agree that "people have to believe in peace," that "strengthening the United Nations" or "giving up the desires for world domination" might do the job. Some express the idea that "peace is freedom," that peace can be secured if "people have freedom to think, work, and play without unfair restrictions."

But not all the young are confident that peace can be secured in their time. The following quotations express their skepticism and even cynicism: "I don't think we can have peace, for if we did we wouldn't know what to do with it"; "No one is peaceful, really. Only the dead are really at peace"; "Dead people are peaceful"; "There is no such thing as a peaceful person."

Erich Fromm distinguishes between "defensive programmed aggression in the service of life . . . and malignant aggression (destructiveness and cruelty), which is specifically human and rooted in the specific conditions of human existence." [7]

The more mature the students, the more they seem to doubt. Some of them expressed their doubts as follows:

Peace is impossible, for man has inherited tendencies which divert his interests to his own pleasurable satisfactions and needs.

The impossible dream! Peace is not possible by the nature of the beast. The day man stops fighting will be the day he dies as a race. The fighting instinct is directly related to the survival instinct.

Some of the older adolescents are without hope. One writes: "It's sad that I can't use this word [peace] without sneering, mimicking, or snickering. We've corrupted, degraded, destroyed it. It's a game, a joke, plastic!" In more or less the same spirit another says: "Well, it would be nice to think of a serene scene, you know, flowers, a cool breeze, but I think of Richard Nixon's peace in Southeast Asia. I think of six years of what I now consider to be futile effort; a large demonstration of uselessness, and beating the old head against the proverbial brick wall." Another response: "Will there be peace in our time? No way, man, no way.

---

[7] Erich Fromm. "Aggression: Instinct or Character?" Letters, *New York Times Sunday Magazine,* March 23, 1972.

No, we like war too much." Still another: "There can never be peace until men look within themselves and . . . on an individual basis rid themselves of selfish ambitions, greed, and the desire to gain material things. The only way is for all to take on a new way of life, free from prejudice and injustice."

Where did the children and teen-agers get their ideas about peace? How soon do small children witness shooting and know that death results? How soon do they see war as a negation of the attempts of parents, teachers, and ministers to affirm the basic supreme worth of the individual and his right to life, liberty, and the pursuit of happiness? Do children experience interpersonal conflict of such severity that they call it war? Many families in our society are in perpetual combat, led by parents who have become enemies of each other and of their children. To many of the young in our society, all adults are "the enemy," and, as adolescence advances, teen-agers seek to escape from the ravages of eternal war at home. They flee, finding refuge in new life styles, in communes based on "love," in other unconventional and possibly antisocial ways of living, in occult religions, or in drug-induced hallucinations.

In most of the schools and colleges from which the participants in the survey came, as well as in most schools across the nation, ruthless competition creates a warlike climate in which the teacher, like every other authority figure, becomes the enemy, cheering on the winners (the "haves" in terms of academic ability) and beating down the losers.

In early childhood, while parents are still the role models for their children, much confusion is created by the difference between what the children see adults do and what they hear those significant others say. One little one said: "My Mom's a Minute Man. She has a gun, and I want one too. I have to learn how to shoot pretty soon, don't I?" Guns come for the little people in Christmas stockings or under the Christmas tree—that symbol of "peace on earth." The shooting soon begins as the Holy Day wears on: "Bang, bang! You're dead!" The obliging adult drops to the floor, dead. Then, when TV brings wholesale killings into the living room—or westerns in which the white men are armed with guns to kill the Indians armed with bows and arrows—the children shriek with glee and, when questioned, say, "But they aren't really dead, you know. They'll be back tomorrow." War is not real. It is only a game. So why worry about peace?

Where do America's young get their ideas about peace? Apparently not often from school. It seems that few of the social studies teachers who helped assemble the papers studied in this chapter had previously discussed international peace with their classes. Few English teachers seem to have considered peace a subject for conversation circles or for themes, compositions, or essays. Perhaps they do not see peace as relevant to the immediate lives of their pupils. Why not? Apparently the history and social studies textbooks, the teachers' guides, and the syllabi gave the subject little attention, a state of affairs not likely to be possible as an aftermath of any of the wars they expect school children to study in detail. And, of course, there are still many teachers who dare not introduce controversial subjects. Is peace controversial? Perhaps the fainthearted might ponder the famous couplet of George Bernard Shaw:

> Some men see things that are and ask, "Why?"
> Others dream things that never were and ask, "Why not?"

Should the teachers of tomorrow's adults be held accountable for failing to stimulate their pupils to dream, to question, to dare to hope for a world at peace?

What of the many books and articles that pour off the presses of the nation, presumably to be used in pre- and in-service education of teachers? For example, to cite at random, in the index of *The Quest for the Dream,* by John P. Roche, there is no reference to peace. Nor is there an article on the subject in *Educational Issues in a Changing Society,* by August Kerber and Wilfred Smith. In *Readings in Curriculum,* composed of 100 articles assembled by Glen Hass and Kimball Wiles, not one selection has to do with education for peace. During the past several years, issues of the most influential educational periodicals have failed to devote their pages directly to peace. In short, peace is not usually included in the behavioral goals of education.

Our readers—presumably teachers of public school and college youth—may well wonder why so little has come from the mouths of so many who answered questions about peace. Why is it so difficult to get meaningful statements about this subject? Perhaps they talk in "body language" more easily than in words. Maybe it is easier for them to pick up signs that someone has tacked to a pole so that it can be held aloft by a member of a protest march—signs that say, "No more war," or, "Get out of Vietnam." It may be easier to lie down on the pavement outside the White House than to answer questions about peace. And few people seem to listen when these protesters engage in violence: "At the University of Wisconsin, more than 3,000 demonstrators marched . . . in a circle around campus buildings, taunting hundreds of city and county policemen, and occasionally *throwing rocks and bottles at them*." [8]

Perhaps running away from the country to avoid going to war is an expression of feelings too deep to be put into words. But do these body-language messages have to do with international peace, or are they an indication that, to use the title of a relevant article written by the vice-president of Brandeis University, "War Is Getting a Bad Name"? [9] Or is the message merely that the young have deep-seated needs to be "in"— to conform to the peer-group pressures to rebel against the Establishment?

"Harvard Center Stormed in New Antiwar Protests." More of the same? "Students pillage offices; smash windows, doors." [10] Is this a "desire for peace," a demand for the rights to life and to be in on decision making, adolescent rebellion, or a perverted idea of what is fun? The teacher had better find some answers!

Is peace an idea whose time has come? Colleges are beginning to see the need for peace studies. Colgate University has a growing interdisciplinary peace studies program which it plans to expand to lead to a major in the field of social science. Paterson State College will soon have a course called Alternatives to Armed Conflict and Social Aggression. Haverford College has a Center for Non-Violent Conflict Resolution. Ohio State University has the Mershon Center, which is devoted to peace research. The Conflict and Peace Group of the University of Pittsburgh is proposing a program that will lead to a certificate. Florida State University offers a seminar on International Law and the Planetary Crisis. And, with this Yearbook, ASCD calls upon the public schools to prepare the young to meet the challenge of peace in our time.

Selected References

"All About the Child: A Special Issue on the Development, Education, and Rights of Children." *Journal of the American Association of University Women* 65 (2): 1–48 (whole issue); November 1971.

Ruth Byler, Gertrude Lewis, and Ruth Totman. *Teach Us What We Want To Know*. New York: Mental Health Materials Center, Inc., 1969.

Margaret Gillespie. *Social Studies for Living in a Multi-Ethnic Society: A Unit Approach*. Columbus, Ohio: Charles E. Merrill Publishing Company, 1972.

[8] *New York Times,* April 17, 1972. Italics added.
[9] *New York Times,* April 18, 1972.
[10] *New York Times,* April 20, 1972.

Allen D. Glenn. "Elementary School Children's Trust in Nations and Acceptance of Foreign Children." Paper presented at the annual meeting of the National Council for the Social Studies, New York, November 24, 1970.

Magnus Haavelsrud. "Teaching About War and Peace." *Bulletin of Peace Proposals.* Oslo, Norway: International Peace Research Institute; Seattle: University of Washington, 1970.

Magnus Haavelsrud. "Views on War and Peace Among Students in West Berlin Public Schools." *Journal of Peace Research.* Oslo, Norway: International Peace Research Institute; Seattle: University of Washington, 1970.

Barbel Inhelder and Jean Piaget. *The Growth of Logical Thinking from Childhood to Adolescence.* New York: Basic Books, Inc., 1958.

John F. Kerr. *Changing the Curriculum.* London: University of London Press, Ltd., 1968.

Muska Mosston. *Teaching: From Command to Discovery.* Belmont, California: Wadsworth Publishing Company, Inc., 1972.

"Ways and Means of Teaching About World Order." *World Law Fund Progress Report,* Vol. 4, No. 1; Winter 1972.

M. E. Wirsing. *Teaching and Philosophy: A Synthesis.* New York: Houghton Mifflin Company, 1972.

Films

Give Peace a Chance. Produced and directed by Gary Keys and Tim Moore. 25 min., 16mm, sound, color. The film reveals the effects of peaceful demonstrations on government officials, as well as on the hopes of the demonstrators themselves.

Rabbit. Produced and directed by Ted Fairchild. 15 min., 16mm, sound, color. A lyrical children's film for adults also. A sensitive study of a nine-year-old boy's first encounter with death.

Song of Innocents. Created by Mark Sadan and Kirk Smallman. 12 min., 16mm, sound, color and b & w. A parable on the nature of violence. We see how innocent people can be moved by violence.

Note: These films are available for rental or sale from Eccentric Circle, Cinema Workshop, P.O. Box 1481, Evanston, Illinois 60204.

*In Bondage**
Claude McKay

*I would be wandering in distant fields
Where man, and bird, and beast, live leisurely,
And the old earth is kind, and ever yields
Her goodly gifts to all her children free;
Where life is fairer, lighter, less demanding,
And boys and girls have time and space for play
Before they come to years of understanding—
Somewhere I would be singing, far away.
For life is greater than the thousand wars
Men wage for it in their insatiate lust,
And will remain like the eternal stars,
When all that shines to-day is drift and dust.*

*But I am bound with you in your mean graves,
O black men, simple slaves of ruthless slaves.*

* From: Claude McKay. *Selected Poems of Claude McKay.* Used by permission of Twayne Publishers, Inc. Copyright 1953 by Bookman Associates, Inc.

Warheads Deliverable by U.S. and Soviet Missiles[†]

Category	United States	Soviet Union
Delivery system	Warheads	Warheads
ICBM	1074	1300
IRBM/MRBM	—	700
Other land-based missiles	(750)	(400)
SLBM	1328	280
Other naval missiles	—	362
Long-range bombers	2250	420
Other aircraft	(2100)	(2200)
Approximate Total	7502	5662

FIGURE 5. *Source: The Military Balance, 1970–1971.* London: The Institute for Strategic Studies, 1970. p. 89. *Note:* ICBM—Intercontinental Ballistic Missile; IRBM—Intermediate-Range Ballistic Missile (1,500–4,000 miles); MRBM—Medium-Range Ballistic Missile (500–1,500 miles). Figures in parentheses are approximate. SLBM—Submarine-Launched Ballistic Missile. The Soviet ICBM SS-9 carries three warheads, each in the 4- to 5-megaton range.

About 6,000 of the U.S. warheads could be delivered to Soviet territory, while only some 2,000 of the Soviet warheads could reach the United States. The U.S. Secretary of Defense said in 1970 that the United States could respond to a Soviet nuclear attack (first-strike) with sufficient force to kill more than 40 percent of the Soviet people and destroy 75 percent of their industrial capacity. Soviet second-strike (response) capacity is not clear, but is believed to be much weaker than the American.

There are at least 50,000 megatons of explosive force in the nuclear arsenals of the United States, Russia, Great Britain, France, and China. Fifty thousand megatons amount to the equivalent of 15 tons of TNT for each man, woman, and child in the world.

[†] William A. Nesbitt. *Data on the Human Crisis: A Handbook for Inquiry.* New York: Center for International Programs and Comparative Studies of the New York State Education Department, 1972. p. 8. Reprinted by permission.

The Heart of the Matter
Theresa L. Held

5

> Rubbishy times create a mountain of rubbishy questions.
> It is the ecological image of Eliot's "distracted from distraction by distraction."
>
> ....
>
> In such times, key questions of decency, justice, peace, the sharing of the world's goods, are lost at the bottom of a cosmic dump.
> A momentous effort of burning, sifting, and removal, if ever the questions of man are to be rescued from the wreckers.[1]

TWO years and two million tons of bombs ago, I proudly accepted an invitation to serve as a member of this Yearbook Committee. My assignment, paraphrased, was to tell teachers in a few pages how they might become more effective teachers of peace. I was well into the chapter I had agreed to write when I was assailed by nagging questions, which I tried to bury by methods familiar to those of us who earn a living selling our talents in the marketplace of ideas. Does the assignment, while it seems to address itself to the burning issue of our times, serve instead to divert our intelligence? Does it summon the ecological image of Eliot's "distracted from distraction by distraction," enabling us to hide the key questions of our times "at the bottom of a cosmic dump"?

[1] Daniel Berrigan. "The Passion of Dietrich Bonhoeffer." In: Kay Boyle and Justine Van Gundy, editors. *Enough Dying! Voices for Peace.* New York: Dell Publishing Co., Inc., 1972. p. 324.

Can I in good conscience give advice to other teachers, when I feel myself to be powerless to influence in any way this country's policy of seeking peace through war? Is this the time to be concentrating on ways of preventing future wars? Perhaps with a little bit of luck and further advances in technology, this war can be kept going forever! Is it not analogous to giving lessons in fire prevention to the victims of a fire while they are still being evacuated from a burning building? Do I believe in my gut that the road to peace can be built with paving stones processed out of lesson plans on ways of preventing war?

To address teachers solely in terms of educating for peace implies that what students learn and feel about war will make a difference. It implies, too, that we can separate problems in foreign affairs from the domestic problems of racism, social inequality, political injustice, poverty, uncontrolled technology. The first assumption is fanciful; the second, naïve at this moment in our nation's history. Educating for peace will not be achieved by literally educating for peace against war. War is the product of a society. Its specific character is dependent upon the organization of society in times of peace.

No aspect of war is intelligible unless it is seen in relation to the organization of society, its technology, its social and political institutions, its material resources, and its morals. Kenneth Keniston in a recent talk suggested that there is a lesson that we might learn by recalling a profession of an earlier day: "We see in retrospect that bleeding was an ineffective cure for the plague, not because the barber surgeons were not good drainers of blood but because they did not sufficiently understand the nature of the disease with which they were dealing."

The heart of the matter is, as I see it, the need to add to the traditional goal of education for socialization the goal of education for politicalization. The challenge is to bring the political process into the main line of education, so that we may cultivate the sophisticated understanding of political power that is required of citizens if democracy in this country is to survive. The problem of achieving and maintaining peace, like the problem of maintaining civil liberties or extending social justice, is a problem of power relationships. It is a problem whose solution will be determined by the outcome of a contest over who is going to determine the means and uses of power. On whom will the responsibility fall for reshaping the uses of power into more democratically responsible instruments, if educators confine their roles in the contest to those of impartial spectators or hard-working cheerleaders?

In one of a series of thought-provoking articles on "politics in the arena," John S. Mann addressed himself to those educators who view politics as a diversion from their main concern of teaching students, who believe that politics should be kept out of the academic world for fear of contamination. He reminded us that the decision is not ours to make; like it or not, we have been pushed into the political arena, and the gates have closed behind us. Mann contended that political power is of major concern to educators in at least three ways:

First, the effort to influence curriculum decisions is an exercise in political power. Such decisions are made, not on the basis of direct inference from definitive scholarly findings, but rather on the basis of a complex interaction of forces representing different interests, values, beliefs, and knowledge systems. Second, since "Political Power" is a ubiquitous fact of societal existence, and since a democracy depends for its vigor and justness upon equitable distribution of power, it is proper that the citizens' schools offer extensive opportunities for learning about how political power operates. Third, there are growing numbers of students who find our schools oppressive, inane, misconceived, and mismanaged, and who consequently are interested and involved in developing . . . political power. . . . [2]

It would be a cop-out not to try to answer, however superficially, the pragmatic questions arising from the theoretical position of Mann's article. It is a position which argues that the goal of teaching for political effectiveness is a satellite goal to that of teaching for peace. How do we teach young people to acquire and use the available levers of power to end war—or poverty or racism or repression or hypocrisy in high places or any of the other ills of our society? What kinds of curriculums do we need, what kinds of teachers, teaching in what kinds of schools? I shall limit myself to a brief description of specific objectives which suggest a promising direction for planning curriculums and a consideration of some teacher understandings and attributes which can be characterized as sociopolitical competencies.

In designing a model for urban schools, Mario Fantini and Gerald Weinstein formulated a set of objectives, in addition to symbolic technical-proficiency skills, which have been extremely helpful to teachers struggling to conceptualize goals designed to help children learn, at an early age, socially desirable ways of being politically effective:

1. To have the children acquire the skills of negotiating with adults

---

[2] John S. Mann. "Political Power and the High School Curriculum." *Educational Leadership* 28 (1): 23–26; October 1970.

2. To have the children devise a variety of strategies for getting something they want

3. To have the children learn to identify the real power sources in their community

4. To have the children develop the skills of organizing people in order to create some change in their immediate social realities

5. To have the children learn to use all forms of media in order to gain support for some social action they intend to take

6. To have the children develop general skills for constructive social action such as

   a. The ability to define clearly the objectives of social action

   b. The ability to evaluate the existing situation, to identify obstacles to the goal, and to identify the available resources for overcoming these obstacles

   c. The ability to analyze and to generate alternative measures for action, and to predict the various outcomes of each alternative

   d. The ability to select the most valuable of these alternatives and to test them through action

   e. The ability to evaluate the tested procedure and to revise strategies, thus beginning the cycle again.[3]

Fantini and Weinstein believe that, if curriculums were developed with such objectives as their focus, we would begin to see a more intrinsic linkage between a teaching task and descriptions of powerlessness.

It is not hard to understand why in the past few years many persons have become more vocal in demanding that our schools make clear their commitment to the goal of a humanist society.

What kinds of teachers do we need to move us closer to that goal? That this question has been raised by every philosopher since the beginning of time—and by every educator of teachers since teacher education was institutionalized—is known to all of us. The question is also the best conversation killer I know, even among concerned intellectuals. The answers that have appeared in print have consumed enough paper to be regarded as a not-too-minor cause of the depletion of our forests. The following comments, I believe, sum up the conclusions we have reached about the kinds of understanding, attitudes, and commitments which our times demand.

- *We need teachers who understand:*

that a profession becomes corrupt and its practitioners irrelevant when it

---

[3] Mario Fantini and Gerald Weinstein. *Making Urban Schools Work.* New York: Holt, Rinehart and Winston, Inc., 1968. pp. 27–28.

limits its concerns to doing better what it has done before without regard to the changing needs and demands of society.

that they must be more than disseminators and accumulators of knowledge; that they must, in the words of Benjamin DeMott, be "grapplers with immediacy, bidding for influence in the shape of public policy even in the act of teaching, laboring to possess the teacher's experience in a new way." [4]

that society is inside man and man is inside society, and that one cannot understand anything about a person, young or old, unless he understands about the world in which that person is living and the forces in his world that have the power to make him what he is and to prevent him from being what he might become.

that we shall never achieve humaneness until we cultivate sincere respect for differences—respect not only for different ethnic groups, cultural groups, age groups, and economic groups but also for different ideas, goals, and life styles.

that as long as there is "murder in the classroom," [5] as long as school is an army game in which students, like teachers, are forced to develop various adaptive attitudes and strategies to survive, we shall not succeed in teaching for peace.

that, if children learn that what are valued most in the classroom are docility and conformity, they will have learned a lesson that can make them obedient servants of malignant authority all their lives. There may be a closer correlation between Lidice and My Lai and the teacher-student relationship in its conventional form, "a form of institutionalized dominance and subordination," [6] than we are willing to believe.

that one of the most important contributions we can make to the development of young people is to help them learn not only what is expected of them by the system but also how they can work in relation to other people to cope with the systems that control their lives.

---

[4] Benjamin DeMott. *Surviving the 70's.* New York: E. P. Dutton & Co., Inc., 1971. p. 25. Copyright © 1971, 1970, 1969 by Benjamin DeMott. Used by permission.

[5] Charles Silberman. "Murder in the Schoolroom." *Atlantic* 225 (6): 83; June 1970.

[6] See: Willard Waller. *The Sociology of Teaching.* New York: John Wiley & Sons, Inc., 1937.

that schools are institutions reflecting the culture in which they exist, and that it may be at least as necessary to work for institutional change as it is to work for changes in pupils or teachers or administrators.

- *We need teachers who are aware:*

of the rationalizations by which we hide unconscious forces in our lives.

of the real possibilities among which we in this country can still choose.

of the consequence of one choice as against other choices.

of the fact that awareness is effective only when it is accompanied by the will to act.

that unquestioning docility and compliance may pose more serious threats than anger and turbulence.

that there is a difference between conflict and violence, and that conflict is an essential ingredient in human relations.

that, before the universal application of higher values can be achieved, the basic needs of life must be met; that it is folly to ask a man to be human if his very existence is in doubt.[7]

that "a merely well informed man is the most useless bore on God's earth." [8]

that, if education is to be a cultural force in shaping attitudes and inciting to action, it must be inspired, colorful, and dramatic.

that, to develop a healthy personality, it is necessary to tip the balance of learning on the side of critical inquiry, discovery, and independence, as opposed to repetition, regurgitation, and regimentation.

- *We need teachers who recognize:*

what their personal needs are, who face up to their own sadistic tendencies and their own fear of standing firm on humane principles against the power of authority.

that the situation in which youth find themselves today is not the same as it was when the teachers were young; that, since the youth are not as

---

[7] Edmund Gordon. "Building a Socially Supportive Environment." In: Alice Miel and Louise Berman, editors. *Educating the Young People of the World.* Washington, D.C.: Association for Supervision and Curriculum Development, 1970. pp. 59–70.

[8] This quotation has been attributed to Alfred North Whitehead.

their teachers were, and since their situation is not one that the teachers experienced, the means by which the teachers were "socialized" may have little relevance for them.

that there are only two possible ways by which they can guide youth: either they try to alter the world in which they live or they try, by understanding that world, to relate students to it and in some sense enter into it.

the value of those few persons who dare to strike boldly at the roots of evil while the rest of us passively look on.

that, whether they know it or not and whether they like it or not, teachers are idealogues, telling their students what they value by what they talk about or fail to talk about, by what actions they take or fail to take.

the indicia of humbug displayed by public officials—paranoid anticommunism, argumentative overkill, selective moralizing, ignorance, contempt of facts—and in turn help their students recognize these.

- *We need teachers who see themselves:*

as motivated inquirers and self-directed, ongoing learners.

as agents of change, rather than as defenders of the status quo, who remember that by their choice of profession they expressed at least a reservation about some of the dominant values in American society.

as advocates for students and parents.

as ombudsmen concerned with control of the quality of the educational process.

- *We need teachers who will commit themselves to:*

constant scrutiny of the purposes for which they are educating and the ways in which content and methods fulfill or fail to fulfill that purpose.

the elimination of all those practices and procedures in our schools which contribute to alienation and dehumanization—segregated classrooms, ability grouping, tracking, discipline through external controls, arbitrary and mysterious criteria of evaluation.

vigilance in reviewing those practices in our society that deny freedom, equality, and justice for all.

the assumption of responsibility to serve as channels through which the passionate yearnings and just grievances of the oppressed anywhere in the world can influence the power structure for good.

What conclusions about teaching to achieve a world without war make sense at a moment in history when even the most sanguine among us recognize that the Pentagon's plan for ending the war in Indochina might end not only the war but also the world?

> Again and once again
> the master pulls the strings
> demands consensus and the puppets dance.
> I tremble for my country
>   ashamed,
> that we must walk with downcast heads,
> And what will history tell of us
> who let such monstrous things go on? [9]

History tells us that we should have done more than train others to think and feel in morally and politically "adequate" ways. Fifteen years ago C. Wright Mills, foreseeing the possibility of a third world war, addressed himself to us in strong language:

> When intellectuals have the chance to speak yet do not speak, . . . when they do not demand that the secrecy that makes elite decisions absolute and unchangeable be removed, they are part of a massive conspiracy to kill off public scrutiny. When they do not speak, when they do not demand, when they do not think and act as intellectuals, and so as public men, they contribute to the moral paralysis that now grips both the leaders and those they lead.[10]

As DeMott concluded, history will tell us that we must "be more, as men, than we're permitted to be by the rule of role and profession and that the life of dailiness and habit, the life that lives us, directs us to the point of suppressing moral conscience and imagination is in truth no life at all." [11] History has taught us that "we need have no fears lest the fairest towers of former days be insufficiently defended. At every crossway on the road to the future there have been placed against us ten thousand men to guard the past. There are men enough about us whose exclusive duty it is to extinguish the fires which we kindle. The least that the timid among us can do is not to add to the immense dead weight which nature drags along." Thus, Maurice Maeterlinck spoke to those who set out to find the bluebird of happiness.

---

[9] Nan Braymer. "Five Day Requiem for Vietnam." In: Kay Boyle and Justin Van Gundy, editors. *Enough Dying! Voices for Peace.* New York: Dell Publishing Co., Inc., 1972. p. 293.

[10] C. Wright Mills. *Causes of World War III.* New York: Simon & Schuster, Inc., 1958. p. 130. Copyright © 1958 by C. Wright Mills. Reprinted by permission of the publisher.

[11] DeMott, *op. cit.*, p. 25.

Selected References

Note: In addition to the following authors and their writings, I am particularly indebted to Professors Edmund J. Gordon, Dan Dodson, Alvin Loving, Noam Chomsky, and Robert J. Lifton, whose articles and speeches have greatly influenced my thinking and the formulation of my position.

Anthony Austin. *The President's War.* New York: J. B. Lippincott Company, 1971.

Richard J. Barnet. *The Roots of War.* New York: Atheneum Publishers, 1972.

Peter Berger. *Invitation to Sociology: A Humanistic Perspective.* New York: Anchor Doubleday, 1963.

Barbara Biber. *Schooling as an Influence in Developing Healthy Personality.* Boston: Harvard University Press, 1965.

Dorothy D. Cohen. *The Learning Child.* New York: Pantheon Books, 1972.

Robert Coles. *Children of Crisis.* Boston: Little, Brown and Company, 1964.

Ryland W. Crary. *Humanizing the School: Curriculum Development and Theory.* Bank Street College of Education Publication. New York: Alfred A. Knopf, Inc., 1969.

Benjamin DeMott. *Surviving the 70's.* New York: E. P. Dutton & Co., Inc., 1971.

Mario Fantini and Gerald Weinstein. *Making Urban Schools Work.* New York: Holt, Rinehart and Winston, Inc., 1968.

Erich Fromm. *The Heart of Man.* New York: Harper & Row, Publishers, 1964.

H. D. Graham and T. R. Gurr. *The History of Violence in America: A Report to the National Commission on the Causes and Prevention of Violence.* New York: Bantam Books, Inc., 1969.

Jules Henry. *Culture Against Man.* New York: Random House, Inc., 1963.

Robert R. Leeper, editor. *Curricular Concerns in a Revolutionary Era: Readings from Educational Leadership.* Washington, D.C.: Association for Supervision and Curriculum Development, 1971.

Harry McPherson. *A Political Education.* New York: Atlantic Monthly Press, 1972.

C. Wright Mills. *Causes of World War III.* New York: Simon & Schuster, Inc., 1958.

Gertrude Noar. *Individualized Instruction: Every Child a Winner.* New York: John Wiley & Sons, Inc., 1972.

L. Raths, M. Harmin, and S. Simon. *Values and Teaching.* Columbus, Ohio: Charles E. Merrill Publishing Company, 1966.

Milton Schwebel. *Who Can Be Educated?* New York: Grove Press, 1968.

Mary-Margaret Scobey and Grace Graham, editors. *To Nurture Humaneness: Commitment for the 70's.* ASCD 1970 Yearbook. Washington, D.C.: Association for Supervision and Curriculum Development, 1970.

Willard Waller. *The Sociology of Teaching.* New York: John Wiley & Sons, Inc., 1937.

Charles A. Willis. *Nixon Agonistes.* New York: Houghton Mifflin Company, 1970.

To You, People
Yevgeny Yevtushenko

Along ulitzas,
    streets,
        along rues
           and *along* calles
you are walking after work,
    pushing one another.
I am joining you
    and don't repent of it.
You've become weary
    You've become nervy
You've grubbed down into the bowels
    of the earth.
        You've reached up to the stars.
But it seems to me—
    You still haven't begun to exist.
In your lips is a Camel,
    a Gitane,
        a Novostj,
and each of you is like
    a separate novel,
a separate heart,
    a separate conscience.
Under every beret,
    cap,
        sombrero,
there is a separate measure for the
    immeasurable world,
separating beliefs into separate
    compartments.
But as you drink your absinthe,
    your vodka,
        your chianti,
just for a moment you cease to be
    separate,
and become mankind in your own eyes.
So you can love one another
    unite your separate novels
into a common novel—
    your separate consciences
into a common conscience.
I would like to predict all this for you,
and in this prediction not discredit
    all that I would like to strengthen
        in life.
No,
    I am not begging to be a prophet,
        or a judge,
but you must forgive me—
    if like a bore I keep on nagging
and repeating to you, the people:
    "We are people.
        We are people.
We are people.
    We argue,
        grumbling and snapping,
at times we jealously trample on
    one another,
but our separateness—
    as you know—is false, in
        general.
We the people
    don't exist separately.
By forgetting others . . .
    you forget yourself,
by killing others . . .
    you kill yourself. . . ."

* From: *Bratsk Station and Other New Poems* by Yevgeny Yevtushenko. Copyright 1966 by Sun Books Pty Ltd. Reprinted by permission of Doubleday & Company, Inc.

Destructiveness of Nuclear Weapons[†]

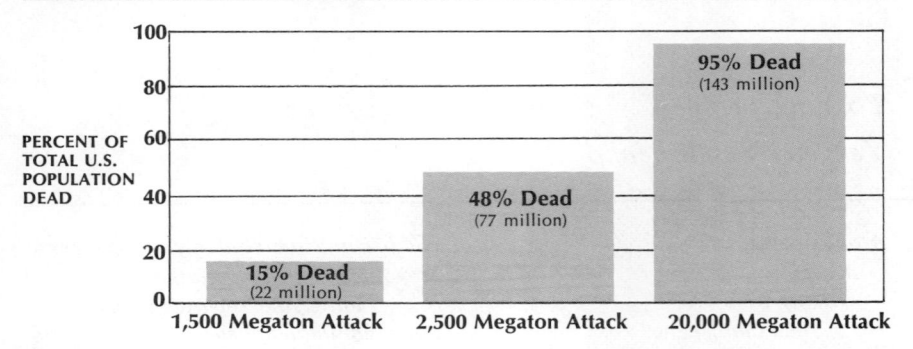

[Bar chart: PERCENT OF TOTAL U.S. POPULATION DEAD]
- 1,500 Megaton Attack: 15% Dead (22 million)
- 2,500 Megaton Attack: 48% Dead (77 million)
- 20,000 Megaton Attack: 95% Dead (143 million)

FIGURE 6. Government study of the effect upon the U.S. population (1950: 150,699,000) from nuclear attack. *From:* Amitai Etzioni and Martin Wenglinsky. *War and Its Prevention.* New York: Harper & Row, Publishers, 1970.

Congressional hearings in 1959 revealed that less than 200 megatons of bombs dropped over American cities could result in over 40 million deaths, with millions more injured. (One megaton is the equivalent in explosive force to one million tons of TNT.)

A biologist, Tom Stonier, in his book *Nuclear Disaster* (World Publishing Company, 1964) provides the following information about a 20-megaton bomb if it were exploded over New York City:

1. About six million out of the eight million inhabitants of the city would die, as would about one million outside of the city.

2. If the bomb were exploded at ground level, it would create a hole 640 feet deep and over 2,700 feet wide.

3. Ordinary brick or wood-frame houses would be completely demolished over seven miles away.

4. The small atom bomb dropped over Hiroshima (20 kilotons, or the equivalent of 20,000 pounds of TNT) caused fires over an area of 4.5 square miles. A 20-megaton bomb, falling on a clear day, could cause fires over more than 1,000 square miles.

5. Lethal levels of radioactive fallout, depending on wind and weather conditions, would spread over an area of 4,800 square miles. (Another authority has stated that the fallout of a 7,500-megaton attack on the United States could so contaminate the land that it would be virtually impossible to grow any safe food. Both Russia and the United States could launch much larger attacks.)

6. Other effects of even a single 20-megaton bomb over New York City would be the spread of infectious diseases, including plagues; severe ecological imbalance over a wide area; long-range genetic damage; increase of cancer, especially leukemia; etc.

7. Social effects for the entire country could include economic collapse, mass hysteria, and psychological damage, and possible political dictatorship.

[†] William A. Nesbitt. *Data on the Human Crisis: A Handbook for Inquiry.* New York: Center for International Programs and Comparative Studies of the New York State Education Department, 1972. p. 4. Reprinted by permission.

International and Cross-Cultural Experiences

James M. Becker

6

OUR educational system has never been free from the conflicts and tensions that divide society at large. In periods of explosive social changes, schools, like other social institutions, are likely to be under conflicting pressures both to reform and to preserve traditional roles. Today the public schools are more and more often drawn into the center of social tumult and are at the same time the object of community protest, taxpayer revolt, and student unrest. Indeed, our public schools have become arenas of struggle for groups advocating competing views of the good society.

The pressures and concerns of contemporary life have already left an indelible imprint on the schools and what they teach. The steady escalation of violence in our generation, the pervasive influence of the military-industrial complex, the controversy over disarmament, racial conflicts, and the growing assertiveness of the poor and the underprivileged have sparked many classroom efforts to deal with the problems of peace, war, violence, conflict, and justice. Yet these are not simply academic issues in the traditional sense. Today's students are often participants in, as well as observers of, many of the social issues being discussed in class. This means that they need to know how to handle not only cognitive issues but also value questions. Furthermore, the goal of "participatory democracy" has elevated the question of school governance to a new significance, so that the issues of what schools ought to teach and how they should be organized and managed can no longer be neatly separated. All this adds up to the fact that individuals and groups advocating curricular change must provide a context that is broad and varied enough to encompass a welter of influences and pressures formerly regarded by many educators as peripheral. The focus needs to be on a social-change strategy rather than merely on a technical-assistance program for teachers and administrators.

THE WORLD AS A DEVELOPING NATION

We are in the midst of what amounts to a global social revolution. Geographically, technologically, and, to a large extent, economically, the world has become a single system—a fact dramatically attested to by the spectacular view of the earth from the moon. Yet, because science has altered both the physical environment and human society so much in such a short time, many of our attitudes, traditions, and institutions have become dangerously outmoded. Man's habits, his thoughts, his actions seem to run counter to his existence. After a few hundred thousand years of evolution, man's instincts and loyalties still seem to be largely tribal. Ethnocentrism and national pride continue to be strong and often destructive forces. In many respects, relations among peoples and nations are conducted today as they were centuries ago.

Today's increased openness about personal feelings and pride in ethnic identification may help man overcome some of the destructive and hostile impulses that underlie ethnocentrism and narrow nationalism. The penetrating influence of technology also serves to undermine traditional ways of thinking and acting, thereby making obvious the need for drastic changes in attitudes and behavior. The "superculture" of airports, expressways, birth control, artificial fertilizers, skyscrapers, space satellites, and universities is worldwide in scope. Science is becoming a common ideology. This condition raises doubts in the minds of many, especially the young, about the relevance of many of our present habits and institutions.

However, the world still has a great deal of ethnic and nationalistic bitterness to live down before better communication, easier translation, and greater understanding of human behavior will make it seem natural for people to react to each other as human being to human being across ethnic and national boundaries. We may be impressed by the evidence of an emerging superculture, but the grim fact remains that some nations have the power to destroy other nations—and perhaps the world—in a matter of seconds.

There is a desperate need for broad public understanding of the natural, political, economic, and social systems that comprise the human environment. An effective basis must be found for cooperative efforts among peoples and nations to enhance the building and maintaining of new outlooks, traditions, and life styles that give meaning and zest to all men's lives. All nations have this need, and no nation has made significant progress toward meeting it. In this respect all countries are "developing nations." This common condition among peoples and nations offers challenging opportunities for collaboration.

A recent report of the U.S. Senate Committee on Foreign Relations suggests that we look upon the world community as a developing nation. It points out that,

> as a composite, the community of nations is much like a developing country. Its government—the United Nations—is embryonic and almost incidental to the needs of its constituency; its distribution of wealth is lopsided and the gulf between its rich and poor increases in near-geometric proportions; its benefits are often wasted on imagined threats; and its vested interests resist meaningful reforms.[1]

Obviously, education cannot furnish the total answer to such a challenge. It can, however, play a significant role, and it is in this context that programs in intercultural and international education need to be developed.

Although this chapter focuses on developing programs in international and cross-cultural experiences in American schools, readers should keep in mind the fact that national programs adequate for today's challenges can be facilitated and perhaps achieved only by transnational cooperation.[2]

EDUCATION TOWARD HUMANITY

If nations could think of education not as the road to power, prosperity, and prestige, but as the road to the full humanity of their populations, the prospects for international and world studies would brighten immensely. In most countries, however, this is far from the case. In the United States, teachers are, in a sense, still seen as part of the nation's defense system. For example, the National Defense Education Act is seen as a means of improving the quality of teaching in selected content areas. Materials available to teachers often contain inaccuracies resulting from our government's strategic considerations. The State Department holds briefings and the Defense Department spends millions of dollars so that foreign policy

---

[1] *The United Nations: The World as a Developing Country.* Washington, D.C.: Superintendent of Documents, U.S. Government Printing Office, June 1971.

[2] ASCD, the World Law Fund, UNESCO, and the International Studies Association are among the groups already much involved in transnational education programs.

and defense policy can be interpreted "correctly" in our nation's classrooms. Civil defense drills, ROTC units, and emphasis on "patriotism" are further evidences of the extent to which our schools are part of the system of threat, power, and prestige in international relations.[3]

Moreover, the emphasis on national prestige and power has made it logical and necessary that schools be judged on the basis of their contribution to nationalistic ambition. Education has thus become synonymous with indoctrination and training. The schools function largely to process, grade, and label students for the market. The net result is often to discard or reject many children as unlikely contributors to the national interest and, therefore, not deserving of education.

The explanation for this phenomenon is not hard to find. It does not, as was once claimed, lie in the inherent incapacity of men of any color, nationality, or social status. Rather, it is attributable to the fact that those in power have monopolized the resources of education to keep the avenues of opportunity and privilege open primarily to themselves.

As long as the framework for international education is based on the notion that education, like military power, is but a means to achieve national ambitions, progress in building better cross-cultural and global relations among peoples and nations is likely to be incidental and haphazard. Education viewed solely as a matter of getting ahead is divisive at local, national, and international levels. The need is to devise a system that educates all comers, rich and poor, foreign and domestic, to full humanity.

FAILURES IN THE NATION-STATE SYSTEM

Violence characterizes much of our life. Crime in the streets, polarization of the races, student unrest, the Vietnam War, tension in the Middle East, police brutality—all are evidence of the lack of peace in the world. Perhaps the most dangerous lag in our time is the failure of nation-states to come to grips with the imperatives of globalism. Man has no plans for conserving the global entity of which he is a part, no organization for sustaining it, no vision of the essential unity of himself and his environment. Instead, he has developed a system of national allegiances and

---

[3] "Children and War." *Newsletter,* Vol. 32, No. 1; September 1971. Publication of the Institute of Administrative Research, Teachers College, Columbia University.

national sovereignties that recognize and serve national interests as the supreme good. This system will have to be changed if man is to survive.

Harold Lasswell has pointed out that "all men are by birth human. They belong potentially to the nation of man. But at birth all men are absorbed into territorial and pluralistic groups whose members may deny the claim of the whole community to have the final word in conflicts among these lesser entities."[4] Erich Fromm tells us that man cannot do without human groups.[5] Self-love or social narcissism is necessary for group survival, but its form may be either benign or malignant. The chauvinistic love of the group merely because it exists is a major obstacle to building and maintaining relationships with other groups.

"Throughout history," John H. Herz has written, "that unit which affords protection and security to human beings has tended to become the basic political unit; people, in the long run, will recognize that authority which possesses the power of protection."[6] Today, however, the power to penetrate or bypass the "protective shell" has rendered obsolete the traditional defense structure of nations. The development of nuclear weapons and modern missile systems with unlimited range, supersonic speed, and automatic guidance has obliterated the relative security of the territorial state, and has thereby generated a totally new set of conditions for world politics. The nation-state is no longer able to provide security for its citizens.

Because of this unprecedented set of circumstances, the most powerful nations may paradoxically also be the most vulnerable. The last three presidents of the United States have as much as admitted that the government cannot defend the American people from nuclear attack. In fact, one might persuasively argue that governments can only endanger people by making them hostages in power confrontations. Much of what is proposed in the name of national security not only fails to protect citizens but actually increases the danger to their lives.

Without the ability to protect its citizens, a national government has lost an important basis for authority—and perhaps its very *raison d'être*. According to Hans Morgenthau, "The nation-state as presently constituted has become the greatest threat to life, liberty, and the pursuit of happiness

---
[4] Harold Lasswell. "Multiple Loyalties in a Shrinking World." Address to National Council for the Social Studies, November 29, 1968.

[5] Erich Fromm. *The Heart of Man*. New York: Harper & Row, Publishers, 1964.

[6] John H. Herz. "Rise and Demise of the Territorial State." *World Politics* 9 (4): 473–93; 1957.

of the individual citizen." He refers to the present situation as a momentous and threatening paradox: namely, that modern technology has made the nation-state as obsolete a principle of political organization as the first industrial revolution did of the feudal system.[7]

Yet, despite its inadequacies, the nation-state is ascendant throughout the world. Nation-states still circumscribe the loyalties and identities of virtually all the world's peoples; and, through the nation-state, mankind is still locked into a precarious structure of rivalry and warfare that, in form at least, represents an archaic holdover from previous centuries.

This highly organized system of nuclear threat and counterthreat, which has infected every aspect of human society, is potentially and indeed actually damaging to millions of persons, even if the missiles and bombs are never used. The turmoil and social disintegration apparent in so many of the world's nations are due, at least in part, to the distorted priorities, unbalanced economies, and warped psychologies created by the system of warfare threat. In rich as well as poor nations, precious human and material resources are diverted from programs designed to support the nourishment of life and the improvement of the environment to those designed to manufacture tools of destruction and death.

The disastrous results of such diversion can be seen not only in the decay of cities and the mounting of tensions between rich and poor, but also in our inability to deal with the technological aggression that is polluting air, water, and land. Our preoccupation with the warfare-threat system has left us powerless to deal with poverty, racism, overpopulation, disease, and deterioration of housing—all major causes of the despair and hatred that explode into violence.[8]

To come to grips with this situation requires nothing less than a redirection of human energy and material resources that is both massive in scale and global in scope. As individuals and societies, we need to achieve a wider and more varied human identity than that provided by the obsolescent nation-state. At the same time, we must act to change the war-threat system that permeates our international and domestic lives. Accomplishing these goals will necessitate dealing with such far-flung considerations as access to worldwide communications systems, uses of the sea bed and outer space, limitation of armaments, and development of

---

[7] Hans Morgenthau. "Are National Self-Interests and World Politics Compatible?" *Social Education* 34 (1): 49; January 1970.

[8] Richard A. Falk. *The Endangered Planet.* New York: Random House, Inc., 1971.

human and material resources. It will also mean restructuring our educational system, which, along with those of many other countries, is so rooted in the war-threat system that it contributes to greater national hostility, not to a recognition of interdependence and the need for cooperation.

Viewed in this perspective, peace education is not so much an idealistic dream as a need to reduce the militarization of our economy and our educational system to the point where problems like poverty and pollution can receive the attention needed to improve man's chances of survival.

ILLUSIONS AND FOLKLORE

There is probably more self-deception, wishful thinking, hypocrisy, and illusion in discussions of peace and war than in considerations of any other concern of modern man. Yet it is potentially riskier to suffer delusions on this subject than on almost any other. Unwillingness to confront the real issues, combined with the inability to perceive the truth about our own motivations and behavior, can lead nations—like individuals—to assume frozen postures of indignation and self-righteousness that are as dangerous in their way as the arms race.

Basic to efforts to grapple effectively with issues of peace and war is a willingness to recognize that human beings are capable of dominating, exploiting, oppressing, enslaving, and destroying one another in a "peaceful" manner. Thus peace as viewed by one group of persons may mean exploitation or oppression to another group. "Peace" in this sense is not always a desirable state of human affairs. In fact, the real issue may not be the choice between war and peace. Peace can be achieved by sacrificing vital interests or even survival. Prisons and cemeteries are logical realizations of such an ideal.

The real dilemma and the real issue is, what kind of peace? Different persons wanting different and incompatible kinds of peace may better explain how conflicts develop than mere claims that some persons want war and others want peace. Political issues and even political "facts" tend to be judged according to the point of view from which they are regarded. This tendency manifests itself in such delusions as, for example, a conviction that one party in a dispute (the "aggressor") is always and necessarily wrong, while the one who fights in defense is always and necessarily right. The result is the seemingly logical but actually misleading conclusion that one who is attacking an injustice is committing a crime of aggression while the one who defends the status quo is fighting for a just cause.

It may be equally illusory to assume that men of good will are always peaceloving while "bad" people are always prone to start wars. Yet in many instances it is impossible to determine who actually "started" a war. Furthermore, the real question may be not who started the war, but what were the important issues and events preceding the outbreak of the conflict.

The truth is that it is often the privileged who are "peace loving" because they want to enjoy their privileges in peace, while the "have-nots" are the troublemakers and aggressors. This is not to argue that violence is an automatic reaction to misery and suffering; but, to the extent that it is effective in reaching the goal that must justify it, violence is rational.[9] Few people react violently to the outbreak of a disease that is beyond the powers of medicine to cure, or to an earthquake, or to social conditions that seem to be unchangeable. Only when it appears that conditions can be changed—but are not being so—is rage likely to come into play. When their sense of justice is offended, most persons react with violence. Ironically, this reaction frequently brings to the fore those who have suffered the least—in revolutions the oppressed and downtrodden are often led by members of the upper or privileged classes.

Another widely accepted illusion regarding peace and war is that appeasement leads to war. A corollary to this argument is the belief that "they" (the enemy) understand only the language of force—a kind of self-fulfilling prophecy that itself breeds hostility and increases the likelihood of conflict. Appeasement may or may not lead to war, but the true statesman must always deal with concrete issues and decide whom, when, and to what degree to appease or not to appease.

It may also be misleading to exaggerate the evils of using one type of power over another—for example, military as opposed to political, economic, or psychological forms of pressure. While it is easier to see a raised fist as more detrimental and more vicious than nonvisible exercises of power, there may be evils inherent in "peaceful" as well as in "violent" means of power. This suggests the need to delve beyond the obvious and seek out the real forms of power and violence, whether or not they are readily apparent.

Violence is commonly thought of as something one person does to another, an overt, physical act causing injury to a person or property.

[9] Hannah Arendt. "Reflections on Violence." *International Affairs* 22 (1): 32; 1969.

This definition enables us to speak of a summer without riots as being without violence—a "cool summer." What it fails to take into account is that many people can suffer the consequences of violence without any overt, physical acts taking place. A social system that forces persons to accept a demeaning role because of their race or ethnic background, condones job discrimination, permits persons to suffer from a preventable disease because they are too poor to pay for adequate health care, or refuses to distribute surplus food to the hungry is a violent system just as surely as if it manipulated them with clubs and guns.

The tendency to institutionalize by law the privileges of the haves and the deprivations of the have-nots is illustrated by the fact that, while it is not illegal for a person not to share his "surplus" food with someone who is starving, it is illegal for the starving person to take "surplus" food from those who have it. If robbing is wrong, should not hoarding also be wrong? Questions such as this need to be faced if schools are serious about teaching about peace, justice, violence, and conflict.

"If peace is the absence of violence, then violence is not only direct personal violence . . . but just as much . . . the indirect, structural violence built into repressive social orders, creating enormous differences between potential and actual human self-realization." [10] Although these definitions are not familiar to many American teachers, they are undoubtedly the basis for much of the protest in our society, whether by the young, the poor, or other minorities.

In international relations, hidden and indirect forms of coercion are also at work. There power operates by implication as well as by application; hence, if a nation enjoys vast strength and resources, it can often impose its will upon other nations by the mere threat of using its power. A weaker nation may have to invoke a less subtle show of force to achieve its goals. And a nation confronting another of relatively equal strength may have to resort to an actual physical contest. There is, therefore, not only a real but also a "moral" advantage that goes with overwhelming power. One need not use it to impose his will; he can appear to be peaceloving and engage in ruthless power politics at the same time. Too few persons seem to realize that words are often being used today (as they probably always have been) to conceal, not to reveal, violence. The rage and alienation of the young may be due as much to hypocritical protestations of peace and benevolence as to the actual injustices perpetrated by

---

[10] Johann Galtung. "On the Meaning of Peace and Violence." *Journal of Peace Research*, No. 5; 1969.

governments and social institutions. Recent events have again demonstrated that even democratic governments can be violators as well as protectors of human rights.

INTERNATIONAL STUDIES AND PEACE EDUCATION

The field of international studies today, like the world it seeks to understand, is in a state of ferment and change. New ideas and concepts are emerging that question many of our most cherished assumptions about international society—for example, that nations are sovereign in their domestic affairs and can be influenced in only very limited ways by foreign powers; that decision makers are not subject to internal tensions and conflicts concerning goals, policies, or definitions of national interests; and that international political processes are unique and differ fundamentally from political behavior within the national or local unit.

Historically, a major justification for the study of international relations has been the need to understand better the problems of war and peace. Today man's potential for self-annihilation lends special urgency to this aim; the area of international studies is no longer merely an academic discipline but, more important, the study of the art and science of survival.

Despite their immediacy and relevance, however, the issues of war and peace have as yet failed to gain the acceptance in the schools that they warrant. From the teacher's point of view the problem may be one of time and energy. Conceptual changes in a single field are sufficient to challenge the most conscientious teacher; when several disciplines are involved, as they are in the realm of international studies, keeping up with change can become an overwhelming task. For those interested in curriculum reform, the difficulties are formidable. Efforts to influence curriculum decisions are exercises in both intellectual and political power. Moreover, the problem is complicated immensely by the fact that one of the basic goals of public school teaching is to help students develop humanistic and democratic values. Effecting curriculum reform thus not only is a cognitive problem but also involves more than a mere reorganization of the traditional disciplines.

There are other reasons that schools have been unwilling to deal with problems of international and intercultural conflict. The issues are controversial and complex. The problems have a deceptively remote appearance. In addition, the widespread belief that only the government knows enough to operate in this field has led to a general abdication on the part of many educators, who doubted—at least until recently—that the schools could play a constructive role.

These arguments no longer justify such a stance. Questions of intercultural and international conflict are crucial domestic issues. Although teachers may be inadequately informed, reluctantly involved, and divided over burning issues, they have an obligation to help prepare students to become better able to grapple with the complex issues that threaten man's survival. Today more educators are beginning to assume some responsibility for the enormous task of building a more peaceful and just world, although many schools still fail, in part because of community reluctance or resistance, to provide students with adequate opportunities to study such issues as the draft, the Vietnam War, the antiballistic-missile controversy, universal membership in the United Nations, and many other issues that involve a conflict of values in our society.

Serious work in education and planning to control international conflict began at the end of World War II, when the specter of the atomic bomb haunted many world leaders. However, the emergence of materials and approaches for dealing with such topics as conflict resolution, deterrence, world law, sovereignty, and control of violence is a much more recent development. Peace education today, limited as it may be, tends to include the related issues of social justice, economic underdevelopment, political exclusion, and ecological imbalance. At present there are few projects or local efforts devoted solely to these topics. Nonetheless, many of the social studies curriculum projects are producing tools which can be used to help students deal with the problems of war and violence.

Rich ingredients for programs or courses focusing on war and peace or conflict resolution can be found in such projects as Ella Leppert's "Sequential Social Science Courses for Secondary Schools" (University of Illinois), which emphasizes "universals in terms of social processes"; the Public Issues Series–Harvard Social Studies Project, which provides insight into such areas as "The Limits of War," "Intervention," and "Revolution and World Politics"; the Foreign Policy Association project, "An Examination of Objectives, Needs, and Priorities in International Education," which establishes a global framework for the study of planet earth, man, his institutions, and society; the University of Minnesota "K-12 Project," especially the twelfth grade course, "Value Conflicts and Policy Decisions"; the "World Order Models" project and other programs of the World Law Fund; and the work of the Center for War/Peace Studies, especially the

Diablo Valley Education project, which deserves the special attention of all educators interested in peace education.[11]

While these projects and other national, regional, and local efforts provide important contributions to the understanding of students' needs in helping create a world without war, "putting it all together" is a real challenge. This is not to argue that there is or should be only one pattern or framework for organizing programs in peace education. But a field that draws on all the social sciences and a number of other disciplines must somehow have a focus or pattern if it is to be articulated. While many teachers may show little concern for the relation of academic disciplines to war-and-peace studies in a theoretical context, most will have a deep interest in the problems of selectivity and organization in the school program. Given the emotional nature of many of the issues, the pressures of time in which to work, and the vast quantities and great variety of available materials, careful consideration of the focus or pattern of peace education is, if only from the standpoint of efficiency, a virtual necessity.

Robert Freeman, of the Center for War/Peace Studies, suggests that coming to grips with these complex issues requires: (a) a sharp focus that can be easily grasped by students and teachers, (b) a commitment to a solid and familiar set of values, (c) an understanding of certain key concepts common to all war-peace problems, and (d) some indication of which war-peace issues warrant our study.[12] These elements are offered as a framework in which progress in this field may be measured.

Freeman believes that our problem is one of finding means other than war for the defense of values and the resolution of conflict. Building institutions to preserve peace rather than seeking an end to conflict may be a more realistic, though still very difficult, goal. In terms of peace education in the schools, such an approach has several advantages. Unlike the approach of many peace groups, it does not allow students to be satisfied with simply condemning military power. It offers a good basis for clarifying the fundamental value conflicts disrupting our society. It does not proceed from a moral vacuum but rather sanctions the teaching of

---

[11] For a comprehensive list of these and related social studies projects, see: *Directory of Research and Curriculum Development Projects in Social Studies Education.* Corte Madera, California: Marin County Social Studies Project, 1971. For an analysis of the materials produced by some of these projects, see: *Social Studies Curriculum Materials Data Book.* Boulder, Colorado: Social Science Education Consortium, 1971.

[12] Robert E. Freeman. *The War/Peace Field in Education.* New York: Center for War/Peace Studies, 1970.

goals, values, and attitudes. And it asks students to apply the same standards to international behavior as to behavior in their own communities; that is, to extend peace and stability—widely supported domestic values—to the world at large.

Since peace and order in our communities are the result of slow, often painful processes involving family, education, and civic and religious activities, building institutions to achieve peace in the world can only be expected to come about in similar ways—through the constant and gradual increment of new attitudes, new institutions, new roles and groups, the acceptance of the goal of making the world safe for conflict, and the willingness to find ways to manage such conflict. Enough is known about political socialization and role identification to suggest how to proceed.

For example, public figures who stand for fair play and stability in domestic life, such as Carl Stokes, former mayor of Cleveland, Ohio; Ralph Nader; John Lindsay, mayor of New York City; Ramsey Clark; and Willie Mays contribute to an ethos that accepts domestic peace and order. On a worldwide scale, the reverse generally holds true. Frequently our heroes are military personalities, such as General Douglas MacArthur and General George Patton, or militant revolutionaries, such as Fidel Castro, Che Guevara, Mao Tse-tung, and Patrick Henry. As a result, students tend to think of international affairs and worldwide social change largely in military terms. It can be argued that we must place more emphasis on the *political* and *diplomatic* roles of our traditional heroes and give more attention to such men as Martin Luther King, Jr., U Thant, Mohandas Gandhi, Albert Schweitzer, and others who have been peacemakers or who have used nonviolent means to bring about change.

The increasing number of careers or positions requiring international roles can also be stressed. The Peace Corps, multinational corporations, communications satellites, world travel, diplomacy, international organizations—all require an increasing number of individuals prepared to play various international roles. Recognition of these developments and identification of the roles involved make more obvious the importance of world peace and order.

SOME APPROACHES

Much of secondary school social studies, backed up by considerable home conditioning, still tends to convey the impression that the West is and always has been superior to all other civilizations. The 19th-century position of dominance over the rest of the world is presented as natural and its continuance into the future as indefinite. Some of the most widely used textbooks still manage to imply that, while civilization may have started in some such unlikely place as Mesopotamia, it failed to improve man's lot until the Israelites and the Greeks took over; they in turn passed it on through the Romans and Christians to the northern Europeans, who brought it to North America and achieved the ultimate.

The past decade has seen many attempts to correct this parochial and dangerous outlook. There is a growing feeling that students need to know more about the various parts of an increasingly interdependent world. Furthermore, intergroup tensions and the polarization of cultural and ethnic groups in the United States have sparked many efforts and programs designed to help students develop the capacity for understanding and working with people whose lives and backgrounds may be very different from their own. There is a growing recognition that this polarization exists on a worldwide scale and involves not only racial and cultural differences but also growing disparities in wealth.

Current events, the study of other nations, international relations courses, and world-problems units or courses have long been used to place international content in the curriculum. More recently the use of area studies has become a popular method of expanding international or cross-cultural awareness, and during the past ten years the study of areas of cultures has replaced or been added to the more traditional, generally chronological study of world or American history, American foreign policy, and international relations.

While the area studies approach is often an improvement over traditional chronological approaches, so far it has been only partly successful in providing insights into the manner in which throughout history all major cultural heritages and their national subdivisions have grown and developed within their own traditions. Even more important, it generally fails to provide a context within which to consider the fact that the acceleration of human mobility and communication greatly increases cross-cultural and cross-national contacts, thereby speeding up and making more complex the process of cultural change.

Unlike the typical current-events approach, which still tends to view the world in the context of U.S. foreign policy issues, the field of area studies at least allows equal time to non-Western cultures. Unfortunately, it also usually reinforces the impression of the world as composed of separate patches of real estate. Likewise, the proliferation of culture studies or units examining the traditional relations of nation-states may prevent students from seeing the world as increasingly interdependent.

Some of the "one world" approaches, on the other hand, have their own imperfections of logic or outlook. The notion of world government as a road to world peace, for example, is based on a stilted analogy with experience in individual nations. Because the United States is a reasonably stable nation with a strong central government, there is a widespread belief that government is responsible for maintaining domestic peace. World peace, in turn, is seen as an outgrowth of world government, conceived as a gigantic replica of the U.S. federal government. This line of reasoning ignores the fact that national governments are as much a result of existing peaceful conditions as a cause of such conditions. It also ignores the fact that many nations have had peaceful external relations without central governmental institutions. Further, it limits the vision and imagination needed to devise new alternatives. While none of these approaches is wrong, all, taken by themselves, are inadequate.

Even if the correct approach can be found, the internationalization of American education is hampered by the fact that world cultures, and in many instances world problems, do not excite students whose vision is limited by the same basic struggle for existence that faces millions all over the world. The ghetto child and his Appalachian counterpart are not likely to be intrigued by poverty in India or tribal struggles in Nigeria unless these problems are demonstrably relevant to his own.

Developing a world view may therefore mean bringing America's "underdeveloped" areas into the classroom alongside similar situations in, for example, Asia or Latin America. While some aspects of social change may be peculiar to this country, the social revolution the United States is undergoing does have parallels in other parts of the world. The black ghettos of America, for instance, are seen by some as colonies struggling for their freedom and independence in ways that resemble Asian and African societies. Sensitizing students to the culture of poverty in their own neighborhoods or in neighborhoods a few miles away and relating them to parallel conditions in disadvantaged nations or world areas may help break down the notion that only distant countries and people have development problems. Such an awareness may also help students recognize the interdependence of human beings, the universality of their needs, and the necessity of coping with threats to human survival on a global basis.

Television documentaries and the many articles and reports have familiarized us with the depressing statistics on illiteracy, population increase, food shortages, and infant mortality. We are now aware, at least intellectually, that the gap between the rich and the poor nations is widening, not shrinking, and we are beginning to see that poverty, not only in economic terms but also in terms of genuine communication, can exist in even the most technologically advanced nations—like our own—side by side with affluence.

The complex and varied issues involved in "development education" are now being recognized as crucial and are receiving increased attention from educators throughout the world. Indeed, there is a universality about today's political and ecological problems that makes them a logical and compelling foundation for international studies in many countries, not just the United States. The interrelated issues of war prevention, social justice, ecological balance, world economic welfare, alternative futures, conflict management, social change, transnational institutions, global political development, and lack of the international cooperation needed to attack these issues effectively may well become the basis for an international curriculum for man, while space exploration and the environmental crisis can provide the immediacy and imagery that will arouse student and community interest. The rationale for such an approach is strengthened by the fact that we now have pictures from outer space that give us a visual representation of what was previously only an intellectual abstraction: spaceship earth. It is no longer unrealistic to think of our planet as a single unit and of man as a single species.

If our schools are to contribute to replacing the war-threat system with a system of trust and conflict resolution, a drastic shift in emphasis must take place in classrooms throughout the country. The results of vast amounts of peace research undertaken by scholars around the world during the past decade will have to become available in a form teachers can use. The results of other kinds of research must also be understood—for example, the work of physical scientists in devising feasible procedures for a ban on nuclear tests; studies in international communication leading to the "hot line"; work in interpersonal bargaining which contributed to ways of defusing the Berlin and Cuban missile crises; and the contributions of economics to multilateral and bilateral aid programs.

Among the scholarly insights and observations that might be considered in planning programs in the areas of peace and war are the following:

1. Despite the fact that governments always justify their warlike acts on the basis of "the other side's" responsibility, the issues underlying conflict are complex and the causes of violence manifold.

2. Stereotyping and labeling enable us to screen out conflicting data so that our images of reality need not change and our actions toward the "enemy" can be accepted as necessary and even praiseworthy.

3. Conflict resolution and peacemaking as interdisciplinary studies are providing useful concepts and generalizations suitable for use with young children.

4. The problems of population, pollution, hunger, and resource depletion are being ignored or intensified owing to the continued maintenance of the war-threat system.

5. War crimes, protests, mass demonstrations against government policies, and hijackings, to mention only a few manifestations, are bringing under public scrutiny the problems of individual rights and responsibilities in the international system.

Until recently, topics such as these have received little consistent attention in the schools. Yet they are the kinds of questions that we can no longer afford to ignore or neglect. Awareness and understanding of the issues of peace and war, conflict and violence are not a matter of idealism; they are demanded by the complexities of democratic decision making today.

SOME GUIDELINES FOR PROGRAMS

In planning for education for the coming decades, we may gain valuable experience by assessing the effect of education on problems of social change in this country. Why, for example, do so many Americans think that more and better police are the answer to riots such as those that occurred in Watts, Newark, Chicago, and Detroit? Why do many Americans think that military power is the only way to solve the problems in Vietnam? How many Americans realize that most other nations think of the United Nations in terms of better food, shelter, and clothing rather than as a peacekeeping organization?

The capability of the police and the military to produce order in either domestic or international arenas may be much more limited than most Americans realize. The goals the American people want most in the international realm—peace and stability—must be considered in the context of the wants of all mankind. It might be a useful exercise to compile an agenda of issues or situations that people around the world believe ought to be handled by an international agency. The list of priorities that would emerge from such a survey would be a useful corrective to our own parochialism and at the same time would raise such important questions as: How well are existing international agencies filling these needs? Why is so little being done? Are there parallels between failure to deal with some of these needs at the world level and failure to deal at the national level with similar problems (for example, poverty, hunger, disease, illiteracy)? Is lack of international solutions likely to create "global riots" such as have occurred in American cities?

Focusing more on problems and less on institutions might encourage citizens and decision makers alike to assign more problems to international agencies or to create new agencies designed to deal with issues for which at present no effective decisional units exist. Such an approach might also enable students to see that problems should be handled by the agency or entity best capable of dealing with them; the criterion of effective problem solving might thereby replace emotional loyalties to state or nation as a way of determining jurisdiction over global problems.

Another field that offers promise is the area of "future studies." Today most teachers use outmoded analytic tools in dealing with data about the past while trying to teach students concepts and skills that they probably will not apply until some time in the future. Social studies education, for example, seldom provides a future orientation that helps students anticipate problems or realize that policy advocacy must always take future change into account.

Future-studies techniques and approaches seem promising in that they treat human behavior as a process of continuous creation, not as an accretion of facts or data from the past, a viewpoint that tends to imprison alternative futures in perceived pasts. Rather than emphasizing what is deterministic and random, the future studies approach affirms the nondeterministic and creative. Rather than stressing feedback-control mechanisms that modify present behavior in terms of past experience, the futures approach concentrates on "feed-forward" mechanisms that experiment with hitherto untried behavior. And rather than taking social control and manipulation of others as a context, this new approach formulates self-manipulative or nonmanipulative systems.

To make the most desirable the most probable, it may be necessary to integrate many approaches. The use of experimental environments, for example, may enable persons to participate directly in defining and creating their own futures; they may thus experience the way it is as well as help create the ways it can be. A public multilogue concerning realities and multiple alternate futures can be a profound step toward creating a more peaceful world. Further, students should be encouraged to design alternative international agencies to handle problems that they anticipate will be important in future agendas. Included might be such issues as population control, uses of the sea bed, demilitarization of space, and environmental health. This approach might prevent images of today's problems and institutions from imprisoning the minds of those who must somehow be prepared to anticipate problems of the future and design effective institutions to solve them.

THE MEDIA AND INTERNATIONAL STUDIES

Proliferating communications media, density of population, and interdependence of persons and nations make inevitable increased interpersonal, intergroup, and international conflicts. The growing awareness of the human and social costs of war and its suicidal nature in an age of nuclear power and supersonic missiles is among the factors that argue for the schools' assuming greater responsibility in helping students learn to analyze and deal with conflict and violence—especially now that the rich yields of peace research have provided the raw materials for approaching these complex issues.

It is against this backdrop that the impact of the media on the teaching of world affairs needs to be considered. A study by Lambert and Klineberg indicates that students name the mass media as "the almost exclusive source of information" about foreign persons. Both children and adults are targets of the same massive communication system, and both are participants in a wide range of common and recurring social interactions. Even the very young child has some exposure to national, international, global, and extraglobal events. The effect of this exposure, however, can sometimes be to overload the individual's capacity for comprehension or retention. There are about 150 countries in the world, and each has its own economic, cultural, historical, and political attributes and relations. Each day brings a fresh supply of data, almost any of which may be considered important, depending upon the context or perspective.

In these circumstances it is difficult if not impossible to devise a single "best" selection of information. Owing to the communications revolution, there simply is no responsible way to tie an adequate world affairs program to a particular body of subject matter. A specific content curriculum, consisting primarily of a selection of subject matter to be studied at a given grade level, is the wrong kind of program for helping students learn to distinguish the important from the trivial or to fit international events into some meaningful framework.

World affairs education should be viewed not as a unique academic compartment with a certain body of information to be mastered, but as a matter of developing skills and insights in information selection and information processing. This approach not only is practical, given the volume of data available, but is a question of human and planetary survival: the learner must be able to discriminate among messages arising from distant sources and be able to decide how and when to respond to the increasing stream of information.

To help students broaden and sharpen their "map of the international environment" to include a rich and varied content and a realistic organization for global developments—and not to teach them a preordained set of international facts—should be the goal of world affairs education.

The importance of providing new maps of the functioning international system has been pointed up by Wesley Posvar. He noted that we already live in a transnational world where political boundaries and jurisdiction of governmental unity are of diminishing importance. For example, "The true map of Germany and Eastern Europe need not be one that traces only political boundaries" but could "be drawn to show peoples with shared ethnic cultural interests, and overlapping social and economic concerns." [13] In a similar vein John Burton has raised the question, "Which is the more representative model of the world—the world of continents, islands, and states or the world of transactions?" [14] Such images and questions are indicative of new perspectives in global studies.

Learning how to use a selection process requires opportunities to make choices. What is needed is a large and diverse body of instructional materials from which both teachers and students can choose in learning the skills of information processing. Here again the communications revolution can be relevant. Not only do the media provide a vast amount of information about world affairs, but also their pervasive influence in

---

[13] Wesley W. Posvar. "Reshaping Our Foreign Policy." *Annals of the American Academy of Political and Social Science* 396: 105; 1971.

[14] John Burton. *World Society*. New York: Cambridge University Press, 1972.

modern society affects the way world affairs are taught. Of course, as is often the case, the technology of communications has far outdistanced society's ability to manage and utilize it; but formal education has been especially unimaginative in its efforts to capitalize on revolutionary changes in the media. If, however, educators can combine a global perspective with the potential of the "media revolution," the task of restructuring international studies education will become at once more reasonable and more practicable.[15]

The scholarly groundwork for a fresh approach to international education has already begun to be laid: a new concept has emerged in international affairs that views the international system as a global set of relationships. Progress is also being made in clarifying goals, needs, and priorities in global education. One such effort has the following goals:

1. Overcoming the Western orientation found in most textbooks and curriculums and helping students achieve a more objective and global perspective on cultural, economic, and political diversity

2. Developing students' empathy toward other cultures and values, both in the United States and worldwide, along with an appreciation of the similarities and differences of human life around the world

3. Increasing students' awareness of the natural ethnocentric bias in the way people see each other and helping them to reduce this bias

4. Helping students develop the independence of thought and the techniques and methods of inquiry necessary to cope emotionally and intellectually with the continuing change, complexity, and ambiguity of human affairs

5. Helping students develop an understanding of the process of decision making in regard to international and global issues

6. Helping students imagine and make objective choices about the world of the future and their probable role in it by emphasizing a global and future-oriented perspective.[16]

Like the "spaceship earth" view of mankind, this approach also emphasizes the oneness of the earth and the interrelatedness of all forms of international political behavior. Both these developments are inherently favorable to international studies education: they give us both a practical reason and an academic framework for educating man for his role in a global society.

---

[15] Keith Tyler. *Television for World Understanding*. Washington, D.C.: National Education Association, 1970.

[16] *An Examination of Goals, Needs, and Priorities in International Education in U.S. Secondary and Elementary Schools*. Washington, D.C.: U.S. Office of Education, 1969. Booklet available from Document Reproduction Service, Educational Resources Information Center, 4936 Fairmont Avenue, Bethesda, Maryland 20014.

Selected References

Robert C. Angel. *Peace on the March: Transnational Participation.* New York: Van Nostrand Reinhold Company, 1969.

Development Bridge to Peace: Introduction to Development. Washington, D.C.: American Freedom from Hunger Foundation, 1970.

"Education on War/Peace, Conflict, and Change." *Intercom,* Vol. 12, No. 3. New York: Center for War/Peace Studies, 1971. 64 pp.

"The Human Person and the War System." *Intercom,* Vol. 13, No. 1. New York: Center for War/Peace Studies, 1971. 72 pp.

Robert M. Hutchins. *The Future of International Relations.* New York: United Nations Institute for Training and Research, 1970.

William A. Nesbitt. *Teaching About War and War Prevention.* New York: Thomas Y. Crowell Company, 1971.

Robert Shaw. *Rethinking Economic Development.* Headline Series No. 208. New York: Foreign Policy Association, 1971.

The Social Science Record: Journal of the New York State Council for the Social Studies, Vol. 9, No. 2; Winter 1972. 100 pp. Special issue on peace education.

"What Should Kids Be Taught About Peace and War?" *War/Peace Report* 11 (1): 3–9; January 1971.

Redeployment (1947)*
Howard Nemerov

They say the war is over. But water still
Comes bloody from the taps, and my pet cat
In his disorder vomits worms which crawl
Swiftly away. Maybe they leave the house.
These worms are white, and flecked with the cat's blood.

The war may be over. I know a man
Who keeps a pleasant souvenir, he keeps
A soldier's dead blue eyeballs that he found
Somewhere—hard as chalk, and blue as slate.
He clicks them in his pocket while he talks.

And now there are cockroaches in the house,
They get slightly drunk on DDT,
Are fast, hard, shifty—can be drowned but not
Without you hold them under quite some time.
People say the Mexican kind can fly.

The end of the war. I took it quietly
Enough. I tried to wash the dirt out of
My hair and from under my fingernails,
I dressed in clean white clothes and went to bed.
I heard the dust falling between the walls.

* From: *New and Selected Poems* by Howard Nemerov. Copyright by the University of Chicago, 1960. Reprinted by permission of the Margot Johnson Agency.

Percent of Civilian War Deaths[†]

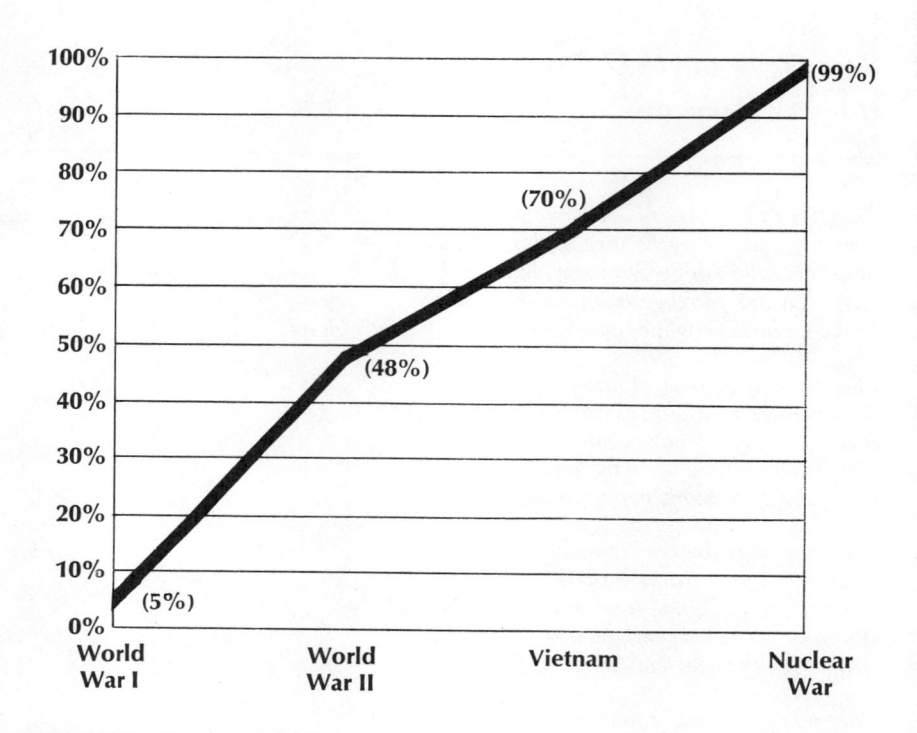

FIGURE 7. Civilian War Deaths.

The numbers of civilians killed in any war is at best a rough estimate.

This is especially true in Vietnam because of the nature of the warfare. Bombing from the air and artillery fire from many miles away mean a heavy civilian toll.

By early 1971, the tonnage of bombs dropped in Vietnam was 2½ times that dropped by both sides in all theaters in World War II.

It is estimated that 1.5 million persons have died in Indochina in 10 years of war, of which the great majority are civilians.

Minimal estimates of U.S. deaths from a Soviet first-strike nuclear attack are put at 50 million persons, of which only a small percent would be military personnel.

[†] William A. Nesbitt. *Data on the Human Crisis: A Handbook for Inquiry.* New York: Center for International Programs and Comparative Studies of the New York State Education Department, 1972. p. 13. Reprinted by permission.

Transformations into Peace and Survival: Programs for the 1970's

Betty Reardon

7

FROM a vantage point early in the 1970's it seems a bit futile to forecast proposals for the decade. Programs for the 1970's should have as their long-range targets not this decade but the next century. Perhaps farsighted programs will help avoid the fruitless kinds of incremental and fragmented change that has characterized the past two decades of American education. Given the current trend projections, educational needs, and various other societal problems, it is evident that drastic changes in educational policy are required. Without such changes we cannot expect the school system itself to survive, much less make any significant contribution to the change of any other system or, indeed, to the survival of mankind. It is that *survival crisis* which programs for the 1970's must face as the key issue in goal formation and strategy planning. It is therefore imperative that survival education become the core of all programs.

The first requisite of survival is peace, a state of order in which tensions and conflicts can be resolved without destruction or lethal violence. (Note: peace need *not* be the absence of tension or conflict but only the nonviolent management of these phenomena.) Educational programs must therefore be concerned with defining and achieving such an order to assure survival in all realms of human experience—as part of a species, or mankind; as members of groups and subgroups, or societies; and as human beings, or individuals.

As we inquire into the definitions and strategies for achievement of the desired order, we must recognize not only the interrelationships among these realms of experience but also the uniqueness of each and the distinctions among them. We cannot, for example, expect world peace to provide "inner peace" for every human being (the ability to handle personal and internal conflicts) any more than we can expect to achieve world peace by gradually bringing "peace of soul" to each member of the human species. Nor can we expect a nonviolent or even a "just" order among nations to resolve all the varied and complex tensions existing within and among other levels of human social organization. We should, however, recognize that some of these domestic and personal tensions do in fact result from the stresses imposed by the "war system" which characterizes present world politics and that any attempt to eliminate them must include efforts to replace that system with a "peace system," a form of politics which reduces and attempts to eliminate organized violence.

Helping to bring such a system into existence should be a primary goal of educational programs in the 1970's. Anything less would be an inadequate response to the petitions of the young reflected in the data in Chapter 4, "Let's Listen to Our Children and Youth." Such a goal requires an education that inquires into three realms of human experience: into social and political structures and processes, with an eye toward understanding and managing institutions and deriving strategies for nonviolent change needed for species survival; into modes to express ideas, feelings, and interpretations of proposed changes, aiming at the kind of exchange among and within groups that will result in intelligent policy formation; and into individual moral growth, intellectual development, and ways of making both personal and political choices on the basis of sound value judgments.

A more comprehensive description of these goals was presented in the Asilomar "Statement of Objectives and Approaches for Improvement of the Social Studies." For the purposes of this chapter, as you read the statement, reproduced below, simply substitute "education" at each mention of "social studies":

> The purpose of the social studies is to educate students toward the development of a world in which all human beings may live in dignity. The goals of learning should be construction of a future world system in which all human persons enjoy material well-being, the benefits of education, access to information, freedom from oppression and violence, participation in making the decisions which affect their lives, and a respectful, nourishing, and fulfilling relationship with all forms of life and their environment. . . .
>
> Learning experiences should be designed to help students understand the processes and causes of change through the careful analysis of all available data. It is imperative that learning experiences equip the learner with the ability to participate effectively in the process of change. This approach should

foster the development of a value system which accords human dignity to all persons and produces empathy with and compassion for other humans of diverse cultures, both in their own countries and in other parts of the world.

The social studies, through social and behavioral sciences and the humanities, should introduce several basic concepts to students of all nations and all cultures. These concepts include the notion that mankind is a single species with basic common needs and that the world is a global system incorporating many human cultures and subsystems. Human and cultural differences should be studied and appreciated as varieties of the total human experience.

Students should be able to recognize and define problems, to gather and apply data in order to understand problems, to conceptualize and plan solutions, to evaluate various plans according to a value system which encourages commitment to action. Students possessing such skills may use them to build a world system in which human life is valued above institutions, freedom is valued above political ideology, and justice is valued above order.

Learning experiences should provide the child with opportunities to select subjects and modes of study and encourage his personal participation in the learning process. Children must be helped to understand themselves and others and permitted to discuss and reflect upon the nature of self and of other selves, such reflections being vital to the child's ability to build his own learning structures and to become a reflective evaluator of his own learning. Content should be based upon the realities of the life of the child, his community, and world society. Controversy, conflict, and serious problems must be as much a part of the child's in-school learning as they are of his out-of-school learning.

Such education implies the need to overcome unnecessary barriers among the disciplines and to create and use knowledge in a way which will contribute to the realization of the desired future world system. The creation and use of such knowledge should encourage the development of the highest levels of cognition, which can produce the kind of affective learning experiences which lead to changes in behavior and to desired social change.[1]

MEETING THE CRISES: A REVOLUTION IN EDUCATION

The question for educators proceeding from the statement above is: What kinds of projects and programs can carry out its purposes? Fortunately there are many possibilities within the growing survival-curriculum movement and also in projects dealing with social issues and human development. Many of these projects have an admitted crisis orientation, an orientation which, far from being a hysterical approach, is a pragmatic

---

[1] Alice Miel and Louise Berman, editors. *Educating the Young People of the World*. Washington, D.C.: Association for Supervision and Curriculum Development, 1970. pp. 107–108.

one. The common orientation is crisis-centered rather than problem-centered because there is a general recognition that our present structures and processes for problem solution are inadequate to meet the current situation. In fact, what differentiates a "crisis" from a "problem" is the inability of the established institutions to deal with the former. A second common characteristic of this growing group of "survivalists" is the search for unprecedented solutions and the concomitant assumption that such solutions will probably require new and radically different institutions, an idea described by Michael Scriven as "survival through revolution." [2]

Scriven was, in fact, the first to put forth a suggestive outline for a survival curriculum which must be developed to replace the "war curriculum" described by Thornton B. Monez in Chapter 2 of this book. Other notable contributions on the relationship between education and survival, together with suggestions for curricular and pedagogical approaches, have been made by William H. Boyer, of the University of Hawaii,[3] and Fannie R. Shaftel, of Stanford University.[4] Although these researchers carry out their work in the tradition of social reconstruction, their writings call for an activist commitment and, indeed, tend to be more revolutionary than reformist in that they document the need for immediate and drastic changes in educational organization and practice.

It is the thesis of this chapter that, while there is a general recognition of the need for educational change of revolutionary proportions, there has been no systematic general diagnosis from which we may project a comprehensive vision of change and design strategies for bringing the vision into reality. Criticism and problems are dealt with separately (if at all), and consequently little or no headway is made toward meeting the real needs of the schools. We must recognize that education is in a systems crisis and requires a drastic system change, a revolutionary approach to meet that crisis.

When we try to sum up all that has been said in the critiques and studies of the schools, the problem of reaching a diagnosis is not so difficult to resolve. Let me posit one possible general diagnosis as a basis for some of the programs to be recommended for the 1970's. The schools are a barometer of the society, revealing the stresses it suffers, demonstrating

[2] Michael Scriven. "Education for Survival." In: G. Kinley, editor. *The Ideal School*. Wilmette, Illinois: The Kagg Press, 1969.
[3] William H. Boyer. "Education for Survival." *Phi Delta Kappan* 52 (5): 258–62; January 1971. Reprints available from the World Law Fund.
[4] Fannie R. Shaftel. "A Survival Curriculum in the Social Studies." Address to the Southern California Social Studies Council, October 1970.

the gap it exhibits between articulated and manifested values, and shaking with the trauma of recognizing the need for change but having no clear and comprehensive vision of what form that change should take. In short, the schools, like most other aspects of society, are oppressive in their atmosphere, product-oriented in their processes, past- and content-oriented in their teaching methods, and hierarchical and elitist in their organization.

For example, the tendency to classify and categorize young people not only in age groups but also in so-called ability groups, and thereby to separate some groups from other groups, undoubtedly contributes to the polarization which afflicts our society. (It is easy enough for the educators to decry the attacks of hard-hat hawkish laborers on the dove demonstrations of students, but they might well recognize that the world view and value system of that group of hard hats were profoundly influenced when they were separated into a "nonacademic" course in secondary school or, even worse, were consigned at a young age to groups with reading or language difficulties, which we know now to be in large part culturally determined.)

At best, the schools' mode of organization and operation is inefficient, and at worst, it is inhumane. Ranging from Silberman, to Denisson, to Leonard, to Rossman, to Goodman, to Firestone, and the feminists, the charge is pretty well documented that delight, exuberance, excitement at the adventure of life, and joy in learning have no place in most American schools.

WORLD-ORDER STUDIES AS SURVIVAL CURRICULUMS

A prescription that would follow from such a diagnosis would include a new school system which is antielitist, person-oriented, inquiry-centered, process-concerned, and future-directed and, God willing, would function in a happy environment in which students could prepare to work toward the survival of mankind on planet earth. In short, a set of conditions should prevail in the schools which peace researchers now refer to as "positive peace," in which peace can be maintained—that is, "a state of assured justice." [5]

Without such an environment no curriculum, even one based on survival criteria, will serve the purpose. Let us keep the goals implied in

---

[5] Bert V. A. Roling. "The Contents of Peace Research." Paper prepared for the 1971 meeting of the International Peace Research Association, held in Bled, Yugoslavia.

this prescription in mind as we seek out substantive bases for survival curriculums. Such goals, I believe, are implicit in programs now being devised to deal with the issues of environment, population, human rights, economic development and welfare, social justice, and war and peace. One particular area of study which combines elements of such issues and works toward a goal similar to that advocated in the foregoing prescription is "world order." After more than ten years of research and development, this topic offers techniques of problem definition, modes of inquiry, and value analysis, as well as particular teaching-learning strategies.

The central concern of the world-order inquiry is peace, a goal described by the discipline as the elimination of organized violence among nations. This central concern with violence has led researchers in the field to see the potential for organized violence arising out of those very problems which individually threaten the survival of man. Working separately in their own regions of the world, but coordinating their efforts through such programs as the World Order Models Project, they have come to see these problems as so closely interrelated that they would be more effectively resolved by integrated programs organized at a world-system level rather than being dealt with as distinct phenomena approached individually by national systems.[6]

World order, therefore, is a comprehensive, integrated, multidisciplinary subject. Researchers have assumed the responsibility of suggesting modes to bring about changes in the world political system to attain the goals of world order. As a result, world order is not merely an academic inquiry into problems of war or peace and survival. It is also a policy science directed at finding viable solutions to those problems. This policy-science orientation makes it a highly appropriate substantive base for educational programs designed to equip and motivate students to act for change.

The basic concern for world peace gives rise to the assumption that the most urgently required change—perhaps, in fact, a prerequisite to changes at other levels of human organization—is that which would radically transform the world political structure by replacing the war system with adequate world institutions to make nonviolent resolution of conflicts among nations both possible and probable. Thus supporters of world-order studies advocate that students inquire into the structures and

[6] Readers interested in specific descriptions of the modes and strategies described here, as well as in the World Order Models Project, may write to the World Law Fund, 11 West 42nd Street, New York City 10036.

processes of the world political system with a view toward transforming it into a true peace system. World order is, therefore, political education for world citizenship. It is a conscious attempt to politicize students responsibly with regard to world problems in much the same manner as Edmund W. Gordon advocated in regard to national problems of race and social justice and student power in the cogent and moving paper he delivered at Asilomar.[7]

Programs such as those advocated by Gordon and world-order educators should have top priorities for the 1970's, not only because of their concern for peace but also because of the related goals espoused as essential to peace—social justice and economic welfare. Such programs would make operational Earl S. Johnson's definition of the "politicization of social knowledge," which is "the purposeful turning of thought and action, collectively and individually, toward the realities of our time—war, the rape of nature, racism, hunger." [8]

World order seeks not only nonviolent solutions to conflicts but, even more important, *just* solutions to conflicts. It is a normative, value-centered discipline which aspires to more than the elimination of war, aiming also at relieving human suffering resulting from drastically disparate distribution of the world's wealth; from the prejudices, discrimination, and oppression which deprive far too many human beings of their rights and dignity; and from the wanton exploitation of the earth's resources by that powerful minority which controls and uses them without regard to the interests of the people of this and succeeding generations. The search for just solutions is expressed by world order as an attempt to achieve five goals:

1. The minimization of violence, or *war prevention*

2. The maximizing of *economic welfare,* or the providing of better standards of living for more people

3. The increasing of *social justice* by relieving discrimination and oppression

4. The broadening of the democratic base of public policy making by increasing the *participation* of minorities and individuals in decision-making processes

---

[7] Edmund W. Gordon. "Building a Socially Supportive Environment." In: Alice Miel and Louise Berman, editors. *Educating the Young People of the World.* Washington, D.C.: Association for Supervision and Curriculum Development, 1970. pp. 59–70.

[8] Earl S. Johnson. "Commentary on Social Studies Curriculum Guidelines." *Social Education* 36 (3): 260; March 1972.

5. The improving of the quality of life through restoration of *ecological balance.*

World order examines these goals by asking some significant questions: What is the present state of the world with regard to peace, economic welfare, social justice, political participation, and ecological balance? If we make no significant changes in the international system, what is the state likely to be in the next generation? If that state is, as most trend analyses indicate, not one likely to achieve peace and the other related world-order goals, what changes in the system would be most likely to do so? How can we bring about those changes?

The methodology of world order encompasses many techniques of inquiry and active learning which offer some hope for improving education on values and public issues. There are five basic steps to this methodology. The first is the *diagnosis:* a summary and analysis of world problems, their causes and their relationship to the . . . values. The second step is a *prognosis* or a projection of the evolution of these problems and the potential for the emergence of other problems over a twenty- to thirty-year period. These two are preliminary to a third step which actually attempts to deal with the future in the *positing of several alternative international systems* designed to resolve the problems defined in the first step. This projection is followed by the *evaluation* of the alternatives and the *selection* of a *preferred system*—the alternative which emerges from the evaluation as the one most likely to achieve peace, economic welfare, and social justice in the world community. The final step, *transition,* plots the strategies and policies needed to transform the present world system into the "preferred world." [9]

It is these processes and questions which should be addressed to all students in every school in terms appropriate to their age and environment. It is the goals implicit in these questions which should form the central purposes of education not only *at all levels* but also *in all subjects.* They are raised in only a few of our schools now; if they are not raised in most schools long before the end of this decade, the schools will have made no contribution to survival or to peace. For these reasons the contributors to this Yearbook assert that these issues and problems should provide the main content of curriculums in the 1970's.

While the central concerns of world-order studies are suitable for programs addressing themselves to the problems of survival, the researchers have not yet directed themselves specifically to problems of personal

---

[9] Betty Reardon. "Prologue." *Media & Methods. Exploration in Education.* 6 (2): 35; October 1969. Copyright © October 1969, *Media & Methods.* By permission. Reprints available from the World Law Fund.

identity and individual fulfillment. These problems have been treated only to the degree to which they affect or are affected by systems and institutions (granted that the degree is arguable and the argument should be an integral part of the general survival inquiry).

PERSONAL IDENTITY AND WORLD CIVILIZATION

The personal realm is a major focus of the rapidly developing human-potential movement, which is another important area of survival programs and one which could well serve to complement world-order studies in programs for the 1970's. In its efforts to help people regain or develop a sense of self, to cultivate, manage, and enjoy emotional responses and aesthetic experiences, the human-potential movement offers much promise of turning us away from some of the dehumanizing aspects of a complex technological society. Certainly the threads of such a movement should be woven into educational programs for survival. Both Shaftel and Scriven argue in favor of such content; Shaftel in terms of reuniting the affective with the cognitive, and Scriven in terms of the potential usefulness of such techniques as encounter groups and Synanon games.

I would, however, while recognizing their promise, recommend the inclusion of such techniques as complements to world order rather than as primary program components, because they have less to offer in terms of immediate crises management and institution building. While learning from these fields may help assure that new institutions may avoid the antihuman elements of the old and encourage the institutions' designers to include the possibilities of human fulfillment as criteria for the desirability of proposed institutions, it does not contribute directly to the design of the structures. That is clearly a systems problem, and systems change is our most immediate survival problem, the crucial component in establishing peace, and the main focus of world-order studies. So, while giving consideration to other program components and full value to all survival levels, the world-systems crisis should be our starting point. Unless some resolutions or new institutions are devised rapidly, there may be no issues of survival in the personal or the social realms.

Another resource for program development in the personal and social realms lies in the field of world cultures and the emerging world civilization. This field has special potential for fulfilling the goals enunciated in the Asilomar Statement, cited earlier in this chapter. Theodore Brameld, for instance, has advocated the establishment of a center for inquiry and study aimed at bringing forth a "world civilization" (a network of common values and human institutions mixed with a plurality of cultures and life styles), the purpose being to aid in the deliberate synergizing of such elements to formulate a community of mankind. Programs such as this will offer us opportunities to study the various philosophies, interpretations of life, and definitions of man which have been devised in diverse cultures and at different periods of human history.

With such a rich variety of resources to call upon, human beings may be better able to develop identities, giving each one full personhood while enabling him to relate fully to his species. A person so identified may be better able to survive crises in the other realms and to adapt and expand his or her identity as his or her community grows. Schools therefore should teach world cultures with this purpose in mind, *not simply as they relate to American culture or compare to each other but as the infinite variety of human qualities, values, and life styles which form the total pool of human resources, the heritage of all mankind.*

If the schools are going to provide this culture pool and permit persons to select from it, they must break out of the tightly structured organization that many now find so oppressive, an organization in which individuals are identified by the system and expected to conform to identities, be they "students," "teachers," or "administrators." Schools must not only tolerate alternative cultures and life styles (those within our own country, as well as those from other countries) but also teach about them, permit students to select freely from among them, and help them develop the skills for making those selections. Certainly such education is required to deal with the antecedents of violence. As Chapter 3 points out, by impositions of roles and behavior the schools themselves can be perceived as perpetrators of violence. And further, since "violence is a solution" resulting from decisions, skills for decision making and for evaluating alternatives are made an even more urgent requirement of survival.

LANGUAGE FACILITY FOR A MULTICULTURAL COMMUNITY

One of the prime requisites for peace is full and accurate communication among peoples. The study of other cultures, therefore, should include immersion in another language, one in which the logic, structure, and harmonies connote thought patterns, sensitivities, and values vastly different from the native culture of the learner. For generations, educated Asians and Africans have learned about the cultures of their conquerers by gaining fluency in French, Dutch, Portuguese, or English. Westerners should become equally fluent in languages, not to command another tool for exploitation but to gain a key to a wider portion of their own human heritage, to come to understand more deeply other members of their species, and thereby gain a wider sphere of identification as part of mankind.

The contrast in the language proficiency of Europeans and Americans has long been cited as an indication of the degree of Americans' culture-bound view of the world. Few Europeans, however, speak Asian or African languages, and their need to learn other European languages was a pragmatic survival mechanism required by a small multicultural geographic region.

The United States, though no small region, without question is multicultural, and therefore the need for us to learn the languages of those who share our region is just as vital to our survival. Societal survival also requires communication. The various black subcultures must learn standard English to protect their interests, but they must also be encouraged to maintain and develop their own modes of expression to preserve their cultural identity. Middle class white Americans should be familiar with this other American language, and both blacks and whites have as much responsibility to learn the third American language—Spanish—as Puerto Ricans and Chicanos have to learn English. Native Americans must be not only permitted but encouraged to learn and to express themselves in their Indian languages. Many more members of the immigrant cultures, from the descendants of the *Mayflower* to recent arrivals from Hong Kong, should have opportunities to study these first American languages.

There is no more effective way to understand our fellow human beings nor a better index of respect than learning their languages. Mutual respect and human dignity for all can only exist in a polyglot global society. Enforcement of one language for instruction and for the economic and political life of a society is a phenomenon of the age of nationalism. If peace and human community building are major goals of education, then the development of multiple language facility should be one of the chief strategies in achieving that goal. If human fulfillment is also one of the goals, there is further need for teaching and learning in various languages, including the nonverbal ones.

The inhibitions on learning, such as those imposed by denying children the right to learn in their mother tongues, have also been imposed through the restrictions on physical activities by which children normally express themselves. Sitting to learn is clearly not the natural order of things. Human expression often attains its most exquisite form in dance and in other art forms freely conceived and executed. The natural and universally human expression of joy is mostly physical—tactile and visual. If learning is to be joyous, these modes of expression must be rekindled and nurtured in our schools, especially if we are seeking to develop some sense of universal human identity. If art is the truly universal language of man, then the humanities must play a vital role in survival education. In the "three grand divisions" of knowledge identified by Earl S. Johnson, such education would fall within "the realm of *poetics* [where] are to be found the myths . . . those things . . . whose endless pursuit has given direction and purpose to . . . lives." [10] Would not the formulation and pursuit of new myths for a mankind community provide a fruitful theme for such programs?

The ability of persons from various cultures, political systems, and ideologies to communicate clearly and accurately will be absolutely essential to formulating new mankind myths, to deriving universal values and projecting, and to establishing new world institutions which will permit survival *on an equal basis* of the many societies and persons to be served by those institutions. It is not efficient in a survival crisis to say everything twice (especially when translations do not always issue identical statements). Nor is it fair for discourse to be conducted in one language rather than another simply because the power and technology of one nation have spread its idiom farther. World institution builders should be able to shift from one language to another, with the same ease and full appreciation of the medium being used as an accomplished musician displays in shifting from one musical mode of composition to another. Multilingual persons are more fully able to enjoy and contribute to varieties of human experience and to expand their identities to include still more groups. Certainly such proficiency should be a major aim of educational programs for human development.

There are also important aspects of individual survival to be benefited by polyglotism. The human rights of minorities have often been violated by states and societies in which power is applied and justice rendered in the language of the governing elites. There should be no room in a human community for such scenes as are now witnessed—

---

[10] Johnson, *op. cit.*, p. 262.

persons being tried in court procedures of which they do not understand a word, in which they are charged with violations of laws imposed on them by an alien culture in a language which to them is utterly "foreign." If the individual is to play an effective role in the world community, he or she must not be limited by the lack of language facility.

DECOLONIALIZING EDUCATION

Planning and implementing such a program will involve other activities which will be enormously helpful in building the human community. Languages are best learned from persons at ease in the language to be mastered and through interactions and experiences in that language. This means that more people are going to have to spend more time living in cultures other than their own. Ideally such an exchange of persons of various cultures will increase in volume and change in character. A change may be expected in the nature of exchange between the "developed" and the "developing" nations. Heretofore students, scholars, and scientists from Asian and African countries have come to the industrialized countries to "receive" expertise and command of technology in much the same way that our young have come to schools to "receive" education. In this way, as Ivan Illich points out, education ceases to be an "activity" and becomes a "commodity," a commodity controlled by specialists and "marketed" to the advantage of the specialists—the professional and technical elites.[11] It is to the advantage of the specialists to maintain this specialization, and the institutions of education and science thus become the bastions of elitism, or, in the terms of Paulo Freire, "the instruments of oppression." [12]

Some of the antidemocratic consequences of specialization and secrecy are brought into focus in Chapter 5, in which Theresa L. Held calls for more adequate political education. To continue to keep most information about these specialties in the hands of a few persons or in only a few Western languages helps to maintain global elitism and to make language another tool of oppression. Such a market economy of education does not offer much promise of producing a democratic human community. We need to shift to something more like bartering or, even better, "sharing." Transfer of technology to the languages of the third world not

[11] Ivan Illich. "The Alternative to Schooling." *Saturday Review* 54 (25): 44–48, 59–60; June 19, 1971.
[12] Paulo Freire. *The Pedagogy of the Oppressed.* New York: Herder & Herder, Inc., 1970.

only would make the benefits thereof available to that part of the globe, but also would make it possible for the first world to understand better the perspectives of the third world on technology and development. Most important, it could break the present technological monopoly of the forces of industry, as well as of the military and scientific elites of the northern tier of nations.

This present "marketing," as defined by Illich, may be termed "training," or initiation into certain levels of specialization. But it cannot be considered education, especially not education for peace or survival. For if peace is a state of order in which conflicts can be resolved without violence, it is also a state which aspires to justice. Injustice and alienation, so characteristic of this kind of schooling, probably nurture more organized violence—that is, warfare—than any other circumstances, and assuredly exemplify the kind of intrasocietal and structural violence George Henderson deals with in Chapter 9. If education is to be an instrument of peace and survival, then it must be a means to overcome injustice and alienation. It must consciously strive toward equal rights for all, including human dignity and equal value of persons. Language facility, therefore, can no longer be the exclusive prerogative of the elites; nor can crucial forms of education, such as the sciences and technology, be formulated and transmitted only in the languages of the powerful.

If the educational system is to respond adequately to the criticisms of Freire and Illich and if justice is to become a goal, then there will have to be a drastic reorganization of the structure of education. It can no longer be merely a conduit for passing on specialization from the initiated to the uninitiated. It must become a fair exchange among equals, or what Michael Rossman [13] calls the "conversation," a sharing of the riches of ability, knowledge, and inquisitiveness, a matching of needs to resources on the basis of justice. Sharing of language and culture is one way of beginning that conversation, that fair exchange. "You teach me your language and I will teach you mine (be it Swahili or nuclear physics). You may learn my perceptions and problems and I will try to learn yours. Together we may find a new perception, and help each other toward solutions."

Such an approach might help to, in Freire's terms, "humanize education"; that is, make it an instrument of freedom. It would at least be a step toward "decolonializing" the schools, a step which is, I believe, a

---

[13] Michael Rossman. "Learning and Social Change." Paper distributed by the National Student Association in 1968, to be reprinted in a forthcoming book under the same title.

more urgent need for survival than "de-schooling" society, as Illich advocates.[14] For, in shifting from interactions between the autonomous and the dependent to an exchange among equals, the colonial relationship would be ended. It would, too, I am convinced, remove the "neocolonial" aspects between the developed and the developing from the educational relationship. It might even help overcome the alienation which Illich attributes in large part to the mystique of specialization.

It is interesting to note that Buckminster Fuller shares Illich's anti-specialization convictions.[15] Fuller believes not only that specialization has been a means of permitting the few to exercise, often unjustly, power over the many, but also that it is a major obstacle to survival. I agree with his conclusions that we need more generalists and that therefore *all* students should receive a basic "general" education. This goal would be one means of combating the social and political polarization currently plaguing our society, a condition which has been reinforced by giving one kind of education to the elites and another to the masses.

SYSTEMS APPROACH AND SURVIVAL SKILLS

Fuller also advocates a "systems" approach to the study of phenomena and problems. In fact, the demystification of specialities may be achieved through the study of systems. If programs incorporate such studies, including inquiry into what systems are, how they came into being, how they operate, and what purposes they serve, we may better come to understand the phenomenon of elitism and work toward the kind of egalitarian and participatory society which many believe would be more conducive to peace and survival. Fuller also tells us that synergism and cooperative and sharing processes are more productive than competitive ones—another factor to consider in education for the establishment of a just and peaceful human community on a planet even now stretching its resources beyond their ability to meet the needs of all its inhabitants.

Even though we grant some validity to the criticism of a systems approach which holds it to be antihuman and amoral, it is nonetheless a highly efficient tool for the study of institutions and processes. It should also be noted that this criticism can be partly answered by much of the

[14] Ivan Illich. *De-Schooling Society*. New York: Harper & Row, Publishers, 1971.

[15] R. Buckminster Fuller. *Operating Manual for Spaceship Earth*. Carbondale: Southern Illinois University Press, 1969.

work being done in natural rather than man-made systems, which are, in fact, the models for Fuller's work. An adequate systems approach would include inquiry into ecosystems and biosystems, emphasizing the life-sustaining aspect and changing nature of systems. It would also demand that all students be given full opportunity for acquaintance with the life sciences. Mathematics and the sciences, like languages, must become agents for equalizing educational experience, rather than means of producing elites. A sufficient variety of teaching-learning strategies must be devised so that no one need be deprived of this essential part of a general education.

We must recognize too that the study of systems, if it is to contribute to survival, must include an inquiry into the human and moral effects of systems. It is in this specific area of inquiry that Scriven has some useful contributions to make to peace and survival programs. He insists that a survival curriculum should raise the fundamental questions of law and ethics, among them, "Why should those who suffer under a system tolerate it?" [16]

Since groups who find a system intolerable may turn to violence to alter or overthrow the system, this should indeed be a core question in the curricula of the 1970's, as should these parallel questions: How can we change systems? How can we establish justice without violence? When legal recourses are inhumanly slow or stacked against the oppressed, what other alternatives can be projected to ameliorate their lot?

Scriven raises his question about systems in his list of recommendations for "survival skills." He also lists as a skill (because he asserts that in part it can be learned) that quality called "creativity," a skill I would refer to as "constructive imagination" or utopianism at its most pragmatic. Unless we can learn to create practical alternatives to violence, there can be no peace and little chance of long-range survival.

The schools of the 1970's should be preparing students to conceive and put into effect alternative systems which are human, moral, and practical. They should be encouraging disciplined speculation on alternative life styles, forms of government, and social orders. They should as well be developing skills of evaluation to aid the young to select from various alternatives their preferences for modes of survival. Further, they should be helping the young to formulate strategies for change, and should be making it possible for them to test their strategies in practical action

---

[16] Scriven, *op. cit.*, p. 35.

programs, such as the Omega program, which was born in a Jesuit high school in New York in the late 1960's and is now spreading to schools in other areas. (Omega students plan and carry out community-development projects, some in their own city, some going as far as Appalachia. They determine their own success by what they accomplish, and they are given academic credit for their work.)

HUMAN VALUES AND MORAL DEVELOPMENT

The Omega program takes its philosophy from the ecumenism of Pope John, with special reference to his encyclical, *Pacem in Terris,* a document which has a mankind focus. Much of the program strategy derives from Paulo Freire's concept of "conscientization," the process of becoming aware of the social and political structure, or "system," of which each individual is a part, and of striving to motivate and equip individuals not to "adapt" to the structures but to "use" them and, where necessary, to change them to meet their own needs. There is a frank and well-conceived moral element to the program, one which might well be emulated by "secular" schools; for, as Scriven asserts, "The survival curriculum is largely about morality in practice." [17]

The late 1960's and early 1970's have heard much about "the new morality," the erosion of "good, old-fashioned virtue," and very serious, if limited, public debate about the morality of foreign policy and the values implicit in a system which uses more resources on weapons than on education, hospitals, and public works combined; spends more of its wealth in pursuit of "national prestige" in the space program than it does on attempts to remove the "national shame" of those dehumanizing social Siamese twins, poverty and racism; and seems more concerned with "law and order" as a goal in itself rather than as a means to justice.

The moral issues imbedded in our survival crises raise questions about the decision-making ability of the American public and consequently about the role of public education in developing a moral basis for such decision making. Justice is clearly a moral issue, as well as a guideline for the evaluation of political and social systems. One of the primary purported functions of our governmental system is to "ensure justice." Indeed, Scriven points out that the Constitution is a kind of moral contract to

[17] *Ibid.,* p. 52.

guarantee equal justice to all citizens, though few recognize it as such. If preparing the public to deal with such issues is part of the job of the schools, then they can no longer avoid the responsibility of education for moral development.

Although moral education is controversial, schools have never hesitated to "moralize." The young have been fed to the teeth with the prevailing kind of moral instruction. "Obey the rules whatever they are!" "Be loyal to your country regardless of its policies!" "Learn about sex, but do not try it!" "Do not take drugs!" "Adjust to reality!" Bright children may or may not be taking drugs, but most do not want to adjust to reality as defined by adults. What they want is to adjust reality to human needs, and that is a sound moral judgment. If, indeed, as the pragmatists tell us, "morality is the intelligent foresight of consequences," much of the demand for revolution is a sign of a rapidly maturing moral sense among many of our young people and growing numbers of educators. There is now a clear and urgent need to respond to that sense and to help such persons develop moral judgment as one of the major skills of change.

There must be in our survival inquiry a careful investigation of the relationship between means and ends. We may at bottom agree with some of the young, and even with some radical educators who see violent revolution as the only means to relieve oppression, and we may want to implement Scriven's recommendation that "curricula at the *moment* should be organized around studying and *creating* the great revolutions of the past, present, and future." [18]

Yet most of us, educators and/or liberals, are caught in the most acute moral dilemma of our time, the tension between the unacceptability of deliberate violence and the intolerability of gross injustice. Discussion of this dilemma should be an integral part of the survival curriculum. Its resolution cannot be left either to those who will act without reflection or to those who reflect without action. To avoid this moral issue would be the greatest cop-out of education, and indeed failure to confront it may make survival impossible.

Much work has already been done in the area of moral development on which suitable programs can be based for all age levels, and also for cross-generational and community inquiries into moral issues. In a speech before the California Council for the Social Studies, Fannie Shaftel eloquently raised the issue in her reference to the morality of a society that

---

[18] *Ibid.* Italics added—and please note that the "moment" was dated 1969.

permitted the occurrence of the Genovese incident, a murder witnessed by many "law-abiding citizens" who did not want to become involved. In her speech on survival curriculum she made two telling points on a subject which should serve as a significant guideline in formulating programs. "Our problem," she stated, "is not so much the result of a lack of available knowledge as it is first of all a *crisis in values*." [19]

> The priorities . . . essential to survival demand a new ordering based upon the valuing of human progress rather than material progress. . . . What will it take to shift the priorities in our economic system from the gross national product to serving the needs of *all* people *in* the ecosphere? . . . *Knowing and caring* is the necessary condition for achieving the results of a survival curriculum. . . . They are crucial aspects of one process. . . . The cognitive and the affective are inseparable.[20]

I suspect that a good deal of the confusion over moral education can be traced to the functional separation of the two domains by many current curriculum programs. If values education is limited to abstract analysis of value conflicts, it may gain the acceptance of those who believe that schools should be apolitical and nonactivist. But it must be recognized that, unless the continuum of analyzing→knowing→feeling→acting is observed, education will have no effect on raising the level of moral behavior and decision making in our society.

Note especially Shaftel's response to the question of approach to social, or, if you will, public, moral issues:

> I see the values component as a product of an affective-cognitive mode of study designed to cultivate feelings and values based on *continual exploration,* through problem-solving processes, of the *consequences of choices.*[21]

In this statement Shaftel nicely ties together several inseparable elements of the survival curriculum: the thought-feeling or valuing-analyzing element with the process of selection from among alternatives; an ongoing process, part of life itself, continued exploration, implying that there will always be social-moral problems and that survival will always depend upon minds developed to function accordingly. A nice case, I think, for the usefulness of a key technique of world-order studies, using

---

[19] Shaftel, *op. cit.,* p. 5.
[20] *Ibid.,* p. 12. Note the similarity of these ideas to those expressed in the Asilomar Statement quoted earlier in this chapter.
[21] *Ibid.* Italics added.

Utopia not as an end but rather as an intellectual tool for constantly reshaping the present in search of a preferred future and also for the utility of the normative perspective which world-order studies bring to that search.

The study of possibilities for a communally preferred future requires that analysis of controversy, value clarification, priority setting, and moral-judgment making become major objectives of the survival curriculum. Many schools are already doing significant work in these areas, basing it on such offerings as those of Hunt and Metcalf, Oliver and Shaver, and Kohlberg.[22]

At the core of Hunt and Metcalf's work is the belief that reflective thinking is the capacity which education should most strive to develop so that values may be clarified and certain areas formerly "closed" to classroom scrutiny or public debate may be opened and fully reviewed in the general interest. Obviously, a survival curriculum could not tolerate the closing of any issues in the three realms of human experience. Full and open inquiry must prevail, and few, if any, taboos can be imposed. Scriven notes that to some people a survival curriculum will seem to emphasize "shock" elements, and he asserts that it is not the content per se which makes it shocking but its unfamiliarity. I would contend that this unfamiliarity is also what makes the "closed areas" so dangerous. (I suggest that readers review Hunt and Metcalf's list of closed areas. War is among them.) Nothing human should be alien or unfamiliar to a graduate of the survival curriculum. One who has mastered skills for analysis of controversy, value clarification, and moral judgment through the examination of formerly closed areas is more likely to be a constructive citizen of a peaceful world community.

DIALOGUES FOR MORAL DECISION MAKING

If nothing human is to be alien to our graduates, then "humanizing" society and its institutions, including the schools, as Freire asserts, should be an aim of education. The method he proposes to achieve that end, "a dialogue between equals," is notably similar to that proposed by Oliver

---

[22] Maurice P. Hunt and Lawrence E. Metcalf. *Teaching High School Social Studies.* New York: Harper & Row, Publishers, 1968; Donald Oliver and James P. Shaver. *Teaching Public Issues in the High School.* Boston: Houghton Mifflin Company, 1966; Lawrence Kohlberg. *Stages in the Development of Moral Thought and Action.* New York: Holt, Rinehart and Winston, Inc., 1969.

and Shaver and also by Kohlberg; and it seems that, even if their aims are not synonymously defined, they are at least in harmony with Freire. Oliver and Shaver advocate dialogue on issues of public controversy, with generous use of analogous cases to clarify value positions. Kohlberg, in his work on moral development, has used the dialogic method to help youngsters raise their levels of moral-judgment making.[23]

Kohlberg's work constitutes a contribution of the highest potential to the survival curriculum. It fulfills most of the criteria posited by Shaftel and Scriven, and also by the U.S. Office of Education study *An Examination of Objectives, Needs, and Priorities in International Education in the U.S. Secondary and Elementary Schools.*[24]

Kohlberg's research base is multinational: it assumes no cognitive-affective split; it relates levels of moral judgment to levels of analysis and asserts that abstract justice as the final criterion for judgment is the highest moral level. Persons making judgments on the basis of abstract justice have also developed abstract reasoning ability; and, even though Kohlberg concludes that persons who make all or most of their decisions at such levels are usually not tolerated by the rest of society (he cites as examples, Jesus, Gandhi, and King), his work should be a source of optimism, for it suggests that capacities for abstract reasoning and intellectually sound analysis can be developed to much higher levels than have been heretofore assumed.

It is only by developing these capacities to the fullest in all human beings that we can hope to move toward a society that is truly democratic and just. Democratic revolutions and various periods of enlightenment notwithstanding, the fundamental egalitarian revolution has yet to take place. Yet now, for the first time in history, we are at least beginning to see what the operational-behavioral components of that revolution are. Education for humanization should embrace as a goal the eradication of the basic hierarchic organization of almost all "human" society. Racism, sexism, favoritism to specialists, all forms of elitism must be subject to thorough critical analysis and moral evaluation. Should not, for example, James Becker's assertion in Chapter 6 that there appears to be a "moral" advantage to power be subject to critical examination in our classrooms? These subjects should be among the main themes of the educational

---

[23] For an account of a project conducted among boys in reform school, see: "Toward Moral Maturity." *Time,* June 28, 1971. p. 48.

[24] This study was completed by the Foreign Policy Association in 1969. See Chapter 6 of this book.

conversation and the foci of the educational revolution as they are of the social revolutions sought by youth, women, minorities, and all the other oppressed. In a sense each of these movements seeks to achieve the goal implicit in a statement by a 19th-century feminist:

> We deny the right of any portion of the species to decide for another portion, or any individual for another individual, what is and what is not their "proper sphere." The proper sphere for all human beings is the largest and highest which they are able to attain to.[25]

In terms of the programs recommended here, the goal is self-definition. Blacks do not wish to have their roles, much less their persons, defined by a white racist society. Nor do women wish to be imprisoned in a definition of femininity emerging from male sexism. And the young will no longer tolerate subservience to age imposed by those who have lived long enough to acquire the power of imposition. Institutions which perpetuate such forms of elitism do violence to the persons oppressed by them and are as guilty of institutional violence as are nations which govern by totalitarianism or states which impose de facto segregation. Recent studies and other data cited in this Yearbook leave little doubt that the school is among such institutions. Schools should be inquiring into these problems, helping to formulate solutions and working to enact solutions.

PROFESSIONAL RESPONSIBILITIES

Professional organizations have a great responsibility for initiating the revolution. This is true, not only because they have access to a significant communications network within a given profession, but especially because they bear a primary responsibility for the development of the kind of dysfunctional specialization described by Illich and for the entrenchment of the elitism which is both an obstacle to dialogue among equals and an impediment to self-definition. Professional organizations in general follow an order of service which must be reversed. They now give service first to the professionals, next to the profession, and last to the clients. This is one of the main reasons that students have remained until now on the bottom perch of the educational hierarchy.

As the hierarchal structure of education must be disassembled and reconstructed into a circular community of equals, so too must the profes-

---

[25] Harriet Mill. Quoted in: *Life* 71 (7): 55; August 13, 1971.

sional organizations reorder their service priorities. They must open themselves to invite and be enriched by others. Professional apartheid impedes the educational conversation and reinforces the disparate and fragmentary nature of learning within the present school structure. Students, parents—in fact, anyone interested—should be invited, at least for periods of time, into the ranks of the professional organizations. Professional as well as national exchange programs should be undertaken. Educators can learn much from scientists, lawyers, artists, and the like, and we have much to offer other professions. Constructive multidisciplinary programs to serve the needs of peace and survival require conversations *among* professionals and *between* professionals and nonprofessionals.

Schools, too, should be opening their doors. As many educators advocate more off-site, experiential learning opportunities, we should also advocate that noneducators participate in school programs, not just as the important resources they may be but also as co-learners with students, parents, and teachers. There should be more opportunity for ongoing education in which the learning experience is shared by students and parents and by teachers and students. We must be striving toward "learning communities" in both senses of those words. Schools should be both communities *for* learning and the centers of communities which *are* learning.

The structures of these learning communities should be truly democratic, striving toward the realization of a set of universal human values and attempting to equip all human beings to participate fully in the global community of mankind. All people should have an opportunity to educate themselves to their ultimate capacities. All should have available the knowledge and techniques of mathematics, the sciences, and the learnings of human experience. They should be helped to express themselves in various languages and art forms. They should be enabled to become significant parts of the political processes that affect them, from the selection of curricula (which is, indeed, the result of a political process) to the reorganization of international institutions.

Just as the world should be brought into the schools, the schools, through the students—those they are designed to serve—should be brought into the world. Why not, for example, organize more work and travel programs, offering students experience in actively contributing to community change and cultural exchange? Let more of them work in development projects and service organizations, go abroad to teach other students their languages and life styles, returning to their schools to share their learnings and insights with others in their communities. By actually practicing survival skills as part of the process of their education, they may help to further refine those skills and to bring new, constructive perceptions to the central issues for education, survival, peace, and justice.

Readers of this book could help initiate the conversations sorely needed: to transform schools from custodial institutions segregating the young from the rest of society to centers for personal, social, and global development; to keep our cities from further polarizing into violence; to reintegrate communities and minorities into the total life of the nation; to heal the wounds of generational conflict; and to reach beyond our nation to the other peoples of the earth—particularly those who suffer deprivation of a fair share of the values of well-being and justice—to structure a world community. To do this we must have help from and interaction with colleagues in all parts of the world, an opportunity now provided through membership in the World Council for Curriculum and Instruction. Let us begin the conversation in each of our communities. Let us endeavor to forge a chain of concentric conversations similar to the concentric communities Elizabeth Mann Borghese recommends for a world political structure.[26]

Let us converse about the themes of survival, peace, and personhood in all realms of human experience—in the world political structure, in the network of human societies, and in every human person. Let the conversations of the 1970's prepare the way for the real survival revolutions of the 1980's and, we hope, an emerging worldwide, peaceful, and just society in the 1990's. Let us use these conversations to develop in ourselves the skills of survival and the capacity for building the community of man. Such conversations may kindle the courage to hope, which, as Shaftel asserts, is the essential component of our programs:

> Erich Fromm in his book *The Revolution of Hope* says that hope is a decisive element in any attempt to bring about social change in the direction of greater aliveness, awareness, and reason. . . . The real problem is whether we, especially teachers, . . . have the courage to be truly hopeful. . . . We must project a survival curriculum in the schools. By a survival curriculum I mean not just physical survival, but survival for living in a humane world community.[27]

---

[26] Elizabeth M. Borghese. "The World Communities." Paper privately circulated in 1971.
[27] Shaftel, *op. cit.*, p. 405.

Selected References

Elizabeth M. Borghese. "The World Communities." Paper privately circulated in 1971.

William Boyer. "Education for Survival." *Phi Delta Kappan* 52 (5): 258–62; January 1971.

Paulo Freire. *The Pedagogy of the Oppressed.* New York: Herder & Herder, Inc., 1970.

R. Buckminster Fuller. *Operating Manual for Spaceship Earth.* Carbondale: Southern Illinois University Press, 1969.

Edmund W. Gordon. "Building a Socially Supportive Environment." In: Alice Miel and Louise Berman, editors. *Educating the Young People of the World.* Washington, D.C.: Association for Supervision and Curriculum Development, 1970. pp. 59–70.

Maurice P. Hunt and Lawrence E. Metcalf. *Teaching High School Social Studies.* New York: Harper & Row, Publishers, 1968.

Ivan Illich. "The Alternative to Schooling." *Saturday Review* 54 (25): 44–48, 59–60; June 19, 1971.

Ivan Illich. *De-Schooling Society.* New York: Harper & Row, Publishers, 1971.

Earl S. Johnson. "Commentary on Social Studies Curriculum Guidelines." *Social Education* 36 (3): 258ff; March 1972.

Lawrence Kohlberg. *Stages in the Development of Moral Thought and Action.* New York: Holt, Rinehart and Winston, Inc., 1969.

Life 71 (7): 55; August 13, 1971.

Donald Oliver and James P. Shaver. *Teaching Public Issues in the High School.* Boston: Houghton Mifflin Company, 1966.

Betty A. Reardon. "Prologue." *Media & Methods. Exploration in Education.* 6 (2): 35; October 1969.

Bert V. A. Roling. "The Contents of Peace Research." Paper prepared for the 1971 meeting of the International Peace Research Association.

Michael Rossman. "Learning and Social Change." Paper distributed by the National Student Association in 1968, to be reprinted in a forthcoming book under the same title.

Fannie Shaftel. "A Survival Curriculum in the Social Studies." Address to the Southern California Social Studies Council, October 1970.

Michael Scriven. "Education for Survival." In: G. Kinley, editor. *The Ideal School.* Wilmette, Illinois: The Kagg Press, 1969.

The Tree of the Great Peace (Iroquois)*   8

I. The Tree (c. 1450)

*I am Deganawidah and with the chiefs of the Five
   Nations
I plant the Tree of the Great Peace. . . .*

*Roots have spread out from the Tree of the Great Peace
the name of these roots is the Great White Roots of
   Peace. . . .*

*If any man of any nation . . . shall
desire to obey the laws of the Great Peace
he may trace the roots to their source and be welcome
to shelter beneath the Great Peace. . . .*

*I Deganawidah
and the chiefs of our Five Nations of the Great Peace
we now uproot the tallest pine
       into the cavity thereby made
       we cast all weapons of war*

*Into the depths of the earth
into the deep underneath . . .*

we cast all weapons of war

*We bury them from sight forever . . .
and we plant again the tree . . .
Thus shall the Great Peace be established.*

---

* From: *The Magic World,* by William Brandon. Copyright © 1971 by **William Brandon**. Originally published in the *36th Annual Bureau of American Ethnology Report* (Washington, D.C., 1921), and the *League of the Ho-De-No-Sau-Nee* (Rochester, New York, 1851). Adapted from translations by Francis La Flesche, William N. Fenton, Paul A. W. Wallace, and Lewis Henry Morgan. Reprinted by permission of the publisher, William Morrow & Company, Inc.

World Military Expenditures[†]
(Billion Dollars, Current Prices) *

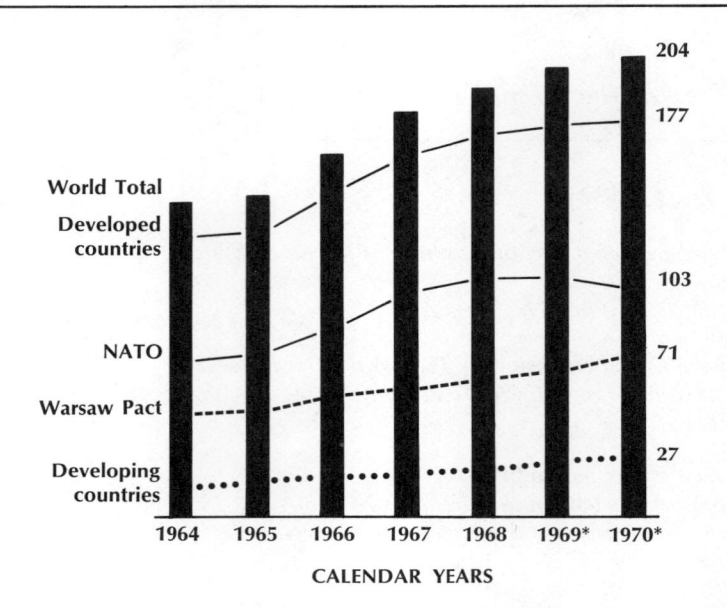

FIGURE 8. Graph based on data from *World Military Expenditures, 1970*. U.S. Arms Control and Disarmament Agency, U.S. Government Printing Office, Washington, D. C. 20402.

The $204 billion spent on arms in 1970 was the equivalent to the annual incomes of the 1.8 billion people in the poorer half of the world population.

Since 1964, military expenditures have risen almost 50 percent, although 3/5 of this rise was the result of inflation. Thus, the real increase was about 20 percent.

NATO spending decreased some 5 percent in 1970, largely because of the reduction in U.S. expenditures. Warsaw Pact spending increased an estimated 1.8 percent in 1970.

Military spending in the developing countries has been rising rapidly, largely in two areas—the Middle East and the Far East. In Latin America, Africa, and South Asia the rise has been moderate. On the whole, the rate of military spending in the developing world has risen faster than GNP (total output of goods and services). In the developed countries GNP has risen faster than military expenditures.

[†] William A. Nesbitt. *Data on the Human Crisis: A Handbook for Inquiry.* New York: Center for International Programs and Comparative Studies of the New York State Education Department, 1972. p. 16. Reprinted by permission.

Children and the Threat of Nuclear War*

Sibylle K. Escalona

8

FOR most of us, it seems to be harder to answer children's questions about the dangers of nuclear war than to talk with them about other difficult facts of life. As parents, we learn to talk with our youngsters about a great many real dangers—accidents, fire, crime, earthquake. We discuss with them sickness, old age, the eventual certainty of death. Why, then, do we have so much trouble explaining fallout, shelters, or drills?

To understand our predicament, we will need to take a look at the actual nature of the threat. What are we dealing with? What makes nuclear danger somehow different from all other hazards?

Nuclear danger is hard to talk about and hard to think about because there is so much that we do not know and cannot imagine. A child may ask, "*Could* there be a war?" and we know the *possibility* exists. A child may ask, "*Will* there be a war?" and no one can be certain. One cannot tell how probable war is. And this is the heart of our problem. Human beings are able to meet with courage dangers and hardships of all sorts. But they can hardly tolerate suspended doubt about whether or not, or to what degree, there *is* a danger.

We have another difficulty: nuclear danger is *unimaginable*. When a child asks, "How big are the bombs?" or "If it happens, where will we go?" nothing in our previous experience suggests an adequate reply. Our

---

* This chapter is reprinted and adapted from portions of a pamphlet published by the Child Study Association of America, Inc., produced in cooperation with the National Institute of Mental Health. Copyright 1962 by the Child Study Association of America, Inc. Reprinted by permission. Schools cannot do the job alone. This article is included to illustrate ways in which parents can teach about war and peace.

imagination cannot grasp what nuclear war might be like. A child wants a simple explanation. But a parent trying to find the answer has disturbing background thoughts like these: After nuclear bombing what kind of world would it be? Who would be in it? What happens to people who stay underground for a long period of time? What would it be like upon emerging? Would food and water be polluted? What would grow? What would be left of community life, law enforcement, the workings of government—and so much else that has regulated the only way of life that we have known?

Lastly, *nuclear threat is all-encompassing.* Most dangers apply only in certain circumstances (drowning, for example, is ordinarily a danger only in deep water). Even major disasters, overwhelming as they are, apply only to a limited number of people or exist for a limited time. But nuclear war threatens us and our children and our children's children. Its effects would be felt by the entire human race for countless future generations. No wonder, then, that a child's questions about war often arouse in us a sense of helpless anxiousness.

What we have said about the difficulties adults encounter in dealing with an overwhelming problem is only half the story. Day in and day out, parents and those who care for children manage somehow to answer their children's questions and to meet their needs. In the following pages, we shall turn to children, to the ways they are affected by an uneasy world, and to some ways adults can strengthen and support their children in the face of much that is distressing.

How much do children know? Apparently a great deal more than we sometimes give them credit for. Children seem so absorbed with their games, their friends, their life at school, that it is hard to believe they pay much attention to grown-up problems. Yet even a young child nearly always seems to know when something really matters to his elders. As soon as American families became concerned over issues of fallout and testing, children also knew about these issues. Signs of their awareness turned up in the questions they asked and even in the games they played.

For example: at times of particularly tense Soviet-American relations, preschool children went right on playing their usual war games. But often the "bad guys" became Russians, and were endowed with all the powers of evil the children could imagine. Again, in October 1961, when renewed nuclear testing aroused worldwide concern, fourth and fifth graders in a New York City school were given a routine assignment. Asked to write one question each about themselves, their school, and the world, 98 percent of these ten- and eleven-year-olds mentioned war or bombs or the possibility that there might not *be* a world.

In short, American children four years old and up are aware of a danger to life. With greater or lesser understanding they connect this danger with the language of nuclear war: fallout, Russia, radiation, H-bomb are all part of their vocabulary.

It is one thing to know about a danger, and quite a different thing to feel afraid. Although a city child knows that carelessness in traffic can lead to serious accidents, he is seldom afraid of cars or of crossing the street. The same is often true of a child's knowledge of nuclear dangers. Children may play at war games or ask about radiation without a sign of fear.

But this is not the whole story. In the winter and spring of 1961–62 many youngsters were frightened by the thought that falling rain and snow contained fallout. Some anxiously followed the weather reports; others told bewildered playmates that the snow was "poisoned" or "bad." Later some four- and five-year-olds showed fears of ordinary passenger planes, believing that they might drop bombs. Still others had nightmares about vague but dreadful images of war.

Why does a child become afraid? As we shall see, a child's awareness of danger may change to fear for many different reasons. The most important one is heightened tension and anxiety among adults. Each time some world event raises the level of concern among grown-ups, there is an increase in the fears of children.

There is another and more subtle way in which children are affected by the threat to survival. Knowing that terrible weapons exist, knowing that shelters and drills are sometimes talked about as dubious protection, even observing that each successful Russian exploration of space is greeted with dismay—all these together may suggest to children an image of the world as an evil, dangerous place. Perhaps the most important challenge to parents lies in this: How can we help our children to achieve a trusting and confident view of life and the future in spite of some dreadful aspects of present-day existence?

HOW CHILDREN COPE WITH THOUGHTS ABOUT NUCLEAR DANGER AND HOW PARENTS CAN HELP

Children of different ages ask different questions and of course need different kinds of answers. At each stage of development, a child responds to danger in ways typical for his age group. More important, at each stage, children have particular ways of protecting themselves from fear and of feeling safe. When parents can fit their answers about nuclear dangers to the ways of thinking most natural to the child, they are likely to be most successful in helping their youngsters to deal effectively with frightening ideas.

Children from About Four to Six Years

Parents know that young children are apt to be afraid of quite a lot of things. They are not usually worried if for a while children are afraid of imaginary monsters, of darkness, of dogs, or of thunderstorms. Yet it is not always easy to feel quite so calm when a child is having nightmares about H-bombs or seems to be afraid of something "bad" in the milk.

Yet it is important to understand that these fears are not all like our own fears of nuclear danger. They are, in fact, much like the preschooler's other fears—an expression of inner emotions. At this stage in his development, a young child is easily frightened by almost anything that is noisy, violent, or suggestive of destruction. This is because, as part of growing up, he is struggling to control very similar feelings within himself. A terrifying TV show or a thunderstorm may evoke in him an echo of his own feelings. If this is more than he can handle, it may then lead to fearfulness.

When a little one is afraid of nuclear danger, it is usually because something has suggested the idea as a symbol for general feelings of uncontrolled violence. Few young children have been frightened by bombs or fallout unless older children have threatened them with the idea ("They'll blow you up!") or unless they have overheard excited grown-up conversations on these topics.

Wise parents know that some fearfulness is normal for the preschool age. They also know that young children have a built-in safety device that makes it possible to calm these terrors. In their heart of hearts, young children believe that their parents are all-powerful and can protect them against all evil. This firm belief is what ordinarily enables them to push aside fearful things—death or accidents, even nuclear danger. Reassurance of our love and protection does most to keep a preschooler feeling safe. For no matter what a preschooler's fear is about on the surface, his real fear is that he may be hurt or lose the protective closeness of his parents.

The young child who asks if fallout hurts or if the bomb is going to drop needs a listening ear and an honest answer. But the answer will be much more satisfying if it is brief and to the point. Detailed explanations are apt to perplex and burden a preschooler. In essence he wants to feel that his parents know all about the problem and that they will take care of him.

It is a good idea to protect young children from too much talk about nuclear danger. Family discussions are best conducted when the youngest members are otherwise occupied. High-powered TV programs on such subjects as nuclear testing might be watched in a room where they will not distress children much too young to understand the nature of the problem. A child shielded from such overly exciting situations is much less likely to choose nuclear weapons as symbols for frightening emotions which come from within.

When a child is having nightmares or is otherwise upset by thoughts of war, two things—explanation and reassurance—very often help.

Almost always, preschool fears are based on misunderstanding. The children are confused and are afraid that something is going to hurt them here-and-now, though in reality the danger is remote. The preschooler needs to be told the simple facts—that the planes do not carry bombs. Yet reasoning alone seldom really comforts a preschool child. A momentarily terrified five-year-old is not calmed by being told "there are no ghosts." What seems to help is a bedtime story, an extra cookie, a nightlight, and the knowledge that mother is not far away.

Even small children understand that nuclear weapons might really be used, on purpose, and by people with intent to hurt. In this respect their fearful thoughts about nuclear war are quite different from fears about monsters or about thunderstorms.

One way parents can help their children is to make it clear that they believe that nations must settle their quarrels peacefully. In general, parents teach children to control their anger, to avoid destruction, and to respect the rights of others. Even a preschooler will sense a "double standard" if we teach one idea for family living and another for life among nations. He will be better fortified against fear and confusion if we can tell him that among nations, too, reason and fairness work better than blind anger.

It is not hard for young children to understand that those on the "good" side have to try to convince others who do not share their views, for they feel the "good" and "bad" impulses in themselves and know it is a struggle.

Children from About Six to Twelve Years

By and large, school-age children are less given to fearfulness than younger ones. They seem well equipped to deal with inner feelings and with outer dangers. Yet, curiously enough, it is just among the eight-, nine-, and ten-year-olds that questions and worries over nuclear danger have often been reported.

To explain this seeming paradox, it is useful to take a look at the underlying sources of fear in middle childhood, and at the ways in which children of this age usually deal with fearful thoughts.

One of the things each child learns as he enters school age is that he must rely on himself. He learns there are many things that even the most loving parent cannot do for him. In school and on the street, he finds that it is he—the child—who must meet the competition, who has to be strong enough to play baseball, and smart enough to learn reading. One underlying fear in school-age children is that they may not be able and strong enough to do all that is required. Even "A" students worry about schoolwork; even splendid little athletes wonder if they can hold their own among the other children.

The second basic source of fearfulness in school-age children is a result of learning about the world beyond the family. Children come to see themselves, their family, their town, and even their country as small parts of a complex universe, subject to large forces. It is no wonder then that children of this age feel threatened by the idea that the world is so big that any one small person can feel lost and of no account.

A school-age child still relies heavily on his parents' love and protection for safety. But by now he has some important new methods of his own to help him feel secure.

School-agers place enormous faith in knowing exactly what lies ahead of them and what they will be expected to do. In encountering something new and possibly painful, often their first reaction is to try to find out all about it in advance. They ask many questions, and by imagining events before they happen, they often can forestall fears. Take, for example, the questions a child asks when he faces an operation. The more he inquires, the more he can anticipate the room, the anesthetic, the stitches, the better are his chances of meeting the experience without undue fear.

Similarly, many a school-age youngster tries to find out all about next year's teacher, or about teen-agers and their doings or any other thing that lies ahead. Children's questions about nuclear war are of the same kind. They ask us about the size of the bombs, about who will be with them, about the speed of missiles, and such questions as, "What do you find when you come out of the shelter?"

It is easy to see why this device of "forewarned is forearmed" fails to work when it comes to nuclear threat. We do not really know the answers, and the child feels his helplessness—even as we do—just because he does not know what to expect.

School-age children learn that confidence comes with knowing how to do a thing, and having the tools to do it with. They are impressed by parents, teachers, older children, public heroes, and all those who seem to them to embody the strength that they themselves still lack. Often they try to be as much as possible like those who most impress them. When children strive to become like the important people in their lives, they feel that they somehow share in the strength and safety of the adult model.

It is entirely healthy and fitting that children, who are not yet ready to find their way without guidance, should rely on the ability and trustworthiness of older persons, and thus on borrowed strength. In children's response to the nuclear threat, we see the same tendency. They admire space heroes, they ask if the President will stop the Russians from making war, and they like to hear about any new and powerful invention by Americans. But they have also asked their parents, "What will *you* do?" or "Will Daddy have to go away?"

This is one of the reasons that a child is helped by knowing that his parents are thinking about these issues and have some definite ideas about them. School-age children cannot judge for themselves the issue of nuclear testing. But they draw strength from an adult who does not shrink from questions and who communicates the feeling that human life and human values are important and worth working for.

Each parent or teacher has his own personal style of talking with children. The suggestions which follow are not intended as rigid rules. They are offered as general principles that parents may find useful in adapting their answers to a child's level of understanding, and to his typical methods of coping with upsetting thoughts. They are followed, in the next section, by some further guides to specific situations parents sometimes face with their school-age children.

Encourage open conversation. In the minds of children, something you must not talk about is easily felt to be something that is bad and frightening. On the other hand, the experience of hearing something spoken of calmly and reasonably is reassuring. It helps to relieve the child from a sense of hidden worry.

Clear up misunderstandings. School-age children do not fully understand all that they hear. Many of their fears rest on partial misunderstanding. For instance, some children are confused about the difference between testing and actual bombings, and there are a host of other ways in which children misinterpret the information they hear and read. It is important to listen closely to what children say; for, at this age particularly, youngsters are apt to take for literal fact expressions that may be general or figurative.

Gauge information to children's understanding. School-age children want more information than do little ones. Yet even ten-year-olds cannot keep in mind all the many sides of complex, controversial issues, such as testing. Parents who go into more detail than a child can keep in mind and understand may unwittingly suggest new dangers of which the child had never thought. With children up to eleven years or so, it is probably best to limit information to those aspects of the situation of which the children are already aware. Youngsters who are encouraged to speak their mind can be trusted to ask further questions, should the first answer fail to satisfy.

Emphasize activities, skills, and resources that exist to combat nuclear danger. Children's own answer to a frightening prospect is to learn the "right way," the proper skill for meeting each situation. Once children know that a danger exists they need to have a concrete picture of what adults are doing for protection.

Parents have different viewpoints about the most effective measures against nuclear danger. Each will select for emphasis those national and civic actions that seem to him most promising. These may include emphasis on government negotiations (and, to most children, government means the President), the United Nations, civil defense, or the work of civic peace groups.

Let children know about the attitudes and values that support friendly regulations among nations. School-age children are interested in other lands and other people. Parents can do a great deal to break down the stereotypes about "foreigners" as hostile and strange beings. Given a chance, children can understand that people in other countries have the same needs and the same human qualities, and they can draw strength from learning that millions of families all over the world are like themselves in that they wish to live in peace.

In school and at home, school-age children can be taught something of the American tradition. They can feel a sense of pride in knowing that we have stood for freedom and equal rights for all human beings. Ten-year-olds are not too young to comprehend the notion that it is possible to stand by one's ideals and to work for them in ways that fit our basic belief in the dignity of every kind of person.

SPECIAL CIRCUMSTANCES AFFECTING THE SCHOOL

Child's Response to Nuclear Danger

So far we have spoken in general terms and have suggested general principles. Yet we know that our description of children's response does not always apply. Parents may encounter problems quite different from those we have already mentioned. The following is a discussion of some of the special circumstances that have a direct bearing on the way in which families experience nuclear danger.

School-age children know quite well that adults disagree on basic attitudes to building military strength. Very often children's questions come about as they hear teachers disagree with parents, or find that the family next door has different attitudes from their own.

Things become more critical when disagreement exists within the family. For example, the mother has joined a women's group to protest testing, while the father does not share her view. Under these circumstances, children will be more concerned than otherwise and may therefore also be more anxious. As in any other family dilemma, children are made uneasy when their belief in one parent seems to imply that they must disbelieve the other.

Explain that parents have a common aim. One thing that grown-ups take for granted needs to be explained to school-age children. Namely, in disagreements of this sort, both parents are equally concerned about the welfare of the child and of all people. Both want their children to be safe. They differ on what is the *best way* of achieving a secure future.

Recognize differences of opinion. Children know when parents will naturally try not to involve the child too deeply; it does not help to act as though there were no difficulty. When parents try to hide their differences, a child will sense concealment. Not knowing the facts, he is apt to imagine something more distressing than a difference of opinion. He may worry (as many children do) that his parents do not love each other any more. It is much easier for him to know that his parents disagree than to worry about the cause of hidden tension in the home. A school-age child will not lose confidence in a mother who says, "Such and such is my opinion, but Daddy thinks differently. We have to talk about it." Because this is something he can understand, it will not make him anxious. And the more secure he feels about his family, the less likely he is to have fearful thoughts about the possible danger of nuclear destruction.

Some families are deeply involved in the social and political issues connected with peace and with international affairs. They may belong to peace groups; they may be active in civil defense; they may take part in any of the organized efforts to better the world situation. No matter what these families' views, to a greater or lesser degree their daily life is permeated by the conviction that danger of war is imminent and real. Children hear a great deal of conversation on the topic; their parents go to meetings and rallies; pamphlets and banners are apt to be in sight.

Children in such homes are keenly aware of public danger. But, more important, they are apt to feel parents' tension and concern. It is not surprising that fear and open worry over the possibility of harm and destruction are more common among children whose parents are most engaged in the struggle for a solution of the world crisis.

This poses a dilemma. The very parents who are most willing to recognize the threat to survival, and who take it as seriously as do scientific and political leaders everywhere, thereby also commit their children to a style of life that brings a greater likelihood of fearfulness. On the other hand, as we suggest later on, the very fact that parents are taking an active role in world affairs can also instill in children a more confident view of the future. In the long run, this may prove of greater basic importance.

We cannot offer easy and complete solutions. We can, however, suggest some ways of preventing *unnecessary* fears.

Do not expose children to overly intense adult emotion. Parents who give much of their time and energy to this issue are people who feel the threat of nuclear danger in an intense and personal way. The problem is so overwhelming that at times adults may feel moved to profound distress, to anxiety, and to a sort of helpless anger. If children bring their questions at such times, it is not easy to navigate between the need for emotional honesty on the one hand and the danger of overwhelming children by the intensity of our feeling on the other.

School-age children cannot reasonably be expected to cope with adult moods of desperation, or with any other very strong emotion. Even as we say of grown-ups that strong feeling can be "overwhelming," so children are flooded and distressed by an emotional intensity that is too much for them.

We do not suggest that parents try to conceal their feelings. When questions are met with answers that are belied by the very tone of voice in which they are given, children will draw their own conclusions and be more troubled than they were before. But it is possible to express honest feeling in a way that is somewhat controlled and modulated.

There are other situations in which parents have occasion to hold in check their feelings in a similar manner—when there has been a death in the family, for instance. At such times children observe their parents' grief and may share in it; yet they are shielded from the most intense moments of feeling among adults.

Be deliberate in the choice of words and examples. In discussing peace and war, adults speaking to one another are apt to use the most graphic phrases they can find, and to use the most telling examples of the horror they wish to guard against. The same is often true of civil defense brochures, and of the literature put out by various peace groups. Parents often report that children who listen to such conversations, and who also read what is in sight, have been disturbed by such graphic language. In one instance, an angry eight-year-old was heard to tease his sister, "Radiation will get you and your fingers will drop off." When she burst into tears, he cited in defense a pamphlet he had read.

It is well to remember that children have a much more vivid imagination than do adults. When we hear a phrase, they often see a vivid inner picture. School-age children also are very literal minded. If someone says, "There is no hope, life on earth will be impossible," a child is apt to envisage total devastation, and at once. Unnecessary fears can be avoided if parents will use care not only in *what* is said in children's hearing but in *how* it is expressed.

Explain what you are doing and why. Children who know that their own parents are taking personal responsibility in relation to nuclear danger may experience this as a source of strength and reassurance. The younger ones especially are apt to feel that if their parents are taking steps to solve a problem, the chances are it *will* be solved, for it is in good hands. Children of all ages are helped by knowing that large numbers of adults are actively engaged in efforts to deal with the nuclear threat. When parents engage in such activity, children come to see the possibility of war less as a shadowy and frightening background terror than as something that can be solved through action, for that is what they see their parents doing.

In this respect, as in some others we have mentioned, what may seem self-evident to parents needs careful explanation to the children. Adults write to Congressmen and go to meetings and take other steps only because they hope and believe that these steps will be effective and really make a difference. Yet children may be more aware of their parents' concern and anxiety than of the positive meaning of these actions. A good way of supporting children against the fear-arousing aspects of the situation is to explain in some detail the positive goals for which their parents work.

Children from Twelve to Eighteen Years

Adolescence can be a stormy period of development. It is not easy to have outgrown childhood and yet not be adult in body or in mind. The concerns and interests of the teen-age set all have to do with the future. They think about jobs and professions, about sex and marriage, about the kinds of people they want to become.

Even at the best of times, the future does not seem a bed of roses to young people. Everyone knows the swings from cheerful optimism to acute discouragement, from silliness to utmost seriousness, and from defiance to harsh morality that are typical of the age. These reflect a kind of tug-of-war that normally goes on in every adolescent. Deep down he wants to grow up, to enjoy adult freedoms, and to find a worthwhile place for himself in the community. Yet he is also loath to give up the pleasures and protection that go with childhood. He is a bit afraid of being independent, and he wonders if the things he wants from life are there for the taking.

In time, most young people settle down, gaining stability and perspective. The single most important force that helps them in their struggle for maturity is the real opportunities for satisfaction that the social environment does offer. It is the promise which the future holds that makes it worthwhile to grow up.

An atmosphere of doubt and dread about the future threatens adolescents at their most vulnerable point. Adolescent conversation shows—and so do many of the essays written for school—that they are not primarily afraid of hardships. Rather it is the thought that there may not be continuity and sense in the life that lies ahead. One high school senior put it thus: "I and my friends know that we cannot live forever, everybody has to die. The only way in which there can be something like reincarnation is in society. I mean, that it would make a difference that we had been alive. If you don't have that, you have nothing."

Adolescents have many different ways of responding to nuclear danger. It seems that *what* it is that causes their distress is much the same for all—it is the fact that nuclear weapons might destroy much of the future they are counting on. Yet *how* they deal with it will vary widely. A description follows of some of the most typical ways of responding.

Some teen-age youngsters claim that there is no point in studying or in taking responsibility, because "the future looks grim." These young people take a very pessimistic view. It is natural for adolescents to see the world as either all good or all bad. The knowledge that there is a threat to survival can so strengthen the "all bad" kind of expectation as to make hard work at studies or care and circumspection seem quite meaningless.

In other cases, parents have the impression that these seemingly defeated youngsters may not entirely believe all of the things they say. Taking chances with exams, with cars, and with dates is what many a teen-age boy and girl would like to do in any case. It is as though the harsh reality gave these young people a ready-made excuse for behaving as they do, and as they might have done in any case. Yet it makes a difference that adolescent pessimism is supported by the facts.

Now as always, adolescents freely criticize the adult world. High school and college students hold long debates about what is wrong with adult values. Since society is far from perfect, they can find much that is disappointing. Many young people take a jaundiced view of anything supported by adult authority, be it religion, politics, or practical advice.

Such healthy youthful skepticism can be greatly exaggerated and distorted as a result of the nuclear crisis. Some teen-agers have come to feel that they cannot trust even the most positive of adult attitudes. It is as though the beliefs of older generations were discredited, for after all they brought us close to world destruction. A scornful adolescent told his exasperated father: "If we stay up all night, whom do we hurt? It's you who made the bomb that's going to blow us up in the end."

Here again, young people's very personal conflicts get mixed up with broader social issues. No matter how absurd the youngsters' way of putting it may be, there is some truth in what these adolescents say. Adults, too, have reason to question some of the established values. It would not be easy—nor honest—to meet adolescent indignation with untroubled confidence in what we have to offer.

Some teen-agers act as though they neither knew nor cared about a threat to their future. When nuclear issues are mentioned, they turn them into a joke, or pay no attention, or become impatient. Some parents are concerned not because their adolescents worry too much about the danger of war but because they seem to show callous indifference.

At first glance it seems as though these youngsters had found an easy way of avoiding fear and discouragement. A closer look at what is happening beneath the surface shows that these youngsters have adopted a somewhat cynical ostrich attitude. In one way or another they express an attitude that could be put like this: "If all these awful things are true, I do not want to know about them."

Whenever people deliberately close their eyes to facts, it means that they feel helpless and fatalistic. As one 15-year-old said, "Nothing can change things, no matter what you do."

Refusal to acknowledge something unpleasant does not do away with it. Disturbing feelings still exist and undermine basic security, even when the adolescent does not admit these feelings to himself. Moreover, we know that a sense of being powerless over one's own fate is one of the most painful feelings in human experience. Somehow, the expressions of unconcern and disinterest do not ring true. They mask the underlying sense of apprehension.

Adolescents are ready to take an interest in world affairs. Some teen-agers have responded by a greater eagerness to learn and to act on their convictions. There are now more student groups (both high school and college) dedicated to discussion and to action than there have been in many years.

In adults, emergencies often bring into the open a strength and energy unlike anything seen at other times. For adolescents, too, the experience of being roused to action can be strengthening and can give an important push to forward development. When young people feel—and many older adolescents do—that grown-ups need the support of youth in a good cause, it can change their feelings about the future. We have seen in many teen-agers, instead of a sense of discouragement, a sense of purpose that makes the future seem exciting and important.

In one way or another, adolescents must react to the fact that survival is at stake. It is all the more important then that, in relation to this crucial issue, parents support positive experiences and be sensitive to the special needs of the young people in their charge. Once again we offer some suggestions that may be helpful:

Take young people into partnership. Conversations between adolescents and their parents are a tricky business. Teen-agers tend to be overly critical of their parents—and to demand of lot of them. Temporarily they may choose to believe and think almost anything—so long as it is different from what their parents stand for. At the same time, they watch their parents closely. If what they see is disappointing, they may react with serious dismay. It is almost as though they feel betrayed when parents do not always meet their highest expectations. The truth of the matter is that anything parents say and do carries special weight with adolescents, even when youngsters act as though their parents' opinions mattered not at all.

Whether a conversation concerns the nuclear crisis or anything else, adolescents are not only overly sensitive to what their parents say but find it hard to accept their parents' ideas or advice. Young people bridle at being told what to think. Above all, they want to be taken seriously as people who can be trusted to form their own opinion.

We cannot always meet the adolescent's need to be treated as an equal, but when it comes to exploring and discussing important world issues, there is every reason to affirm young people's budding sense of independence, and to take them into partnership.

In talking with young people, it is especially important to let them know just what the grown-up thinks and feels. Teen-agers feel the strength of a parent who "sticks by his guns." When parents hesitate to share their own point of view, a teen-ager can easily misunderstand. He may feel that his parents are indifferent to him and *his* opinion, or indifferent to issues that vitally affect *his* life. Strangely enough, this is just as true for boys and girls who reject their parents' point of view as it is for those who want to share it.

Provide opportunities for exploration away from home. Young people often can learn from relative strangers, or from their fellows, what they cannot accept at home. This is so because any interchange between parents and their adolescent children is charged with the very personal emotion that each has for the other.

Parents and teachers can see to it that adolescents have a chance to discuss nuclear threat and the various ways of combating it, and to do so in ways that are congenial to the age group.

This means debates at school. A youngster scheduled to debate disarmament will "bone up" on his subject. And when it is a contest among peers, the young audience will listen with absorption to what would seem "dry facts" at other times.

It also means encouraging young people to see and hear authorities express their views. Adolescents are especially responsive to direct contact with individuals who can serve as symbols of maturity. Scientists, political leaders, renowned scholars—they all represent positive adult models. Adolescents can view such figures on TV, but that is a poor second best. The experience of being addressed as part of an adult audience, sensing the interest and excitement aroused in people in the room—all this conveys a sense of sharing the life of the community. This is what adolescents need. It strengthens the ties that bind them to the world about, and lends excitement to the prospect of maturity.

Parents can also encourage youngsters to make their own discoveries and explorations. Articles and books can be put where they are hard to overlook. They have a good chance of being read if others in the family have already found them exciting. Parents can clip newspapers for notices of lectures, special TV programs, and meetings to which they themselves might like to go.

In most of this, the parents' role in helping teen-agers come to grips with the world they live in is partly indirect. Through the PTA and local school boards, through churches and neighborhood centers, and through public channels, parents can provide the opportunities we have mentioned. In general, an attitude of inviting participation without urging it will be the most helpful.

Parents' attitudes are important even when youngsters do not seem interested. We know that it is easier to make suggestions than to carry them out. We have said, for example, that it is important for parents to share their point of view with adolescent children. Yet often enough, young people will cut short their elders' explanations. Or discussion groups may be organized, and many a youngster would rather spend his time on something else. Books and lectures may be plentiful, but the young hopeful in the house may studiously ignore them.

And yet it makes a difference if parents can maintain a readiness to involve their children in the adult concern with the nuclear danger. It feels very much better to turn down an invitation than never to have been asked.

At the very least, parental attitudes of the kind we have described will make adolescents feel that they are not excluded from adult affairs. Rather, they will see that parents expect and welcome a sharing of responsibility.

THE SUM AND SUBSTANCE

In this chapter we have put together what is known about children's reactions to nuclear danger. Based upon our understanding of child development, and of parent-child relationships, we have pointed to some ways in which parents can help children of different ages deal with a threat that is entirely new to human experience.

Children are influenced first and foremost by the attitudes of adults. This is one reason why, throughout the chapter, we have stressed how important it is for children to know that the adults whom they trust have thought about the nuclear threat and what it implies.

We believe that what parents and educators think and do at the present time can play a vital role in determining the future. Whenever a species or a civilization is confronted by a change in circumstances which threatens survival, one of two things must happen. Either patterns of behavior unsuited to the new conditions of life do not change in basic ways, and the particular civilization disappears from the face of the earth. Or the civilization has the resourcefulness to adapt to altered circumstance, to change itself in such a way as to survive under new conditions. The existence of nuclear power within a pattern of social life that has always led to warfare is nothing less than such a threat to the survival of human civilization as we know it. Our children must learn to develop attitudes and beliefs and patterns of living that make possible some sort of peaceful regulation and control of human affairs.

We, ourselves, learned our basic attitudes from our parents. And what we learned is not in all respects adapted to survival in the nuclear age. If our children are to make the vital shift toward new patterns of existence, parents and all concerned with children must be the ones to point the way. We must be willing to give up some familiar patterns of thought and action.

This is a difficult and painful task. We have not tried to minimize the difficulty, but we think the challenge can be met.

We are the first generation to hold a veto power over continuing human life on earth; but we are also the first to be so fully capable of deciding our future. We have knowledge, experience, technological skills, communications systems, and resources never before available. We can know people in other countries, and learn to understand them as our ancestors could not dream of doing.

What we are saying is that child rearing and education are not an entirely private matter. At this time especially, *child rearing is a way of making history.* Helping children to help themselves may require of us that we come to terms with broader social issues.

Selected References

The Effects of Nuclear Weapons. Revised edition. Washington, D.C.: Superintendent of Documents, U.S. Government Printing Office, 1962.

Foreign Affairs Bibliography: A Selected and Annotated List of Books on International Relations. 3 volumes. Published for the Council on Foreign Relations. New York: Harper & Brothers.

International Atomic Energy Agency Catalog. New York: United Nations Bookshop.

An International Bibliography on Atomic Energy. Vol. 1: *Political, Economic, and Social Aspects.* New York: United Nations Bookshop.

U.S. Disarmament Administration. *A Basic Bibliography: Disarmament, Arms Control, and National Security.* Washington, D.C.: Superintendent of Documents, U.S. Government Printing Office.

U.S. 86th Congress. *Biological and Environmental Effects of Nuclear War.* Hearings before Special Subcommittee of Joint Committee on Atomic Energy, June 22–26, 1959. Washington, D.C.: Superintendent of Documents, U.S. Government Printing Office.

U.S. Senate Committee on Foreign Relations. *Disarmament and Security: A Collection of Documents, 1919–1955.* Washington, D.C.: Superintendent of Documents, U.S. Government Printing Office.

Let America Be America Again
Langston Hughes

Let America be America again.
Let it be the dream it used to be.
Let it be the pioneer on the plain
Seeking a home where he himself is free.

(America never was America to me.)

Let America be the dream the dreamers dreamed—
Let it be that great strong land of love
Where never kings connive or tyrants scheme
That any man be crushed by one above.

(It never was America to me.)

O, let my land be a land where Liberty
Is crowned with no false patriotic wreath,
But opportunity is real, and life is free,
Equality is in the air we breathe.

(There's never been equality for me,
Nor freedom in this "homeland of the free.")

Say who are you that mumbles in the dark?
And who are you that draws your veil across the stars?

I am the poor white, fooled and pushed apart,
I am the Negro bearing slavery's scars.
I am the red man driven from the land,
I am the immigrant clutching the hope I seek—

And finding only the same old stupid plan
Of dog eat dog, of mighty crush the weak.
I am the young man, full of strength and hope,
Tangled in that ancient endless chain
Of profit, power, gain, of grab the land!

* Reprinted by permission of Harold Ober Associates, Incorporated. Copyright 1938 by Langston Hughes; renewed.

Of grab the gold!
Of grab the ways of satisfying need!
Of work the men! Of take the pay!
Of owning everything for one's own greed!

I am the farmer, bondsman to the soil.
I am the worker sold to the machine.
I am the Negro, servant to you all.
I am the people, worried, hungry, mean—
Hungry yet today despite the dream.
Beaten yet today—O, Pioneers!
I am the man who never got ahead,
The poorest worker bartered through the years.

Yet I'm the one who dreamt our basic dream
In that Old World while still a serf of kings.
Who dreamt a dream so strong, so brave, so true,
That even yet its mighty daring sings
In every brick and stone, in every furrow turned
That's made America the land it has become.
O, I'm the man who sailed those early seas
In search of what I meant to be my home—
For I'm the one who left dark Ireland's shore,
And Poland's plain, and England's grassy lea,
And torn from Black Africa's strand I came
To build a "homeland of the free."

The free?

A dream—
Still beckoning to me!
O, let America be America again—
The land that never has been yet—
And yet must be—
The land where every man is free.
The land that's mine—

The poor man's, Indian's, Negro's ME—
Who made America,
Whose sweat and blood, whose faith and pain,
Whose hand at the foundry, whose plow in the rain,
Must bring back our mighty dream again.
Sure, call me any ugly name you choose—
The steel of freedom does not stain.
From those who live like leeches on the people's lives,
We must take back our land again,
America!

O, yes,
I say it plain,
America never was America to me,
And yet I swear this oath—
America will be!
An ever-living seed,
Its dream
Lies deep in the heart of me.
We, the people, must redeem
Our land, the mines, the plants, the rivers,
The mountains and the endless plain—
All, all the stretch of these great green states—
And make America again!

$167 Billion Appropriated by Congress in 1970†

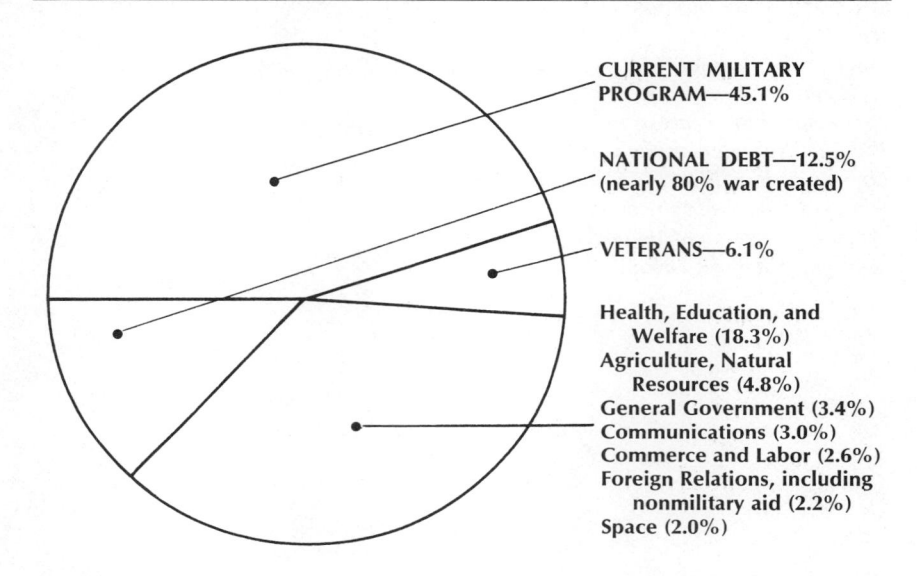

```
CURRENT MILITARY
PROGRAM—45.1%

NATIONAL DEBT—12.5%
(nearly 80% war created)

VETERANS—6.1%

Health, Education, and
   Welfare (18.3%)
Agriculture, Natural
   Resources (4.8%)
General Government (3.4%)
Communications (3.0%)
Commerce and Labor (2.6%)
Foreign Relations, including
   nonmilitary aid (2.2%)
Space (2.0%)
```

FIGURE 9. Graph based on data from Friends Committee on National Legislation, 245 Second Street, N.E., Washington, D.C. 20002.

Over 61 percent (over $100 billion) of the money appropriated in Congress during 1970 went to pay for national defense and past and present wars. Included is not only over $75 billion for present military and defense activities but over $10 billion for veterans of past wars and Vietnam and nearly $17 billion interest on the national debt, which is largely the result of borrowing to pay for wars.

The Senate Majority Leader said in 1970 that the government requested over $375 in military defense for every man, woman, and child in the United States, but only $7.50 for elementary and secondary education.

In *The Economy of Death* (New York: Atheneum Publishers, 1970), Richard J. Barnet said: "The American people are devoting more resources to the war machine than is spent by all federal, state, and local governments on health and hospitals, education, old-age and retirement benefits, public assistance and relief, unemployment and social security, housing and community development, and the support of agriculture. Out of every tax dollar there is about 11 cents left to build American society."

† William A. Nesbitt. *Data on the Human Crisis: A Handbook for Inquiry.* New York: Center for International Programs and Comparative Studies of the New York State Education Department, 1972. p. 21. Reprinted by permission.

Peace: Today and Tomorrow*
George Henderson

PEACE means many things to many people. It can mean the inner tranquillity which comes to those who live in harmony with their personal universe. And it can mean the absence of war, of force or the threat of force, in relations between nations. Peace should also mean opportunity for the human race to meet the physical threats of gnawing hunger, of agonizing disease, of the expanding problems of population and pollution. Opportunity to meet the moral challenges of racial strife, of callousness to suffering and death, of hate and greed and all their ugly kin.[1]

The closer we get to the year 2000, the more our thoughts turn to the future. Some writers believe that we are moving irreversibly toward the antiseptic societies of *1984* and *Brave New World*. Others foresee chaos and an uninhabitable planet. The future will be what we make it—no more, no less. It is my hope that our future will be peaceful.

OUR VIOLENT PEOPLE

No society can exist without order. Violence is a result of the breakdown of social order. Social order is maintained, and violence is prevented, by the effective functioning of legal, political, and educational institutions—especially the agencies of law enforcement and public education. Individuals can form communities, but only through social institutions can

---

* This chapter is expanded upon in: George Henderson. *To Live in Freedom: Human Relations Today and Tomorrow*. Norman: University of Oklahoma Press, 1972. Reprinted by permission of the University of Oklahoma Press.

[1] *To Free Mankind*. Washington, D.C.: World Federalist Youth–U.S.A., 2029 K St., N.W., n.d.

they form nations. As a nation, communities solve their joint problems collectively and thereby become civilized. Though we are civilized in terms of institutions, it appears that we are not yet civilized in our interpersonal relations. As a nation we are afflicted by a kind of institutional paralysis, and we seem incapable of peacefully solving our rapidly growing national and international problems.

Even though ours is a violent history, most Americans are ignorant about violence.[2] We perpetuate childlike fantasies and smug assumptions that violence is bred by some unknown "bad guys" who will be destroyed by some unknown "good guys." Commissions are appointed, research is conducted, and books are written to reassure the public that justice will triumph. But the basic public attitude remains unchanged. Few people care enough to become actively involved in combating the conditions leading to violence.

There seems to be something sadistically fascinating about violence. The word "violence" has a menacing, disturbing quality. It implies something dreaded, powerful, destructive, or eruptive. It startles, frightens, and horrifies us. Yet violence is also exciting and dramatic. Reading about it and sometimes participating in it give many people a tingling pleasure. On television screens there appear for our amusement scenes of fighting, beating, torturing, and killing. We are a Pow! Crash! Ugh! Bang! nation. We are even willing to write off the agony that is a part of war, the ultimate violence, as a cheap price to pay for securing "peace" throughout the world.

Much of the movie violence is portrayed semirealistically, even romantically. Jesse James, Billy the Kid, Al Capone, Bonnie and Clyde, Ma Barker, and other criminals are remembered, often with admiration. The superhero who emerged in the 1960's was James Bond, a machinelike man who was licensed to kill and destroy and who was even more violent, callous, and aggressive than old-style criminals. Heroes like Bond allow us to experience violence from the safe distance of our movie or television seats. The fake quality of this kind of violence gives the impression that being beaten, kicked, and cut, while unpleasant, is not really very painful or serious. Such physical treatment may incapacitate a weakling—but not our movie hero. After being knocked down or shot, our hero rolls over, opens his eyes, jumps up, rubs his chin, grins, and moves on. This is one of the lessons children learn by watching movies.

[2] James Campbell *et al. Law and Order Reconsidered.* New York: Bantam Books, Inc., 1970.

Even sweet little old men and women may peek at violent orgies when they get a chance. To accommodate them and others, entrepreneurs promote bloody sports spectacles. People pay large amounts to see their particular champions of violence perform. Crowds come alive when a man is hit hard over the heart or head, when blood gushes from his nose and eyes, when he wobbles under the attack, and when his pursuer continues to smash at him with devastating impact; and they cheer when the loser falls. Athletes participating in these public spectacles are much like the ancient gladiators who risked their lives for a public that would cheer their victories.

We are becoming increasingly aware of our national characteristic of violence and are beginning to recognize it as a social problem. Once aware of the violence in our land, we tend to try to alter the facts to suit our definitions of the situation, responding as it were to our own fears. Some people maintain that we must meet force with force: an eye for an eye and a life for a life. The number of weapons purchased in this country for purposes of self-defense (that is, to have the power to kill or maim another human being) is, to say the least, frightening. At the national level the emergence of the United States as a great power was accompanied by a growing commitment to violence as a technique for implementing international policy.

In 1970 there were 16,000 criminal homicides in America—one every 33 minutes. We continue to be the leading Western nation in the rate at which its citizens destroy one another. Crime officials estimate that there are 115 million privately owned guns in the United States, almost one for every male between the ages of 14 and 65. Guns are used in 65 percent of all killings in the United States, and knives are used in 20 percent of the killings.

But violence is not unique to our country; throughout the history of the Western nations violence has been a technique of those who are committed to social change and political control.

Children become acquainted with the uses of violence early in life. Many of their games and toys stimulate violence, rather than instilling in them the belief that it is immoral to injure another person or to take a human life. Such toys also teach children to use violence to suppress violence. Our penal system offers other illustrations of violence employed to suppress violence. At one time or another every concerned person—seeing policemen's drawn guns, soldiers firing on the "enemy," hunters stalking the nation's wildlife—is shocked into the awareness that as a people we greatly value instruments made for the purpose of killing. The easy access that children, the mentally disturbed, and professional criminals have to weapons of destruction is alarming. Yet scores of bills to establish gun controls have been defeated. Americans spend about two billion dollars a year on guns, and each year the federal government disposes of about 100,000 guns at bargain prices.

Today the pattern of violence appears to be changing. In 1967 there were 83 riots in which 83 people were killed and 2,000 people injured. Property damage—almost all of it in central cities—totaled $61 million. Since 1967 riots have been replaced by bombings, assaults on the police, and other random acts of violence. During the fifteen-month period ending in April 1971, there were at least 4,330 bombings, 1,475 attempted bombings, and 35,128 threatened bombings in the United States.

What effective counter is there for violence? It will surely have to begin with motivating more people to seek an end to behavior that triggers violence. At the same time we must find ways to curtail individual acts of violence through education, medical treatment, counseling, and training. Such programs may be successful in most cases, if they are undertaken in time. Our penal systems and courts of law do little to curtail violence. We are still using 19th-century methods in our prisons and early 20th-century codes of conduct in our courts. Basic human rights to dignity, fair trial, and opportunity for rehabilitation are neglected.

But we should be concerned with violence beyond the local level. What counter is there for structural violence which results in 4 percent of the world's population utilizing 60 percent of the world's resources? Hunger, disease, short life expectancy, deplorable working conditions, and limited health facilities are but a few of the factors which fan the fires of violence throughout the world.

LAW AND ORDER

One of the most important issues in political campaigns of the past several years has been law and order. Federal, state, and local governments have appointed commissions to study problems attendant on maintaining order. Millions of words of copy have appeared in the press, and countless hours of rhetoric have been devoted to the subject. But crime rates continue to spiral upward. Public concern grows, but not public understanding.[3]

[3] Erle Stanley Gardner. *Cops on Campus and Crime in the Streets.* New York: William Morrow and Company, Inc., 1970.

Every year policemen are presented citations for outstanding achievement, often for capturing or killing dangerous criminals. To most policemen and to many civilians, these citations and the brave deeds they symbolize are the sum total of law and order. But citations are an inadequate approach to this complex problem. Somehow we must make it unnecessary for people to break laws in order to survive.

Far too often the issue of law and order tends to be used as a defense of the status quo. Few advocates of law and order note that laws must be just if they are to be supported. Laws must be legitimate in the sense that they must proceed from the needs of the people whose lives they are to regulate.

The concept of law and order as involving the preservation of the family, the prevention of cruelty by government regulations, and the restructuring of nonresponsive institutions such as public schools and welfare agencies is foreign to most Americans. Yet this aspect of law and order is tremendously important. Law and order must be accompanied by *justice*—moral rightness.

There are hopeful signs. In October 1971, the black and the white citizens of Hancock County, Georgia, surprised the people of surrounding counties by calling an end to their weapons race. At a time when hostility was at its peak, leaders on both sides began to ponder the future of human relations in their county. In a rare mood of sanity they decided not to pursue the weapons stockpiling that was likely to lead to several deaths. Perhaps other counties—and nations—will follow their example.

The May 26, 1972, strategic arms limitation agreement signed by President Richard Nixon and Soviet Communist Party Leader Leonid Brezhnev signaled the beginning of a new era in international relations. For the first time in modern history, two superpowers signed a written agreement to try to use the threat of mutual devastation as a deterrent to war between them. This was a hopeful first step toward what may eventually lead to world peace.

THE POOR

Despite our great national wealth, millions of American children grow up in circumstances which deny them the opportunity to achieve satisfying, productive lives. In this nation dedicated to freedom and equality, many of our citizens still struggle for survival on a day-to-day basis. The poor of the urban ghettos are the most brutalized and unprotected of the nation. Without a doubt slums breed violent people, and, with our cities rotting at the core, a contagion of violence is spreading throughout them. Until the basic needs of the poor are met in a peaceful and orderly fashion on a long-term basis, violence will continue.

Fortunately, there are several organizations—including the National Urban League, the National Association for the Advancement of Colored People, the Society of Friends, and the Southern Christian Leadership Conference—committed to improving societal conditions by using nonviolent means. The efforts and achievements of the men and women who comprise these organizations offer much-needed encouragement during periods of pessimism.

The poor of all races have more legal problems than the rest of society. They cannot afford expensive legal counsel, bond, or retrials. The recent increases in efforts on their behalf, such as store-front legal-aid services, only emphasize their unmet needs in our system of justice.[4] From birth to death the curse of poverty weighs heavily on the slum dweller, and the law gives little relief. The poor seldom have access to lawyers. Strategies to help the poor include abolishment of court costs and long-range reforms of laws and institutions that work unfairly against them. But long-range strategies are not enough. The poor need adequate legal redress for their grievances today. To be poor and denied justice is intolerable.

Poverty is not restricted to the big-city slums. It is a curse of rural areas as well, particularly among migrant workers. Very much as in the sweatshops of the 1930's, there is much abuse of child labor on farms employing migrant workers. A 1970 study by the American Friends Service Committee concluded that child-labor abuse is not only tolerated but encouraged in America. Though the employment of children as industrial laborers was outlawed in 1938, one-fourth of the farm workers in 1970 were under sixteen (some were as young as six). Their pay ranged from 12 cents a crate for strawberries to an average hourly wage of $1.12.

All children need clearly defined legal rights and accessible legal procedures to enforce these human rights:

1. *The right to be well born.* Every child has the right to be born of a mother who has had adequate nutrition and prenatal care, who has been educated in the subjects of pregnancy and birth, and who has borne her child

[4] Melvin M. Belli. *The Law Revolutions.* Hollywood, California: Sherbourne Press, 1968.

without the use of unnecessary drugs or procedures which may be dangerous to her or her child.

2. *The right to shelter.* Every child has the right to live in a home where he is protected from adverse environmental conditions and diseases, malnutrition, and injury to the spirit.

3. *The right to a humanistic education.* Every child has the right to be taught to respect himself and other people and to learn to be a productive member of his society.

4. *The right to liberty.* Every child has the right to be protected from abuse and to be given the same legal safeguards which are extended to adults.

Poverty affects all of society, not just the poor. The average citizen, the "Forgotten Man," is not poor enough to qualify for free legal service, and he is not wealthy enough to afford expensive legal counsel. To make matters worse, every day he reads about proposals to increase taxes to provide more "free" assistance to the poor. Such proposals make him angry, and he is becoming angrier every year. In his anger and resentment he listens to racists, superpatriots, and demagogues.

SOCIAL ORDER

Social order is not maintained without effort. We must consciously work at not destroying each other. Yet all around us we see men destroying men. Cavemen used clubs; modern men use words. In many ways physical aggression is less brutalizing than verbal aggression. The modern casualties are walking dead; they are the socially and psychologically destroyed members of society.

As societies grow and become more complex, the methods of maintaining social order have also become highly complex, impersonal, and structured. Indeed, when a society becomes highly complex, mobile, and pluralistic, the beneficiaries—and also the victims—of technological changes need more protection, not less. The influence of the traditional stabilizing institutions, such as the family and the church, has decreased as we have become more dependent on systems of law and government to maintain social order.

We have moved to a point where legal procedures and correctional institutions occupy a preeminent position in the preservation of social order. Whether for good or ill, we are committed to formal legal institutions as the primary agencies of social control. The "rule of law" and its corollary, "respect for the law," reflect the idea that people should recognize the legitimacy of the law as a means of ordering and controlling the behavior of all people in a society. The incongruity of our commitment to legal order is that many people do not really want law enforcement officials to follow the letter of the law when their own freedom is being restricted. They want officials to be lenient with them—to give them "armchair equity" or "fireside justice"—but to prosecute with vigor people whom they do not know or like. There are two clear lessons to be learned from the maintenance of social order in America:

1. Social order requires that our political and social institutions be able to improve themselves and respond more effectively to the legitimate complaints of minority groups within our society who are currently pressing their claims upon the larger public.

2. Social order demands a modern system of criminal justice which will effectively control deviant behavior in a fair and humane manner.

In the past two decades many people have publicly supported the idea that civil disobedience and even violent acts in violation of existing laws are justified to achieve social or political goals. Cases in point include the white majority in the North and the South who resist enforcement of the public school rights of nonwhites. Other examples are the policemen who brutalized the demonstrators in Chicago during the Democratic National Convention in 1968. The same idea—that acts of disobedience to laws are justified if the social cause is moral—has been expressed by militant college students, blacks, and others pressing for social change. They cite the Boston Tea Party and other historical acts of civil disobedience as justification for their behavior. "Violence," they say, "is as American as apple pie."

It is the latter acts—the illegal and violent activities of minority groups—that have been most perplexing and disturbing to the great majority of white Americans. They have prompted an intense interest in philosophical questions about man's obedience to the state. Business luncheons and suburban cocktail parties have come to sound like university seminars in philosophy. Middle Americans are preoccupied with the rightness or the wrongness of "what the kids and the blacks are doing." In fact, most Americans are experiencing a conscience crisis. The tactics of the minority-group demonstrators have encountered stiff opposition, but many white Americans sympathize with the goals sought by the angry demonstrators. "If I were black," some whites say, "I'd riot too."

To most whites, however, a radical black militant who bombs a college building or takes public officials as hostages or attacks a policeman is not an ordinary protester—he is a *black* protester. He is different. Social scientists say that he is acting out of a profound alienation from society; he believes that the existing social and political order in America is perpetuating his "colonial bondage" with an organized "imperialist force." Accepting this rhetoric, a growing number of blacks interpret their acts of violence as prerevolutionary acts to gain freedom, not as crimes. It is psychologically easier for groups to use violence against the police and other symbols of authority when they define their acts as legitimate.

America's social problems, of which radical black militancy is but one aspect, are grave and deep. We are finally being forced, as a nation, to understand the awesome dimensions of these problems and what they have done to our people, both white and nonwhite. When enough of us realize that we must transcend our history and create new institutions, new customs, and new attitudes and lay to rest the old self-validating judgment of white supremacy and nonwhite inferiority—then we will achieve racial peace and justice.

It is an established fact that we learn our values, attitudes, and behavior from formal and informal social institutions. Whether institutional experiences are planned or just happen, they become the basis for our accepting or rejecting people who are culturally different. For this reason, the quality of our interpersonal and intrapersonal activities within schools significantly affects our readiness to live peacefully in a pluralistic society. With few exceptions, the public schools bring together a greater number and variety of cultural backgrounds than any other social organization. They also bring together a greater number of human relations problems.

The ultimate goal of a school's human relations emphasis should be to help each student become aware of and achieve his optimum individual and social growth. This includes freedom to be and to express oneself as long as it does not violate or infringe upon the inalienable rights of others. Specifically, all students should learn that cultural and racial differences are not valid reasons for rejection. Children should be taught to live with and accept cultural differences. Schools, then, should teach "peace" by being peaceful places.

When we suggest that schools educate for peace, we do not equate peace with quiet, harmony, order, or perpetuation of the status quo. Instead, educating for peace means preparing students to respond maturely to frustration and conflict. Frustration and conflict are necessary conditions for social and psychological growth. Therefore, students should learn reflective skills that will allow them to understand the causes of conflict, as well as nonviolent methods for resolving conflict. Finally, education for peace consists of teaching students to assume responsibility for their behavior.

Because we learn what we live, the major training emphasis in our schools should be upon living good human relations. We must learn to live together. Learning about other people is not enough; we must also learn to live with them. For this reason, interaction is the best medium for communicating appropriate behavior. Dynamic leadership is needed within schools if we are to prevent modeling intergroup and intragroup violence. Therefore, we should not retreat from the battle to desegregate and humanize our schools.

The following essay clearly illustrates the need to become consciously aware of the effects of our behavior on other people. But being aware is not enough. We must model behavior that is humane.

WANTED: A HUMAN RELATIONS APPROACH TO EDUCATION[5]

Although many phases of American society might fittingly be described by the phrase "man's inhumanity to man," none seems more worthy of this designation than our public schools. Six years ago I would not have made that statement; then, I would have denied it vehemently. But then I was a young, first-year high school teacher, glossy and polished with the pride and confidence that I would be the best teacher my students had ever known. Now I am older and wiser, dulled by a system that doesn't really care but only pretends to, a system in which textbook is topdog and student is underdog, a system which dehumanizes humans.

I entered my first teaching assignment never questioning that I knew what education was all about. I had trained to teach the English language; that was what the students needed, and that was what they were going to get. (Never did I stop to consider then that many of them had a fourth-grade reading level or a hatred for school or alcoholic parents or little money with which to buy a notebook.)

So English I taught—from informal essays to Shakespearean drama, from short stories to the medieval sonnet. I followed the traditional school rules of, "Below 70, give an F," and "Fix all grades in an accurate curve" without question. I lowered averages for talking, for acting up in class, for failing to get homework, and for chewing gum.

One time an overweight, self-conscious sophomore girl refused to stand up in front of the class and practice our unit on etiquette (etiquette! to a class

---

[5] Jacqueline Peters. "Wanted: A Human Relations Approach to Education." Unpublished paper, University of Oklahoma, Norman, 1971.

whose meals meant jelly glasses rather than china and crystal, to students whose "May I introduce" would receive derisive laughter at home). So I forced her to participate, saying that it was her duty to the class and to me to do what the rest of the students were doing! When a freckle-faced, implike boy talked back to me, I made him stand up for 15 minutes while the class and I sat and looked at him.

For four years I taught this way, really feeling that I was a good teacher, not knowing then that I was playing a big part in the "man's inhumanity to man" role. I liked my students, but I didn't try to get close to any of them; my main aims were to keep them relatively quiet and to finish the textbook by the end of the year. These were the criteria absorbed from my teacher education classes, and doubting them never entered my mind.

Now I know I was wrong.

This discovery came not in the classroom, however, but as a result of my decision to become a counselor. During the course of that specialized training, I began to realize for the first time that each student in every classroom is a unique individual, with hopes, dreams, problems, and needs which form the basis for his classroom behavior. (As a teacher I may have known this, but I was too wrapped up in textbooks, grades, and school rules to care.)

Through counseling I found that there was a whole human world inside that school which had never been visible to me before; in comparison, my English content became irrelevant. For example, I had been preaching simile and metaphor to a girl whose father had been having sexual relations with her since the sixth grade. I was urging nouns and verbs on a boy who had a butcher knife hidden under his bed in wait for the right moment to kill his stepmother. I was assigning book reports to a 16-year-old common-law wife whose "husband" was stealing food for them at night and molesting small girls during the day. I was forcing *Julius Caesar* on a boy who believed that men from outer space were communicating with him and asking him to kill the President of the United States and anyone else in authority. These were the kids I was telling to spit out their gum, sit up straight in their seats, and practice introducing their parents to their friends properly.

The incongruity of it all was appalling.

Following my counseling training, I was again placed in an English classroom, only to find that, although I had changed, the educational system had not; now that I saw the possibilities and necessities for humanizing education, I found that rules and traditions bound me in. When I arranged my 36 desks in two semicircles rather than the traditional rows, the janitor complained that my room was too hard to sweep. When I used small-group interaction, other teachers complained that my classes were too loud. When I suggested to the scheduling adviser that one of my students was enrolled in a course which he had already taken and passed (the boy had asked me what he should do about it), I was told to quit trying to be Jesus Christ in the classroom and to tell the boy that if he kept quiet in the course for the first semester he might get out the second semester.

When a student came to me with a personal problem, I could rarely talk with him because teachers were constantly advised not to leave their classrooms unsupervised.

As I began to be more and more student-aware, I found myself becoming more and more disillusioned by the little box in which I was supposed to fit, and less and less inclined to want to fit there. I found that humanizing education was not the game we were playing. So I became a teacher dropout.

Now that I am outside the public school system rather than in it, I can more clearly see what is happening: the educational system seems designed to hinder rather than help a child fulfill his basic human needs. These needs, as listed by Abraham Maslow in *Motivation and Personality*,[6] are:

1. *Physiological needs.* These are needs for air, food, water, and physical comfort, which must be met before the other needs can be satisfied.

2. *Safety needs.* Using children for an example, Maslow finds that they have a desire for freedom from fear and insecurity. Safety needs relate to the avoiding of harmful or painful incidents.

3. *Belongingness.* Needs for belonging are the first of the higher-order needs. Maslow means that the human personality wants security. The human being wants to be somebody, even though it is in a small group.

4. *Love needs.* Man has always had and will have the desire to love someone else and be loved in return.

5. *Self-esteem needs.* Man wants to feel that he is worthwhile, that he can master something of his own environment, that he has a competence and an independence and a freedom and a feeling of being recognized for some kind of endeavor.

6. *Self-actualization needs.* These are the highest needs, as Maslow considers them. They involve the needs for recognition and for aesthetic reality. Man has a strong desire and a need to know and understand not only himself but the world about him.

If these are the basic needs that school children, as human beings, have, then the school should, in the course of its systemization, be attempting to fulfill them. A brief analysis will indicate that it is not.

First are the *physiological needs*. Although many cities have new, showy classroom facilities and buildings, many more do not, especially in small rural towns and inner cities. A dark, gloomy hall, a moldy room with stale bathroom smells, an unappetizing cafeteria tray or a can of pork and beans brought from home (or no lunch at all), a light bulb dangling from a frayed cord in the ceiling—is this the way the most affluent society in the world meets the physiological needs of its most precious human beings, the children?

Next are the *safety needs*. Do our children feel safe in our schools? This means freedom from fear, insecurity, harmful and painful incidents.

---

[6] Abraham Maslow. *Motivation and Personality.* New York: Harper & Row, Publishers, 1954. pp. 80–92.

How can they? Many of them live in mortal terror (little ones and big ones alike) of threatened or actual punishment with a teacher's paddle, ruler, or rubber hose. They fear being shaken, slapped, scorned, ridiculed, lambasted, and ignored. They fear those inconsistent giants called teachers who can so mercilessly mete out punishment with the flick of the wrist or a slash of the tongue. It is no wonder that assaults on teachers increased 800 percent between 1964 and 1968. The children have finally decided to show the teachers what it is like to feel a need for safety.

There is also a *belonging need*. Of course, our schools consider the belonging issue to be important—haven't we all heard teachers say, "He belongs in jail," "She belongs in the slow group," or "I'm glad that one doesn't belong to me"? No one ever considers where the child *wants* to belong; no one helps him *feel* that he belongs. Instead, on their own biases, teachers issue out a kind of segregated belonging: "*You* belong with the rich, and *you* with the poor; *you* belong with the blacks, and *you* with the whites; *you* belong with the smart, and *you* with the dumb." In essence they are saying, "You belong where I put you, and whether you like it or not, that's where you are going to stay." Since statistics show that more than one-third of all students drop out of the public schools before graduation, it is obvious that one place they feel they do *not* belong is in school.

Fourth are the *love needs*. This set of needs is truly ignored in the educational process. Who has ever heard of expressing, or feeling, love in the classroom? The formal, scientifically structured educational process seems aimed at avoiding admittance of such a need. Even when affection is displayed by students in the halls between classes, teachers—feeling that school is not the place for love—intervene.

Next are the *self-esteem needs*. These are needs that the schools seem especially adept at denying. This denial often takes the form of grading. The teacher, playing the game God in the classroom, looks down on the efforts of the underlings below and passes a value judgment on them. He dares to say, "That is poor work—F work—even if you did do your best. You will just have to try harder." He takes an artificial yardstick and uses it to measure a human endeavor; he never gives self-esteem a chance. What the teacher is really doing is fulfilling his own self-esteem needs by playing Almighty with the Gradebook. Whom does the school exist for—the teacher or the student?

The highest of all human needs is *self-actualization*. Well, here is the big one, the need that theoretically does not even reveal itself until the others have been met. Then why discuss it? Because somehow the teachers and the schools are confused. They think that this need, because it is the highest, should be dealt with first. They assume that all students have, or should have, an intense desire to know things, a need for abstract thoughts and aesthetic experiences. Therefore, they jam textbooks in students' faces and facts down students' throats. They disregard security, belonging, love, and self-esteem in their fanatic worship of knowledge, not realizing that the needs they are so casually tossing aside must be met first.

Can our schools become places where basic human needs are met first and where facts are put into second place? Can schools help a child feel secure, loved, and important, instead of afraid, unwanted, unloved, and unnecessary? Can the child come first in education?

THE YEAR 2000

No one can deny that we are changing our environment with fantastic rapidity. The implications of these changes defy even the best scholars. Only one thing seems certain: wherever we are going, we are going with great speed. In the past century, we have increased the speed of communication by a factor of 10^7, the speed of travel by 10^2, the speed of data handling by 10^6, energy resources by 10^3, the power of weaponry by 10^6, the ability to control diseases by 10^2.

We are a nation of *mobicentric* people. Our lives are centered on motion—arriving, doing, and becoming. One out of every five Americans changes his residence every year. The implication is clear: to adjust to this new form of existence, we have to learn to develop relationships quickly. Along with mobility comes the challenge to find a few people with whom we can be intimate.[7]

There are, in our society, four basic sources for change: technology, diffusion, structural development, and the relationship of the United States to the rest of the world. The basic technological changes are likely to grow out of the new biochemical engineering, the computer, and weather control. Diffusion of goods and privileges in society can do much to equalize health, education, and welfare opportunities for all people. Structural developments—especially in politics, education, and industry—are already moving us into a postindustrial society. Finally, our relationship to the rest of the world will determine whether we will even have a world in the year 2000.

The newness of our scientific breakthroughs is seen in the following statistics:

1. Approximately 90 percent of all scientific achievements have been made in the 20th century.

2. The gross national product of goods and services in the technologically advanced nations of the world is doubling every decade and a half.

---

[7] Eugene Jennings. "Mobicentric Man." *Psychology Today* 4: 35–36, 70–72; July 1970.

3. Until the mid-19th century, the speed of transportation never exceeded 20 miles an hour. Today rockets carry astronauts at more than 20,000 miles an hour, and the speed of some airplanes exceeds the speed of sound.

4. The number of scientific journals and articles is doubling every 15 years, with a current output in excess of 20 million pages a year.

In their book *The Year 2000,* Herman Kahn and Anthony Wiener identified what they call "the basic long-term manifold trend." They warned that, as we gain technological power over the world and become more affluent, alienation—cynicism, emotional distance, and hostility—rather than contentment will characterize our lives.[8]

Moving further into the future is not likely to be without negative consequences. However, these consequences need not be as negative as some futurologists imagine. We can intervene and alter the direction of cultural growth. Our world is becoming a global culture, but this fact alone is neither good nor bad. By providing an extended range of common experiences through the facility of transmission-shared symbols and attitudes, the societies of the world are becoming more similar in norms and behavior. But it seems unlikely that a single political ideology will emerge. If the world is to survive, it will require prodigious talents and also considerable skill in human relations. Specifically, the quality of life in the future will depend on how those who control education and technology today use their power. What, then, can educators do?

In *Education in World Affairs: A Realistic Approach to International Education,* Kenneth Melvin asked educators several thought-provoking questions about peace, including the following:

1. Is the management of America's educational and cultural interests abroad properly lodged in the State Department?

2. Have we any consistent theory of education which accommodates the revolutionary role? Or is all Western education necessarily reactionary?

3. In preparing our own people to think globally rather than parochially, teachers may be encouraged to intellectualize politics, but are they permitted to politicize education?

4. Should teachers encourage children to consider the ideals found in American documents as moral imperatives for interpersonal behavior?

5. Can the peace proposition be advanced by violence of any kind, in any sphere, or in any relationship?[9]

[8] Herman Kahn and Anthony Wiener. *The Year 2000.* New York: The Macmillan Company, 1967.
[9] Kenneth Melvin. *Education in World Affairs: A Realistic Approach to International Education.* Lexington, Massachusetts: D. C. Heath & Company, 1970.

The necessity for educators to join social scientists and natural scientists involved in planning social change should be evident. It seems certain that the misfit between traditional patterns of social relationships and social control on the one hand and technology and industrialization on the other hand will not disappear if we simply pretend that it does not exist. The need for planned social change is inherent in the conditions of industrial cultures. However, the best guarantee of democratic social planning (social engineering) is based on a methodology of planned change which unites the principles of democracy with the skills of group dynamics.

In democratic social planning each person is treated as an end, and social arrangements are judged by their effects on persons influenced by them. For this to happen, schools must foster an atmosphere which permits each person to make his unique contributions to his school and his community. Even more so than today, students of tomorrow will need to learn the skills of contributing to collective thinking, and their teachers will need to master the skills of eliciting and facilitating effective communication across lines of prestige and power.

It is also important that we learn to communicate common values needed for world-community survival. This involves a world-order approach to the study of the international system. Specifically, it involves an inquiry into the ways and means of achieving three basic goals: limiting and eliminating international violence, raising the standards of economic welfare enjoyed by all mankind, and expanding the degree of social justice within political communities in world society.[10]

ETHICAL CONCERNS FOR THE FUTURE

In the growing concern about the future of man, traditional beliefs are being questioned, including the notions that (a) scientific progress is automatically good, (b) what is medically beneficial for one man is necessarily good for society, and (c) scientists know how to improve humanity.

In 1969 the Institute for Society, Ethics, and the Life Sciences was organized in New York to study the ethical questions involved in the areas of population control, genetic engineering, death and dying, and behavior control. A similar organization, the Institute of Religion, was organized

---

[10] Gary Thorpe and Betty Reardon. "World Order and Simulation." *High School Journal* 55: 53–62; November 1971.

in Houston, Texas. The purpose of this institute is to explore the ethical problems that arise out of medicine and medical research, including heart transplants. Smaller institutes with similar purposes include the Center for Human Values in the Health Sciences, in San Francisco, and the Institute for Theological Encounter with Science and Technology, in St. Louis. All these groups have interdisciplinary teams consisting of representatives from the humanities, theology, and the social and physical sciences.

The range of questions these groups discuss is broad: Does an individual have a right to his uniqueness? Does a dying person have the right to ask not to be treated? Where do the rights of society enter when physicians, funds, and hospital beds needed for terminal patients are in short supply? Should criminals be forced to accept rehabilitation that would involve direct electrical and chemical stimulation of their brains or even brain surgery? What would be the societal effects of using a drug that would raise the general level of intelligence of all citizens?

Implicit in the questions being discussed is the assumption that change for the sake of change is not a commendable goal. Those changes which seem to promote a more humane society are the ones we should support. Indeed, the problems of tomorrow are likely to be closely related to our solutions to today's problems in human relations. A racist nation will pass on racism to the future generations unless steps are taken to alter traditional patterns of segregation and discrimination.

In 1971, in an address at the annual conference of the American Psychological Association, Kenneth B. Clark proposed the creation of new drugs that could routinely be given to persons, especially leaders holding great power, to subdue hostility and aggression and allow more humane and intelligent behavior to emerge. The full implications of Clark's proposal could and should be the subject of study by an association of education, behavioral, and neuropsychological scientists. Among the many questions inherent in the proposal is whether science can enhance man's empathy and kindness without destroying his creative, evaluative, and selective capacities.

An equally challenging question grew out of a 1972 report of the Federal Commission on Population Growth and the American Future. The majority of the commission members concluded that women should be free to determine their own fertility and that the matter of abortion should be left to the conscience of the individual concerned, in consultation with her physician. Dissenting, Commissioner Paul B. Cornley stated that "such moralistic monism, simplistic as it is, at bottom fails to consider the freedom of the unborn child to live."[11] The following data were presented in the majority report:

1. According to a 1970 national fertility study conducted by the Office of Population Research of Princeton University, between 1966 and 1970 there were 2.65 million births that never would have occurred if the couples had had fertility controls.

2. If blacks could have the number of children they want and no more, their fertility rate would probably be similar to that of whites.

3. In more than two-thirds of the states, abortion is a crime except to preserve the life of the mother.

4. Medically safe abortions have always been available to wealthy women.

5. It is estimated that from 200,000 to 1,200,000 illegal abortions are performed each year in the United States.

In summary, do the various prohibitions against abortion stand as an obstacle to the exercise of individual freedom—the freedom of women to make difficult moral choices based on their personal values, the freedom of women to control their own fertility, and the freedom from the burden of unwanted childbearing?

Bringing children into the world gives rise to a wide range of questions, especially those which focus on their human rights. At the other end of the life spectrum is old age. Currently there are twenty million Americans who are 65 years of age and older—one-tenth of our population. With birth rates declining and life expectancy increasing, the aged will constitute an even larger proportion of the U.S. population in the year 2000. Will the senior citizens of tomorrow be like those of today, plagued by ill health and social-financial insecurity? The aged are mainly unwanted; they are pushed aside, thrown away, and often stranded in socially sterile environments built especially for "old folks." What must our society become so that "old age" as we know it will be nonexistent?

Between youth and old age lie what are sometimes referred to as the "most productive years." This is the time when our energies are likely to be devoted to preventing or abating the problems of hunger, disease, pollution, population, war, sexism, and ethnic strife. The major domestic problem is black-white relations. What can be done to help black and white citizens live together voluntarily when some are still unwilling to sit next to each other on buses, trains, and airplanes? Will the members of ethnic groups of the future be taught or conditioned peacefully to go to

[11] "Abortion Report Abstracts." *The New York Times,* March 17, 1972.

school together, live in the same neighborhoods, and work together on the same jobs? Or will we become the Separate States of America? If we cannot solve our domestic problems, how can we solve our international problems centering on war and peace?

Ideally we will reshape our education and physical and social sciences to improve the quality of our human relationships. Yet more than that is needed. The physical and social sciences must combine with the other disciplines, especially with education, to create a humane world. If the special abilities of human beings are the creation, transmission, understanding, reordering, and re-creation of symbols, then we should be able to improve greatly our definitions of life and their cultural, biological, and ethical realities. Indeed, freedom and equality along with the attendant rights and responsibilities can become our primary reason for being:

> Man has tried halfhearted measures to solve the problems of war, of poverty, of injustice, and [he] has failed. Now he must build a system of peace which has the capacity to attack these problems and move along the road to their solution. This requires more than faith and hope and love, much as these things help. It requires, in short, a Government for Man.[12]

Each year more students are doubting the ability of their teacher models to be humane persons. Perhaps teachers and administrators are ceasing to be significant models for students who are rebelling because the students have discovered that these adults have lied to them. Some rebelling students have learned that money, clothes, cars, houses, and educational concepts are not, as many educators would lead them to believe, more important than people. Some rebelling students discover that the concept of "race" is a myth, existing only in the imagination of the classifiers. They learn that love need not be restricted to those within the family.

When students stop reaching out to teachers and administrators for facts and instead start reaching out for understanding, they find most teachers and administrators woefully inadequate. I am speaking not of a generation gap but of an empathy gap—empathy is not a function of age.

For these and many other reasons our students are not so much angry at us as sorry for us. They are sorry that we have forgotten the impatience of youth. They are sorry that we seem no longer committed to sweeping social changes. And they are sorry that we have forgotten how to laugh at ourselves and with other people. A four-year-old girl got to the essence of it when she asked, "Daddy, does it hurt to be an adult?"

[12] *To Free Mankind, op. cit.*

"Yes, my love," her father answered. "It hurts very much at times. But I pray that you will live in peace, freedom, and happiness." That, I believe, is a necessary beginning for all our tomorrows.

Selected References

David Abrahamsen. *Our Violent Society*. New York: Funk & Wagnalls Company, 1970.

Hannah Arendt. *On Violence*. New York: Harcourt, Brace & World, 1970.

George W. Ball. *The Discipline of Power*. Boston: Little, Brown and Company, 1968.

Kenneth E. Boulding. "Education for the Spaceship Earth." *Social Education* 32: 650; November 1968.

George I. Brown. *Human Teaching for Human Learning: An Introduction to Confluent Education*. New York: The Viking Press, 1971.

Blanche Cook. *A Bibliography on Peace Research in History*. New York: Clio Press, 1969.

Ryland W. Crary. *Humanizing the School: Curriculum Development and Theory*. New York: Alfred A. Knopf, Inc., 1969.

William Theodore De Barry. "Education for a World Community." *Liberal Education* 50: 437–57; December 1964.

Dave Dellinger. *Revolutionary Nonviolence*. New York: Anchor Books, Doubleday & Company, 1971.

Theodore Draper. *Abuse of Power*. New York: The Viking Press, 1968.

Mario D. Fantini and Milton A. Young. *Designing Education for Tomorrow's Cities*. New York: Holt, Rinehart and Winston, Inc., 1970.

Orville L. Freeman. *World Without Hunger*. New York: Frederick A. Praeger, Inc. Publishers, 1968.

Morton Fried *et al.*, editors. *War: The Anthology of Armed Conflict and Aggression*. New York: Doubleday & Company, Inc., 1968.

J. William Fulbright. *The Arrogance of Power*. New York: Random House, Inc., 1967.

Hans-Georg Gadamer. "Notes on Planning for the Future." In: Stanley Hoffman, editor. *Conditions of World Order*. Boston: Houghton Mifflin Company, 1968.

George Henderson. *To Live in Freedom: Human Relations Today and Tomorrow*. Norman: University of Oklahoma Press, 1972.

Robert D. Hess and Judith V. Torney. *The Development of Political Attitudes in Children*. Chicago: Aldine Publishing Company, 1968.

Ralph E. Lapp. *The Weapons Culture*. New York: W. W. Norton & Company, Inc., 1968.

Harold M. Long and Robert N. King. *Improving the Teaching of World*

Affairs. Bulletin 35 of the National Council for the Social Studies. Washington, D.C.: the Council, 1964.

Kenneth Melvin. *Education in World Affairs: A Realistic Approach to International Education*. Lexington, Massachusetts: D. C. Heath & Company, 1970.

Carl R. Rogers. *Freedom To Learn*. Columbus, Ohio: Charles E. Merrill Publishing Company, 1969.

Lionel Rubinoff. *The Pornography of Power*. New York: Quadrangle Books, Inc., 1968.

Harold Taylor. *The World and the American Teacher*. Washington, D.C.: American Association of Colleges for Teacher Education, 1968.

Robert Ulich, editor. *Education and the Idea of Mankind*. New York: Harcourt, Brace & World, 1964.

F. Champion Ward. *From Manpower to Mankind*. New York: Ford Foundation, 1967. Reprint.

Harmon Ziegler. *The Political Life of American Teachers*. Englewood Cliffs, New Jersey: Prentice-Hall, Inc., 1967.

Appendix A
Data on the Human Crisis: Teacher's Guide[1]
William A. Nesbitt

ASSUMPTIONS

1. The combination of problems that now beset the global system seriously threatens improvement of the quality of life in the future; indeed, most scholars studying the evidence are concerned about a future of worsening poverty, pollution, drastic resource shortages, and conflict in which nuclear destruction cannot be ruled out.

2. Problem-oriented education should be given—in fact, *must* be given—more emphasis if optimistic hopes for the future are to have any chance for realization.

3. Inquiry approaches are desirable for enhancing learning, encouraging critical thinking, and changing attitudes. Use of data, especially when presented graphically, can aid the use of the inquiry method.

INQUIRY

The term "inquiry" is used here to refer to a process that includes at least the following steps:

1. Data are presented.
2. Students are encouraged to ask questions of the data.
3. The questions may lead to the formation of hypotheses.
4. Hypotheses are submitted to analysis: Are there exceptions to the proposition? Are there enough data available to substantiate the hypotheses, or must the hypotheses remain tentative?
5. Additional data may be gathered where required.
6. Hypotheses may be further analyzed in light of additional data.
7. Generalizations may be formulated. (For an overview of inquiry, see: Rodney Allen and others. *Inquiry in the Social Studies: Theory and*

---

[1] Excerpted from: William A. Nesbitt. *Data on the Human Crisis: Teacher's Guide* (1972). Reprinted by permission of the Center for International Programs and Comparative Studies of the New York State Education Department, Albany, New York 12224.

Examples for Classroom Teachers. Social Studies Readings No. 2. Washington, D.C.: National Council for the Social Studies, 1968.)

Below are suggested questions that might emerge from data sheets and possible hypotheses. Of course, it is better, insofar as possible, for students to find questions and develop their own hypotheses; but in some cases teachers may want to "prime the pump" to help students get at significant questions and possible hypotheses.

AN EXAMPLE OF COMPARATIVE USE OF DATA SHEETS IN INQUIRY

1. The most significant inquiry exercise in which data sheets are compared is one that gets at the question, "Given various world problems and their projections, what are the prospects for mankind in the future?"

Data sheets from every category can be used.[2] The teacher might use a data sheet on number of warheads. Students may examine the hypothesis that nuclear war is so destructive that such wars will not happen. On the other hand, the students may analyze the proposition that world problems will become so critical that desperate measures, even national suicide by launching a nuclear attack, cannot be ruled out. . . .

SUGGESTED TECHNIQUE

Teachers may find it advantageous to present the graph part of the data sheets on an overhead projector as an initial part of the inquiry. Of course, this requires making a transparency, at which time the written information can be blocked off. Or a transparency can be made of the whole data sheet and the written part covered over with blank paper for projection; then the blank paper can be removed at an appropriate time if the teacher wishes to have the class read the written information from the overhead projector screen.

POSSIBLE QUESTIONS, FOLLOWED IN PARENTHESES BY POSSIBLE HYPOTHESES AND FURTHER INFORMATION FOR THE TEACHER

1. a. The graph can show wars between states. What other kinds of war are there? (Need to consider civil wars and wars between groups across borders. Students may attempt a definition of interstate war. They need to distinguish between brawls, riots and other civil commotion, and war. They need also to consider the meaning of guerrilla warfare, including urban guerrilla warfare, in the context of war.)

b. How often do periods of large-scale warfare seem to occur? (About every 20 years.) How is the 20-year cycle explained? (One hypothesis

---

[2] Yearbook editor's note: Examples of data sheets are found at the beginnings of Chapters 2 to 9 in this Yearbook.

is that people "need" a war to vent aggressive feelings, let off steam, or because they get bored with peace, and that after the fighting is over they need a period of recovery. Such a hypothesis makes an assumption about human nature for which there is little scientific evidence. Teachers should have students consider the "human nature" question. Are individuals subject to cycles of tension, aggressiveness, and so on? And, even if so, does this explain why national governments go to war?)

c. Why have some countries, particularly European ones, fought more wars than others? (There are many hypotheses possible: (1) geographic factors—possible friction owing to close proximity of potential enemies, lack of natural barriers to enemies; (2) desire to acquire economic resources of other nations; (3) belligerent national value system with a highly regarded military class; (4) lack of national cohesiveness and "need" to externalize internal problems; (5) desire to annex territory of another nation inhabited by people of the same ethnic background; (6) desire to "proselytize" an ideology; etc. Each country should be considered separately, with much additional evidence needed to verify any hypothesis.)

d. Why has the United States not fought as many interstate wars as other nations? (The United States is a relatively young nation; separated from potential enemies by two oceans; rich in natural resources; peace-loving.)

e. What is the effect upon a country of being either a frequent "loser" or "winner" in war? (Leader of "winning" nation would not want to be first head of state of his country to lose a war; "losers" might, on one hand, develop enormous fear of further wars, or, on the other, risk another war to repair past damaged prestige.)

f. What does winning or losing really mean? Might not a country lose a war but gain a great deal in the long run? (Japan, for example, lost World War II but has emerged as a vastly greater economic power than it was before the war.)

2. a. Will the destructiveness of weapons continue to grow? (Nuclear nations are not upping megatonnage per warhead; instead they are looking for greater accuracy in delivery and greater numbers of warheads. If one or two 10-megaton bombs are enough virtually to destroy a city, why build heavy 100-megaton bombs?)

b. Would thermal and blast effects be the only effects? (Radioactive fallout would cause serious long-term damage. Students might research fallout effects. Some may be able to discuss such effects from having seen the movies *On the Beach* or *Hiroshima* or having read the books from which the movies were made.) How useful would fallout shelters be? (Further data are necessary, but students may be able to discover that all oxygen would burn in the firestorm area, turning shelters into incinerators. They may also consider extreme damage to shelters for many miles from blast and heat. Students should also consider the conditions those who survived in shelters would find above ground when they emerged from their shelters.)

3. How large an attack could the United States survive? (Students need to consider not only loss of lives and material damage but also the psychological effects on survivors. They may find it useful to compare the effect of Black Death in 14th century Europe with that of a nuclear attack.) What might be the main target of a nuclear attack, people or industry? (If industry were the target, millions of people would unavoidably be killed. If the attack on industry failed to bring the enemy to surrender and the principal target became human beings, virtual extermination would result. However, when people are subjected to terrible destruction, they often are driven to fight on; witness during World War II the spirit of the English during the bombing of Britain or the Germans during the fire bombings of Dresden and Hamburg, or the Japanese who were forced to surrender only after the atom bombing of Hiroshima and Nagasaki. If the Japanese had had the atomic capacity to retaliate, would they have surrendered then?)

4. What can the graphs suggest about what might be the limits in numbers of warheads for an attack upon the U.S.S.R.? (The discussion might center around the principal purpose of an attack—first-strike or retaliation.) How can we explain that increasing the number of warheads does not proportionately increase the percentage of industry destroyed? (Concentrated industry is vulnerable to attack.) Why is it that percentage of people killed increases proportionately to warheads? (Blast, heat, and radioactive fallout, especially the latter, can eventually reach people even in rural areas.) Could the Russians and Americans virtually eliminate each other's populations? Do the data suggest that it may not be necessary to stockpile more and more weapons?

5. Is there any correlation between the unpopularity of a war and battle deaths or economic costs? (Requires research into popularity of wars. World War II was a popular war but most costly. Duration and gains need to be considered; for example, Vietnam has been the longest U.S. war with the fewest clear gains.) How do original war costs compare with the costs of veterans' benefits and interest on war loans? (Students might compute the original costs, which seem to be an increasingly smaller proportion of the total; that is, people are only beginning to pay for a war when it is over.)

6. Why is there a marked increase in the percentage of civilian war deaths? (A strategic objective of war is to destroy the enemy's capacity to continue fighting by attacking industries and cities. Weapon technology permits enormous destruction from great distances. Wars have become total, with whole populations against whole populations and not just armies against armies. Students may imagine the difference between a medieval battle and the Battle of Britain during World War II. They may also consider the fact that a small, 20-kiloton atom bomb—equivalent to 20,000 tons of TNT—killed some 100,000 civilians in Hiroshima.)

7. Which countries are the big military spenders, and why? (Students will soon realize that a key figure is missing—percentage of GNP spent on the military; but math buffs can compute these figures. Students might be surprised

to discover that in 1970 the United States spent nearly 8 percent [in 1968 it was 9.3 percent] of total GNP on the military, whereas Italy spent about 3 percent, Sweden 3.7 percent, and Switzerland 2.1 percent. Another useful figure students might research is the percentage of total national government budget that is spent on the military.)

8. How can it be explained that developing African nations spend more on education and health than on the military, whereas the reverse is true in the United States? (Hypotheses might include: the United States has worldwide defense obligations, the United States can "afford" the "luxury" of heavy military expenditures, African nations place a greater value on social services, and so on.) Why has U.S. foreign aid been reduced in recent years even though the rich-poor nation gap is growing? (The United States is returning to isolationism, Americans are fed up with giving to foreigners who are not grateful, it is easier for Congress to cut the budget for foreign aid than for other programs. An important point is that most of the money in foreign aid bills submitted to Congress has been for military aid. Many Congressmen have voted against the foreign aid bills because of the military emphasis, not from objection to economic aid to developing countries.)

9. What is the significance of the heavy and increasing arms expenditures by the United States and the U.S.S.R. in the Third World? (Rivalry develops between the superpowers over their extension of influence in underdeveloped areas, involving not only ideology but also the need to maintain access to raw materials, markets, and so on.) Might not such arms exports by major powers fuel war rather than prevent it? (There is need for more data. The Israeli-Arab conflict is perhaps a good example for considering a possible hypothesis: Does U.S. aid to Israel and Soviet aid to Egypt keep peace or encourage war?)

10. Is the United States spending too much on national defense, the Vietnam war, military aid, and other military programs? (Additional data are required. Arguments in Congress in the fall when appropriations bills are brought up can provide much data. *The Readers Guide to Periodical Literature* or the *New York Times Index* can help in finding articles.) Approximately what percentage of the U.S. budget goes to pay for past wars? (The percentage includes expenditures for both veterans and the 80 percent of the national debt which is the result of borrowing to pay for defense and past wars.)

11. Is it fair to compare military and social cost equivalents? (One aspect of the question is whether money saved by reduced military expenditures can simply be transferred to social needs. Another consideration is that military expenditures are necessary for preserving freedom, which is at least as essential as the building of hospitals and schools. An inquiry may consider possible savings by collective security, or disarmament with peacekeeping forces under an international organization.)

Appendix B
Selected Bibliography on International Education[1]

GENERAL BACKGROUND READING FOR TEACHERS

International Studies

Richard Barnet. "The Game of Nations." *Harper's* 243: 53–59; November 1971. Examines the mentality behind Americans' belief that in order to be the number-one nation you have to be able to do what you want, when and where you want to do it.

James M. Becker and Howard D. Mehlinger, editors. *International Dimensions in the Social Studies*. 38th Yearbook of the National Council for the Social Studies. Washington, D.C.: the Council, 1968. Offers a setting and a framework for international studies. Emphasizes the need for new perspectives in many related areas.

Lincoln P. Bloomfield. *The UN and World Order*. Headline Series No. 197. New York: Foreign Policy Association, October 1969. Examines the role of the UN in the efforts to create world order in the 1970's.

Helene Castel. *World Development*. New York: The Macmillan Company, 1971. A book of readings that raise questions about basic goals and values of development and attempt to place the development process in a context of human dignity and justice.

Barry Commoner. *The Closing Circle: Nature, Man, and Technology*. New York: Alfred A. Knopf, Inc., 1971. A lucid description of ecology and suggestions for some needed changes in economic thinking if man is to survive.

Richard Falk. *This Endangered Planet*. New York: Random House, Inc., 1971. Argues that preoccupation with the warfare-threat system has kept us from dealing with poverty, racism, overpopulation, and diseases; calls for massive redirection of human energy and material resources.

Roger Fisher, editor. *International Conflict for Beginners*. New York: Harper & Row, Publishers, 1969. A handbook on the analysis of recent inter-

---

[1] Compiled and annotated by the Diffusion Project, Social Studies Development Center, Indiana University, Bloomington 47401. A slightly different version of this material was published as ERIC Clearinghouse for Social Studies/Social Sciences Education Interpretive Series No. 6, and also is available from the Superintendent of Documents, U.S. Government Printing Office, Stock No. 1780-1064. See also Appendices C and D.

national affairs; uses current problems in presenting ideas; a pragmatic, nonmoralistic approach emphasizing "Yesable Propositions."

Leon Gordenker. *The United Nations in International Politics.* Princeton, New Jersey: Princeton University Press, 1971. A number of experts provide answers to such questions as: How can we understand the United Nations? How can we assess the prospects for the future of the UN?

Arthur Hoffman, editor. *International Communication and the New Diplomacy.* Bloomington: Indiana University Press, 1968. Specialists in various fields discuss what their respective disciplines can bring to the study of interpersonal and intergroup relations across national boundaries, and what the diplomat can learn from their findings.

Robert M. Hutchins. *The Future of International Relations.* New York: United Nations Institute for Training and Research, 1970. The author argues that nations should think of education as a means to full humanity for their populations rather than as a means to power, prestige, or wealth.

Irving L. Janis. "Groupthink." *Psychology Today* 5 (6): 43–46, 74–76; November 1971. Argues that the drive for consensus at any cost helps explain foreign policy disasters in Vietnam, Cuba, and Korea.

Leonard Kenworthy. *The International Dimension of Education.* Washington, D.C.: Association for Supervision and Curriculum Development, 1970. A report on efforts to incorporate the international dimension of education into the total learning experience of students at all levels; includes practical suggestions for teachers.

John P. Lowell. *Foreign Policy in Perspective.* New York: Holt, Rinehart and Winston, Inc., 1970. An introduction to some of the complexities of the foreign policy process in the United States. Provides a useful guide for making independent assessment of foreign policy.

Sidney I. Rolfe. *The Multinational Corporation.* Headline Series No. 199. New York: Foreign Policy Association, February 1970. Examines various facets of the multinational corporation, its economic and political consequences, the political demands it makes, and national responses to it.

Bruce M. Russett. *What Price Vigilance? The Burdens of National Defense.* New Haven, Connecticut: Yale University Press, 1970. A dispassionate, objective analysis of why expenditures for national defense are so high and what some of the consequences are for American politics, economy, and society.

Robert Shaw. *Rethinking Economic Development.* Headline Series No. 208. New York: Foreign Policy Association, 1971. 64 pp. Outlines a new strategy for development emphasizing employment. Examines implications of this focus for the rich countries.

Reginald Smart. "The Goals and Definitions of International Education: Agenda for Discussion." *International Studies Quarterly,* December 1971. Identifies several different widely accepted goals for international education and demonstrates the need to face the implications honestly. Such goals are national power, mutual understanding, permeation of ideas, and national development.

Harold Taylor. *The World and the American Teacher.* Washington, D.C.: American Association of Colleges for Teacher Education, 1968. Examines teacher education and recommends that, through an arranged series of appropriate experiences in intellectual, cultural, and social affairs, the teacher would be better able to understand himself and others and teach more effectively.

The United Nations: The World as a Developing Country. Report to the U.S. Senate Committee on Foreign Relations. Washington, D.C.: Superintendent of Documents, U.S. Government Printing Office, June 1971. Focuses on the "sea bed" and "development" issues.

Max Ways. "More Power to Everybody." *Fortune* 81 (5): 173–75, 290–99; May 1970. Argues that wider distribution of power and broadening of participation by individuals in controlling their own lives are creating a new social vigor.

Ralph K. White. "Selective Inattention." *Psychology Today* 5 (6): 47–50, 78–84; November 1971. Using Vietnam as an example, the author points up how, once an activity is well under way, the tendency is to retain thoughts in harmony with it and discard others.

G. Vann Woodward, editor. *The Comparative Approach to American History.* New York: Basic Books, Inc., 1968. Using a chronological framework of traditional topics, 22 historians attempt to reinterpret the American Revolution, the frontier movement, world wars, and several other topics within a comparative framework.

James D. Wright. "Life, Time, and the Fortunes of War." *Transaction* 9 (3): 42–52; January 1972. The report of a study of whose opinions are more manipulated by the mass media, those of the common man or of the upper-middle class elites.

Global and Future Studies

"American Business Abroad: The New Industrial Revolution." *Saturday Review* 52 (47): 31–56; November 22, 1969. A series of articles dealing with the impact of the multinational corporation in rich and poor nations.

Robert C. Angel. *Peace on the March: Transnational Participation.* New York: Van Nostrand Reinhold Company, 1969. Explores the effects of increased transnational participation on hopes for achieving international accommodation.

Ben H. Bagdikian. *The Information Machines: Their Impact on Men and the Media.* New York: Harper Colophon Books, 1971. An insightful treatment of the nature of the information machines and how they will influence our lives.

Victor Basiuk. *Technology and World Power.* Headline Series No. 200. New York: Foreign Policy Association, April 1970. A review of the impact of technology on different nations and speculation on possible implications for further developments within these nations.

Paul Bohannan. "Beyond Civilization." *Natural History* 80: 10, 50–67; February 1971. A look at the requirements for survival and ironies in the post-civilization culture. Sees "phase 2" as a new opportunity to understand the mysteries of life and culture.

"Cleaning Humanity's Nest: The New Planetary Priority." *Saturday Review* 53 (10): 47–66; March 7, 1970. Includes articles on "Prospects for Spaceship Man," "The Politics of Ecology," "Earth Watch," and "Environment Bookshelf."

Norman Cousins. "Needed: A New World Theme Song." *Saturday Review* 51 (28): 20; July 13, 1968. An appeal for a change in emphasis in international and cross-cultural contacts.

Robert Disch, editor. *The Ecological Conscience: Values for Survival.* Englewood Cliffs, New Jersey: Prentice-Hall, Inc., 1970. A series of articles by experts, scientists, poets, educators, and engineers, designed to promote an awareness of the interrelatedness of all things, including values, actions, and visions.

René Dubos. *Reason Awake: Science for Man.* New York: Columbia University Press, 1970.

René Dubos. *So Human an Animal.* New York: Charles Scribner's Sons, 1968. Both books warn that man is in danger of losing his humanness to his mechanized surroundings. A science of human life is proposed as a way to stop the trend toward dehumanization.

"Education and Futurism." *Futures* 4 (5): 191–230; December 1970. Includes survey of courses in the future being developed at various North American universities. (*Futures* is a publication of the World Future Society, P.O. Box 19285, 20th Street Station, Washington, D.C. 20036.)

Education for the Revolutionary World of the Future. Albany: University of the State of New York, State Education Department, 1969. A call for action and new perspectives to meet today's social and technological problems and to prepare to meet the future.

Loren Eisley. *The Invisible Pyramid.* New York: Charles Scribner's Sons, 1970. Argues that man, the creator of culture, must preserve and reenter the world of nature if he is to survive.

Amitai Etzioni. *The Active Society.* New York: The Macmillan Company, 1968. Outlines political and social processes which would constitute a self-developing advanced industrial society.

Victor Ferkiss. *Technological Man: The Myth and the Reality.* New York: George Braziller, Inc., 1969. Concludes that technological man is more myth than reality but that survival may require such a development, as well as a new philosophy and a new naturalism.

R. Buckminster Fuller. *Operating Manual for Spaceship Earth.* Carbondale: Southern Illinois University Press, 1969. Recommends "general systems theory" as a form of technical expertise for better piloting of spaceship earth.

Huey D. Johnson, editor. *No Deposit—No Return: Man and His Environment, A View Toward Survival.* New York: U.S. National Commission for UNESCO, 1970. A primer for environmental awareness; a collection of papers from a UNESCO conference on man and his environment.

John McHale. *The Future of the Future.* New York: George Braziller, Inc., 1969. Discusses some likely characteristics of the impending planetary society. Includes discussions of life styles, cultural diffusion, individual participation, and work.

Margaret Mead. *Culture and Commitment: A Study of the Generation Gap.* New York: Doubleday & Company, Inc., 1970. An analysis of the search for a new commitment by today's youth. Suggests that there are new resources and approaches available.

"Peace." *Journal of the American Association of University Women* 63 (4): 153–208 (whole issue); May 1970. A series of articles by experts suggesting some approaches to furthering the cause of peace.

"Political Conflict: Perspectives on Revolution." *Journal of International Affairs,* Vol. 23, No. 1; 1969. Provides different theoretical frameworks for studying revolution as an important force in politics.

Mark Terry. *Teaching for Survival: A Handbook for Environmental Education.* New York: Ballantine Books, Inc., 1971. An ethical and practical plan for transforming the educational system, with the idea that humanity can be measured against man's treatment of the nonhuman world.

William Irwin Thompson. "Planetary Vistas." *Harper's* 243: 71–78; December 1971. Looks toward a future transformation of civilization to "planetization" with a mystical view of reality to guide mankind.

Alvin Toffler. *Future Shock.* New York: Random House, Inc., 1970. A revealing, exciting treatment of the processes of rapid change. Provides suggestions for future-shock observers.

Raymond Vernon. *Sovereignty at Bay: The Multinational Spread of U.S. Enterprises.* New York: Basic Books, Inc., 1971. Provides insight into the problems posed by business and government to this new kind of enterprise.

Warren W. Wager. *Building the City of Man: Outlines of a World Civilization.* New York: Grossman Publishers, Inc., 1971. An analysis of the failings of modern civilization and proposals for a radically restructured world order for the future.

D. D. Wallia, editor. *Toward the Twenty-First Century.* New York: Basic Books, Inc., 1970. Stresses the need for efforts to preserve human values in our technical society. Argues that it would be suicidal to let technology overshadow ecology.

APPROACHES AND METHODS

Adventure on a Blue Marble: Approaches to Teaching Intercultural Understanding. Atlanta: Southern Association of Colleges and Secondary Schools, 1969. An attempt to assist teachers in their efforts to help students accept and appreciate others for what they are and to value the rich and varied contributions of all cultures. Includes case studies and bibliography.

Alfred S. Alschuler, Diane Tabor, and James McIntyre. *Teaching Achievement Motivation: Theory and Practice in Psychological Education.* Middletown, Connecticut: Educational Ventures, Inc., 1970. Aimed at helping the classroom teacher, a "do-it-yourself" book. Describes how to go about enlivening a classroom and improving teacher performance.

Arno Bellack and others. *The Language of the Classroom.* New York: Teachers College Press, 1967. An analysis of classroom discourse using a framework based on pedagogical functions. Provides examples and protocol material.

Barry K. Beyer and Anthony N. Penna. *Concepts in the Social Studies.* Bulletin No. 45. Washington, D.C.: National Council for the Social Studies, 1971. A useful discussion and guide for those seeking to develop a concept-centered course or unit.

James S. Coleman. "The Children Have Outgrown the Schools." *Psychology Today* 5 (9): 72–75, 82; February 1972. Argues that the pluralism of sources of information and impressions available to students creates a need for more emphasis on "information-management" skills and experience in working in groups on real issues.

"Education on War, Peace, Conflict, and Change." *Intercom,* Vol. 12; Fall 1971. An overview of many of the factors influencing international studies today. Includes a brief description of a number of special projects and programs.

Paul Ehrlich. *How To Be a Survivor: A Plan To Save Spaceship Earth.* New York: Ballantine Books, Inc., 1971. Uses principles of spaceship operation to suggest what needs to be done in such areas as population, hunger, governmental reforms, and justice if our planet is to survive.

"The Human Person and the War System." *Intercom,* Vol. 13, January/February 1971. Features a series of articles representing different approaches to the problems of modern war. Includes suggestions for teaching, bibliographies, and film lists.

International Understanding at School. Circulars No. 21 and No. 22 of the Department of School and Higher Education, UNESCO. Paris, France: UNESCO, April and October 1971. Contain reports of projects being carried out by UNESCO Associated Schools around the world, as well as descriptions of other projects of interest to teachers of international understanding. (The Department of School and Higher Education, UNESCO, is situated at Place de Fontenoy 75, Paris 7, France.)

Richard Jones. *Fantasy and Feeling in Education.* New York: Harper & Row, Publishers, 1968. A handbook with many suggestions related to developing approaches which recognize feelings as a crucial factor in learning.

Bruce Joyce. *New Strategies for Social Education.* Chicago: Science Research Associates, Inc., 1972. Part of an innovative packaged approach to teaching which includes filmstrips, audio tapes, pamphlets, and an instructor's guide. Presents examples of recent developments in social, scientific, and humanistic education as they relate to the classroom.

David Kellum. *The Social Studies: Myths and Realities.* New York: Sheed & Ward, 1969. An interesting essay on how and why people should teach social studies. Not a methods book, but one filled with suggestions for those seeking to become better teachers.

Leonard Kenworthy. *Social Studies for the Seventies.* Toronto: Blaisdell Publishing Company, 1969. A guidebook for teachers with many suggestions, checklists, bibliographies, and outlines relating to objectives, learning themes, and classroom practices.

David C. King. *International Education for Spaceship Earth.* New York: Thomas Y. Crowell Company, 1970. Based on an extensive study conducted by the Foreign Policy Association, this paperback provides sample units, bibliographies, and lists of games and resources for developing a global approach in the social studies classroom.

Herbert R. Kohl. *The Open Classroom: A Practical Guide to a New Way of Teaching.* New York: Vintage Books, Random House, Inc., 1969. Explains how a teacher can survive in a bureaucracy while maintaining an open and exciting classroom in which students are treated as people.

Roger F. Mager. *Developing Attitudes Toward Learning.* Palo Alto, California: Fearon Publishers, Inc., 1968. A "how-to" book that helps teachers in their efforts to interest students in their "courses." Also offers a way of measuring success in this endeavor.

Byron G. Massialas and C. Benjamin Cox, editors. *Social Studies in the United States: A Critical Appraisal.* New York: Harcourt, Brace & World, 1967. A useful survey of much that goes on in social studies and a critical review designed to help in a rethinking of the basis for many traditional programs.

William A. Nesbitt. *Interpreting the Newspaper in the Classroom: Foreign News and World Views.* New York: Thomas Y. Crowell Company, 1968. Intended to assist teachers in their efforts to help students make better use of messages they receive from the media. Includes classroom exercises and a collection of readings.

William A. Nesbitt. *Simulation Games for the Social Studies Classroom.* New York: Thomas Y. Crowell Company, 1968. Seeks to answer such questions as: What are educational games? How can they be used effectively? How good are they? Where can teachers get them?

William A. Nesbitt. *Teaching About War and War Prevention.* New York: Thomas Y. Crowell Company, 1971. Provides a framework for classroom consideration of questions about causes of conflict, violence, and war. Contains suggestions for classroom exercises and a selected bibliography.

Norris M. Sanders. *Classroom Questions: What Kinds?* New York: Harper & Row, Publishers, 1966. A practical guidebook for teachers interested in improving the quality of classroom discussions.

Seymour B. Sarason. *The Culture of the School and the Problem of Change.* New York: Allyn and Bacon, Inc., 1971. Offers a way of thinking about the culture of the school involving viewing overt behavioral and programmatic regularities in a nonjudgmental way.

Stanley Seaberg. *Teaching the Comparative Approach to American Studies.* New York: Thomas Y. Crowell Company, 1969. Uses case studies to demonstrate a way of viewing societies or issues in a comparative framework. Cases include nationalism, the American Revolution, and interventionism.

Fannie Shaftel and George Shaftel. *Role Playing for Social Values: Decision-Making in the Social Studies.* Englewood Cliffs, New Jersey: Prentice-Hall, Inc., 1967. A framework, with examples, for using role playing in a classroom setting. Suggests many practical, interesting, and useful ways of helping students become more involved in their learning.

Fred Smith and C. Benjamin Cox. *New Strategies and Curriculum in Social Studies.* Chicago: Rand McNally & Company, 1969. A useful review of learning theory, curriculum design, and other factors shaping the social studies projects and reform efforts of the sixties. Includes examples drawn from a number of projects.

Social Studies Today: Guidelines for Improvement. Harrisburg: Pennsylvania State Department of Education, 1970. A source book especially useful for supervisors and department chairmen. Lists projects, materials, and objectives and includes suggestions for planners.

"Teaching Topic: Media." In: *The World and the School.* London: Atlantic Information Centre for Teachers, February 1971. Deals with the problems created by the impact of mass media on the formation of a coherent view of world events. Includes articles on the media, classroom implications of media viewing, and a selected bibliography.

Teaching Toward Inquiry. Washington, D.C.: Center for the Study of Instruction, NEA, 1971. Outlines, describes, and provides examples of teacher and learner behavior in inquiry-focused classrooms.

Theory into Practice: Concepts and Concept Learning. Columbus: College of Education, Ohio State University, April 1971. Explores the nature of concept learning and its challenges for curriculum planning.

Keith Tyler. *Television for World Understanding.* Washington, D.C.: National Education Association, 1970. Treats the relationship between television and international understanding. Includes plans and strategies for using television to improve world understanding.

MATERIALS FOR THE CLASSROOM

Art and Man. Published eight times a year by *Scholastic Magazine* in cooperation with the National Gallery of Art. The program includes slides and other visuals. Topics for 1971 and 1972 include issues on Japan and Africa.

Pat Barr. *Foreign Devils.* New York: Penguin Books, Inc., 1970. The story of the meeting of East and West from the 16th century to the present day. Well illustrated and told with wit and wisdom.

Jerry Brown. *A Plan for an Instructional Unit on Population Dynamics.* Bloomington: Social Studies Development Center, Indiana University, 1971. Presents a comprehensive rationale and detailed plan for developing a unit on population. Includes a population-dynamics inventory.

Jerome Bruner. *Outline for "Man: A Course of Study."* Cambridge Massachusetts: Seminar for Teachers, Education Development Center, 1968. Focusing on the question "What makes man human?" this guide suggests ways teachers can use the materials developed for this course and student responses to these materials to promote learning.

Case Studies of Developing Nations. Boston: Houghton Mifflin Company, 1967. Twelve booklets covering problems of poor nations and the impact of relief efforts on human beings.

Children in Other Lands and *Teacher's Kit.* Boston: Allyn and Bacon, Inc., 1970.

Concern: Extremism; Race; Poverty; Revolution. Morristown, New Jersey: Silver Burdett Company. A dramatically illustrated series of pamphlets, each dealing with a different topic.

"Declaration of World Citizenship," 1971. Available from: United Nations Association of Minnesota, 55 South 8th Street, Minneapolis, Minnesota 55415. State of Minnesota declaration, printed on parchment, suitable for framing.

Development Bridge to Peace, Introduction to Development. Available from: American Freedom from Hunger Foundation, 1717 H Street, N.W., Washington, D.C. 20036. A unit for classroom and community use emphasizing the many-faceted nature of development issues.

Mary Jane Dunstan and Patricia W. Garlan. *Worlds in the Making: Probes for Students of the Future.* Englewood Cliffs, New Jersey: Prentice-Hall., Inc., 1970. Challenges students to become aware of their values, to seek new meanings in the changing present by exploring, imagining, and evaluating the future. Includes problems, probes, and projections to stimulate the reader and open his vision to new possibilities.

Families Around the World and *Teacher's Guide.* Minneapolis: Project Social Studies Center, University of Minnesota. Uses studies of family patterns to deal with such concepts as culture, role, and socialization. Provides a basis for subsequent study of community, political systems, and cultural values.

William R. Fielder. *A Rationale: Holt Data Bank System.* New York: Holt, Rinehart and Winston, Inc., 1971. An explanation of the assumptions, chief components, and teaching strategies of the data-bank approach. Clearly outlined and illustrated with concrete examples.

Four Communities Around the World and *Teacher's Guide.* Taba Social Studies Curriculum. Menlo Park, California: Addison-Wesley Publishing Company. A series of curriculum guides and teaching units, interdisciplinary and planned for sequential development of skills and attitudes, as well as knowledge.

Geography in an Urban Age and *Teacher's Guide*. New York: The Macmillan Company. A new approach to the teaching of high school geography using simulations. Topics include "Japan," "Cultural Geography," "Political Processes," and "Habitat and Resources."

Great Decisions 1972. New York: Foreign Policy Association, 1972. Concise summaries and discussion of questions relating to eight current foreign policy or world issues. Topics include "China," "Population," "Chile," and "The Soviet Union."

History as Culture Change: An Overview. Anthropology Curriculum Study Project. New York: The Macmillan Company, 1970. A sample kit of materials designed to demonstrate how anthropologists study society, outlining some comparative analysis models for use in studying historical data.

How Should the United States Handle Conflict in the 1970's? Unit based on the UNA-USA *Controlling Conflict in the 1970's*. Available from Marion Scott, P.O. Box 1127, Ames, Iowa 50010.

Leonard S. Kenworthy. *Studying the U.S.S.R. in Elementary and Secondary Schools*. New York: Teachers College Press, 1970. Comprehensive resource guide providing lists of materials and services. Similar guides are available on Latin America, Africa, and the Middle East.

Lessons from the Moon: A Teaching Guide to the Multi-Media Archive. New York: New York Times, 1969. Provides insight into and raises questions about the implications of man's exploration of space for life on earth.

Barbara Long and Thomas E. Linehan. *100 Curriculum Ideas*. New York: Herder & Herder, Inc., 1970. A variety of imaginative suggestions for interesting students in art and human behavior. Contains many illustrations and examples.

Barbara Long and Thomas E. Linehan. *The Road Game*. New York: Herder & Herder, Inc., 1970. An interdisciplinary exercise seeking to integrate verbal and visual behavior and designed to help students become better observers of human behavior.

Barbara Long and Thomas E. Linehan. *The Value Game*. New York: Herder & Herder, Inc., 1970. A game designed to reveal differing value systems.

Byron G. Massialas and Jack Zevin. *World Order*. World Order Through Inquiry Series. Chicago: Rand McNally & Company, 1970. A concept-oriented unit dealing with how conflicts have been and might be handled.

Media Supported World Affairs Seminars. Chicago: Association of School Librarians, 1971. A report on the use of the seminar method in high school classes studying current world affairs issues. Contains actual dialogue. Issues include "America's Position on China," "Allende Election in Chile," "Arab-Israeli Conflict," and "Detente in Europe."

Perspectives. Set of 12 booklets on a single theme. Available from: American Universities Field Staff, 3 Lebanon Street, Hanover, New Hampshire 03755. Topics include "The Impact of Modernization on Traditional Societies" and "The Impact of Population on Society."

Social Studies Curriculum Materials Data Book. Boulder, Colorado: Social Science Education Consortium. Designed to help teachers select and evaluate innovative materials for their social studies classrooms.

Sociological Resources for Secondary School. Boston: Allyn and Bacon, Inc., 1970. Based on selected sociological concepts, such as culture, stereotypes, ideology, and values, these materials emphasize the process of sociological inquiry. Includes episodes (short units) and readings which can be used to supplement problems of democracy in other social studies courses.

Tradition and Change in Four Societies: An Inquiry Approach and *Teacher's Guide.* New York: Holt, Rinehart and Winston, Inc., 1968. An examination of traditional society, the impact of Western institutions, technology, and selected ideas on South Africa, Brazil, India, and China. Problems studied include race relations and their implications in Brazil and South Africa.

Mary Jane Turner. *Materials for Civics, Government, and Problems of Democracy: Political Science in the New Social Studies.* Boulder, Colorado: Social Science Education Consortium, 1971. An analysis of almost 50 packages of materials produced by more than 40 social science curriculum projects. Describes the materials with regard to content selection, organization, instructional techniques, and appropriate grade level.

Samuel Yares and Cia Holdorf, editors. *Big Rock Candy Mountain: Resources for Our Education.* New York: Dell Publishing Company, Inc., 1971. Excerpts, exercises, "eye-catchers," and bibliographical resources dealing with a great variety of new and imaginative materials and approaches. A "whole-earth catalogue" approach to educational materials.

CURRENT ISSUES

Civic Leader, teacher edition of *American Observer.* Available from: Scholastic Magazines, 902 Sylvan Avenue, Englewood Cliffs, New Jersey 07632. Published 17 times during the school year.

Current Affairs and the Social Studies. Medford, Massachusetts: Lincoln Filene Center for Citizenship and Public Affairs, Tufts University.

Futures. Periodical available from: World Future Society, P.O. Box 19285, 20th Street Station, Washington, D.C. 20036.

Great Decisions. New York: Foreign Policy Association. An annual publication that provides up-to-date analysis of foreign policy topics.

Headline Series. New York: Foreign Policy Association. Published five times a year. Each issue treats a different topic and is written by an expert.

Intercom: A Resource Guide and Program Catalyst on World Issues. New York: Center for War/Peace Studies. (See Appendix D.)

Internationalist. Available from: Peter Adamson Communications, Ltd., 744 High Street, Wallingford, Berkshire, England. Published three times a year.

The New York Times School Weekly. Available from: New York Times School Division, 229 West 43rd Street, New York, New York 10036.

The Newsweek Magazine Educational Program. Available from: Newsweek, Inc., 444 Madison Avenue, New York, New York 10022.

Orbit. Available from: Ontario Institute for Studies in Education, 252 Bloor Street West, Toronto, Ontario, Canada. Designed to keep teachers up to date on new ideas in education. Published five times a year.

Social Education. Available from: National Council for the Social Studies, 1201 Sixteenth Street, N.W., Washington, D.C. 20036. Monthly journal. See the November 1968 issue, "International Education for the Twenty-first Century"; see also the January 1970 issue.

Social Science Record. Available from: New York State Council for the Social Studies, 412 Maxwell Hall, Syracuse University, Syracuse, New York 03210. Published three times a year.

UNESCO Courier. Available from UNESCO, Place de Fontenoy 75, Paris 7, France. Published 11 times a year.

VISTA. New York: UNA-USA. Published bimonthly.

War/Peace Report. New York: Center for War/Peace Studies. Published 10 times a year. (See Appendix D.)

The World and the School, a review for teachers of current international affairs, and *Crisis Papers,* an ad hoc series analyzing current crises, including comment from newspapers and journals of several countries. Available from: Atlantic Information Centre for Teachers, 23/25 Abbey House, 8 Victoria Street, London SW 1, England; or from: American Institute of College Teachers–National Association of Secondary School Principals, 1201 Sixteenth Street, N.W., Washington, D.C. 20036.

TELEVISION

Prime Time School Television, Suite 1208, 100 North LaSalle Street, Chicago, Illinois 60602. Provides information about forthcoming TV programs of interest to teachers, as well as guides and suggestions for classroom discussion of selected programs.

SOURCES OF INFORMATION AND MATERIALS

Africa

The African-American Institute, 866 United Nations Plaza, New York, New York 10017.

Professor Richard B. Ford (chairman of the Committee on Teaching about Africa), Africa Studies Association, Department of History, Clark University, Worcester, Massachusetts 01097.

Project Africa, Baker Hall, Carnegie-Mellon University, Pittsburgh, Pennsylvania 15213.

Asia

Asian Studies Project, Ohio State University, Columbus, Ohio 43210.
The Asia Society, 112 East 64th Street, New York, New York 10021.
The Japan Society, 250 Park Avenue, New York, New York 10003.
National Committee on U.S.–China Relations, 77 United Nations Plaza, New York, New York 10017.

Latin America

Center for Inter-American Relations, 680 Park Avenue, New York, New York 10001.

Middle East

American Friends of the Middle East, 1605 New Hampshire Avenue, N.W., Washington, D.C. 20009.
Institute for Mediterranean Affairs, 1078 Madison Avenue, New York, New York 10028.
Middle East Institute, 1761 N Street, N.W., Washington, D.C. 20036.

United Nations

UNA-USA (United Nations Association of the United States), 833 United Nations Plaza, New York, New York 10017.
UNESCO, Place de Fontenoy 75, Paris 7, France.

World Affairs

American Friends Service Committee, 160 North 15th Street, Philadelphia, Pennsylvania 19102.
Center for International Education, School of Education, University of Massachusetts, Amherst 01002.
Center for the Teaching of International Relations, Graduate School of International Studies, University of Denver, Denver, Colorado 80210.
Center for War/Peace Studies, 218 East 18th Street, New York, New York 10003.
Foreign Area Materials Center, State Education Department, University of the State of New York, 60 East 42nd Street, New York, New York 10017.
Foreign Policy Association, 345 East 46th Street, New York, New York 10017.

Lincoln Filene Center for Citizenship and Public Affairs, Tufts University, Medford, Massachusetts 02155.

World Law Fund, 11 West 42nd Street, New York, New York 10036.

Future

Institute for the Future, Riverview Center, Middletown, Connecticut 06457.

Resources for the Future, Inc., 1755 Massachusetts Avenue, N.W., Washington, D.C. 20036.

Development

American Freedom from Hunger Foundation, Inc., 1717 H Street, N.W., Washington, D.C. 20006.

MIND (Management Institute for National Development), 230 Park Avenue, New York, New York 10017.

Organization for Economic Cooperation and Development, Publication Center, 1750 Pennsylvania Avenue, N.W., Washington, D.C. 20006.

Overseas Development Council, 1717 Massachusetts Avenue, N.W., Washington, D.C. 20036.

Voluntary Committee on Overseas Aid and Development, 69 Victoria Street, London SW 1, England.

Newsletters

Challenge for Change Newsletter, National Film Board of Canada, Montreal 101, Quebec.

Commitment, quarterly service bulletin designed to help nongovernmental organizations in development assistance activities, DSIS/UNDP, United Nations, New York, New York 10017.

CTIR Newsletter, Center for Teaching International Relations, Graduate School of International Studies, University of Denver, Denver, Colorado 80210.

Education USA, weekly newsletter published by National School Public Relations Association, 1801 North Moore Street, Arlington, Virginia 22209.

Focus on Asia Studies, Service Center for Teachers of Asian Studies, Association for Asian Studies, Ohio State University, 29 Woodruff Avenue, Columbus 43210.

News and Notes on the Social Sciences, Coordinator for School Social Studies, 101 Lindley Hall, Indiana University, Bloomington 47401.

SCEWA Newsletter, Society for Citizen Education in World Affairs, 3300 University Avenue, S.E., Minneapolis, Minnesota 55414.

SSEC Newsletter, Social Science Education Consortium, 855 Broadway, Boulder, Colorado 80302.

Appendix C
Additional Resources[1]

BIBLIOGRAPHIES

William A. Nesbitt. *Teaching About War and Its Control: A Selective Annotated Bibliography for the Social Studies Teacher.* Available from: Studies in International Conflict Project, Center for International Programs and Comparative Studies, State Education Department, Albany, New York 12224. A bibliography prepared especially for the use of secondary school teachers.

Arthur Newman. *A Select Bibliography on International Education.* Available from the author, University of Florida, Gainesville 32601.

Robert Pickus and Robert Woito. *To End War: An Introduction to the Ideas, Books, Organizations, and Work That Can Help.* Available from World Without War Council, 1730 Grove Street, Berkeley, California 94709. This bibliography, recently revised, is now a standard in the field, covering the substantive aspects of war-peace issues.

Gordon V. Webster. *An Annotated Bibliography on War and Peace.* Available from War, Peace, and Conscience Project, Box 731, Stony Brook, New York 11790.

INSTRUCTIONAL METHODS

CTIR Newsletter. Available from: Center for Teaching International Relations, University of Denver, Denver, Colorado 80210. Offers suggestions on such issues as racism and development.

Social Science Record. Special issue on peace education. Available from the World Law Fund. (See Appendix D.)

FILMS, MUSIC, OTHER MATERIALS

Brandon Films, 221 West 57th Street, New York, New York 10019.

Richard D. Burns. *American Protest Songs of War and Peace: A Selected Bibliography.* Series No. 1. Available from: Center for the Study of Armament and Disarmament, California State College, Los Angeles 90032.

---

[1] Compiled and annotated by Betty Reardon. See also Appendix D.

Churchill Films, 622 North Robertson Boulevard, Los Angeles, California 90069.

Lucy Dougall. *The War/Peace Film Guide.* Available from: World Without War Council, 1730 Grove Street, Berkeley, California 94709.

Films, Inc., 1144 Wilmette Avenue, Wilmette, Illinois 60091.

Indiana University Audio-Visual Center, Bloomington 47401.

National Peace Corps Tape Bank, Leyden High School, 2400 Rose Street, Franklin Park, Illinois 60131.

Social Studies School Services. Provides 8mm films, filmstrips, games, and a range of other materials from various publishers. Available from: Social Studies School Services, 10000 Culver Boulevard, Culver City, California 90230. This is the only distributor at present with a specific listing on peace studies.

NATIONAL SERVICE ORGANIZATIONS AND AGENCIES

APGA Peace Commission, 1607 New Hampshire Avenue, N.W., Washington, D.C. 20009. Among other services, provides the *Peace in Action Directory of Activities, Organizations, Careers, and Studies for the Promotion of World Peace.* An excellent all-round resource.

Canadian Peace Research and Education Association, 25 Dundana Avenue, Dundas, Ontario, Canada. Provides information about local and regional peace-education centers and groups.

Appendix D
Consortium on Peace Research, Education, and Development (COPRED)[1]

The Consortium on Peace Research, Education, and Development was founded in May 1970 to meet the growing demand on college and university campuses across the country for assistance and support in developing peace studies and peace research programs. In addition to campus-based activities, it has concerned itself with the inventorying and practical use of peace-related knowledge.

PROGRAMS

COPRED's first task has been the development of a communications network for the peace research/education/action community. Over 70 institutions are associated with it, ranging from purely research groups such as the Mershon Center to program organizations such as the World Law Fund and the American Friends Service Committee. Through its secretariat, newsletters, regional conferences, and annual meetings, the Consortium informs its members of recent developments in the field and ties them in with transnational organizations such as the International Peace Research Association and UNESCO. It is also working to develop student and faculty exchanges among universities.

Another major activity in COPRED is the development of peace studies as a legitimate academic field. Through consultative conferences at colleges and universities seeking assistance in creating formal peace and conflict studies curricula, COPRED supports innovative methods of teaching the determinants of peace. In connection with its campus consultations, it has produced a guidebook that will be published commercially and is available for groups wishing to initiate or improve programs. In addition, it works with professional associations to develop peace studies/research emphasis in the various behavioral science disciplines by cosponsoring peace-related sessions at national meetings of these associations. The Consortium also collaborates with other organizations in developing peace and conflict education for primary and secondary schools.

The third major COPRED thrust concerns the organization and facilitation of policy-relevant research. This involves creating a demand among policy

[1] Institute of Behavioral Science, University of Colorado, Boulder 80302. Prepared by Elise Boulding.

makers and legislators, a research inventory for scholars committed to peace-related research, and a policy advisory group to link policy and research.

PARTIAL LISTING OF PEACE STUDIES PROGRAMS AND INSTITUTES

CENTER FOR NONVIOLENT CONFLICT RESOLUTION, Haverford College, Haverford, Pennsylvania 19041. Founded: 1968.

CENTER FOR PEACE STUDIES, University of Akron, Akron, Ohio 44304. Founded: 1970.

CENTER FOR PEACEFUL CHANGE, Kent State University, Kent, Ohio 44240. Founded: 1971.

CENTER FOR TEACHING ABOUT PEACE AND WAR, Wayne State University, University Center, Detroit, Michigan 48202. Founded: 1965.

CENTER FOR WAR/PEACE STUDIES, 218 East 18th Street, New York, New York 10003. Founded: 1966.

COMMITTEE ON CONFLICT RESOLUTION AND PEACE STUDIES, Department of Sociology, University of Pittsburgh, Pittsburgh, Pennsylvania 15213. Founded: 1971.

CONFLICT STUDIES COMMITTEE, 268 Condon Hall, University of Washington, Seattle 98105. Founded: 1968.

GRADUATE GROUP IN PEACE RESEARCH, Department of Regional Science, University of Pennsylvania, Philadelphia 19104. Founded: 1970.

INSTITUTE FOR THE STUDY OF PEACE, 336 Champlin Hall, St. Louis University, St. Louis, Missouri 63103. Founded: 1970.

MASTER'S PROGRAM IN PEACE STUDIES, Earlham School of Religion, Richmond, Indiana 47374. Founded: 1971.

MISSOURI PEACE STUDIES INSTITUTE, 813 Maryland Avenue, Columbia, Missouri 62501. Founded: 1968.

PACEM IN TERRIS INSTITUTE, Manhattan College, Bronx, New York 10471. Founded: 1966.

PEACE AND CONFLICT STUDIES PROGRAM, University of Hawaii, 2500 Campus Road, Honolulu, Hawaii 96822. Founded: 1970.

PEACE STUDIES INSTITUTE, Manchester College, North Manchester, Indiana 46962. Founded: 1948.

PROGRAM ON PEACE STUDIES, Center for International Studies, Cornell University, Ithaca, New York 14850. Founded: 1970.

STUDIES IN NONVIOLENCE, ESIN Chapel House, Syracuse University, Syracuse, New York 13210. Founded: 1970.

WORLD LAW FUND, 11 West 42nd Street, New York, New York 10036. Founded: 1961.

Notes About the Authors

JAMES M. BECKER is Director of the Diffusion Project, Social Studies Development Center, Indiana University, Bloomington. He has taught at the secondary school and college levels. For five years he was Director of School Services for the Foreign Policy Association, and he is currently adviser to the Center for War/Peace Studies, New York City, New York. He was coeditor of the 1968 Yearbook of the National Council for the Social Studies. He has contributed articles to many professional journals, including *International Studies Quarterly, American Education, Social Education,* and *World and the School.*

JULIETTE P. BURSTERMANN is Professor of Education, Eastern Connecticut State College, Willimantic. She serves on several national and Connecticut state committees concerned with teacher education and mental health. She has also served as Visiting Professor of Education at Winston-Salem State University, Winston-Salem, North Carolina, and Brooklyn College, Brooklyn, New York. Her articles have appeared in *Progressive Education, School and Society, Negro History Bulletin, Educational Leadership, North Carolina Parent,* and *Norfolk Journal and Guide.*

SIBYLLE K. ESCALONA is Professor of Psychology, Albert Einstein College of Medicine, Yeshiva University, New York City, New York. She has conducted research and has written extensively in the areas of child development, infant psychology, and early personality development. She is former Director of Research with the Menninger Foundation. Among her many writings are *The Root of Individuality* (1968) and, with Grace M. Heider, *Prediction and Outcome* (1959).

AUBREY HAAN is Professor of Educational Administration, Dean of the School of Education, and Chairman of the Department of Educational Administration, California State University, San Francisco. He is a member of many organizations dedicated to improving the quality of human life. In addition to being a national consultant in higher education, he is the author of a number of books, including *Elementary School Curriculum: Theory and Research* (1961), *Education for the Open Society* (1962), and, with Norma Haan, *Readings in Professional Education* (1963).

THERESA L. HELD is Director of the Graduate Program in Counselor Education, Bank Street College of Education, New York City, New York. Previously she served as Director of the Sarah Lawrence–Bank Street Program for Continuing Education in Counseling and Guidance. She has also served as a consultant to the U.S. Office of Education and as a high school assistant principal and counselor. She is the author of articles that have appeared in *Journal of Secondary School Principals, Country Beautiful, Civic Education,* and *Bulletin for Social Studies.*

GEORGE HENDERSON, Editor of the ASCD 1973 Yearbook, is Goldman Professor of Human Relations and Professor of Education and of Sociology, University of Oklahoma, Norman. He is a member of the Executive Committee of the Consortium on Peace Research, Education, and Development. He was formerly Assistant to the Superintendent of the Detroit Public Schools. He has written a number of articles and is the author or editor of four books: with William B. Ragan, *Foundations of American Education* (1970); with Robert F. Bibens, *Teachers Should Care* (1970); *America's Other Children: Public Schools Outside Suburbia* (1971); and *To Live in Freedom: Human Relations Today and Tomorrow* (1972).

LOUIS S. LEVINE, to whom this Yearbook is dedicated, was Professor of Psychology, California State University, San Francisco. At the time of his death in 1971 he was conducting research and writing in the area of the preservation and enhancement of human rights and liberties. In addition to contributing many articles to professional journals, he was the author of *Personal and Social Development: The Psychology of Behavior* (1963). Although he did not contribute a chapter to this Yearbook, his ideals inspired the other committee members.

THORNTON B. MONEZ is Professor of Education and Coordinator of the Sixth Year Program in Supervision and Administration, Richmond College of the City University of New York, New York City, New York. He was previously Superintendent of the Caldwell–West Caldwell Schools in New Jersey, where he also served as a teacher, a supervisor, a secondary school principal, and Assistant Superintendent for Instruction. He has devoted his career to humanizing instruction in the public schools. He was a contributor to the ASCD publication *Humanizing the Secondary School* (1969).

WILLIAM A. NESBITT has been devoting most of his time for the past two years to the Studies in International Conflict project of the New York State Education Department. Among the materials he has developed for the project is *Data on the Human Crisis: A Handbook for Inquiry,* excerpts from which appear in this book. He has been a history teacher and is currently teaching part-time at the Wooster School, Danbury, Connecticut. He was formerly an editorial director for the Foreign Policy Association, and during that time he wrote *Teaching About War and War Prevention, Simulation Games for the Social Studies,* and *Interpreting the Newspaper in the Classroom* (1971). He is also the author of a simulation game, *Guns or Butter.*

GERTRUDE NOAR is a national consultant in education. She has been an elementary and secondary school teacher, a high school principal, and a university professor. For several years she was National Director of Education for the Anti-Defamation League of B'nai B'rith. She has had a long and distinguished career devoted to improving human relations and working for human rights. In addition to many articles and pamphlets, she has written a number of books, including *Living with Difference* (1965), *The Teacher and Integration* (1966), and *Individualized Instruction: Every Child a Winner* (1970).

BETTY REARDON is School Program Director for the World Law Fund and has been involved in the development of peace-education programs since 1963. Before joining the World Law Fund, she taught social studies in secondary school. She was a participant in the World Conference on Education at Asilomar, California, in 1970, and she is a charter member of the World Council for Curriculum and Instruction. She has contributed articles to many publications, including the 1968 Yearbook of the National Council for the Social Studies, *High School Journal, Teachers College Record,* and *Media & Methods.*

ASCD 1973 Yearbook Committee Members

GEORGE HENDERSON, *Chairman and Editor;* Goldman Professor of Human Relations and Professor of Education and of Sociology, University of Oklahoma, Norman

JAMES M. BECKER, Director of the Diffusion Project, Social Studies Development Center, Indiana University, Bloomington

JULIETTE P. BURSTERMANN, Professor of Education, Eastern Connecticut State College, Willimantic

AUBREY HAAN, Professor of Educational Administration, Dean of the School of Education, and Chairman of the Department of Educational Administration, California State University, San Francisco

THERESA L. HELD, Director of the Graduate Program in Counselor Education, Bank Street College of Education, New York City

LOUIS S. LEVINE (d. 1971), Professor of Psychology, California State University, San Francisco

THORNTON B. MONEZ, Professor of Education and Coordinator of the Sixth Year Program in Supervision and Administration, Richmond College, City University of New York, New York City

GERTRUDE NOAR, National Consultant in Education, former National Director of Education for the Anti-Defamation League of B'nai B'rith

BETTY REARDON, School Program Director for the World Law Fund, New York City

ASCD Board of Directors
as of November 1, 1972

EXECUTIVE COUNCIL, 1972-73

President: JACK R. FRYMIER, Professor and Chairman, Department of Curriculum and Foundations, College of Education, The Ohio State University, Columbus

President-Elect: HAROLD G. SHANE, University Professor of Education, Indiana University, Bloomington

Immediate Past President: ALVIN D. LOVING, SR., Assistant Dean, School of Education, University of Michigan, Ann Arbor

O. L. DAVIS, JR., Professor of Curriculum and Instruction, The University of Texas, Austin

BENJAMIN P. EBERSOLE, Director of Curriculum and Instructional Services, Board of Education of Baltimore County, Towson, Maryland

MINNIE H. FIELDS, Educational Consultant, 1032 Joe Louis Street, Tallahassee, Florida

RICHARD L. FOSTER, Superintendent of Schools, Berkeley Unified School District, California

JOHN U. MICHAELIS, Professor of Education, University of California, Berkeley

AUDREY NORRIS, Director, Tomorrow's Educational Systems Today, Cincinnati, Ohio

EDWARD G. PONDER, Research Associate and Professor of Education, New York University, New York City

ELIZABETH SCHMOKE RANDOLPH, Director, ESTA Activities, Charlotte–Mecklenburg Schools, Charlotte, North Carolina

GLENYS G. UNRUH, Assistant to the Superintendent for Curriculum and Instruction, School District of University City, Missouri

JEFF WEST, District Superintendent, North Central District, Miami Springs, Florida

BOARD MEMBERS ELECTED AT LARGE

Mitsuo Adachi, Arizona State University (on leave), Tempe (1974); Louise M. Berman, University of Maryland, College Park (1974); Leslee J. Bishop, University of Georgia, Athens (1976); John E. Codwell, Houston Public Schools, Texas (1975); O. L. Davis, Jr., University of Texas, Austin (1973); Grace S. Epps, Robeson County Schools, Lumberton, North Carolina (1975); Marie Fielder, University of California, Berkeley (1974); Richard L. Foster, Berkeley Unified School District, California (1974); Robert S. Fox, University of Michigan, Ann Arbor (1975); C. Glen Hass, University of Florida, Gainesville (1976); Daisy M. Jones, Arizona State University, Tempe (1973); Frances R. Link, Curriculum Development Associates, Washington, D.C. (1973); Wilma S. Longstreet, University of Michigan, Flint (1975); James B. Macdonald, University of North Carolina, Greensboro (1974); Barbara T. Mason, City University of New York, Flushing (1976); John E. McGill, University of Illinois, Urbana (1975); Dwight Teel, Milwaukee Public Schools, Wisconsin (1973); Vincent R. Rogers, University of Connecticut, Storrs (1976); Jeff West, North Central School District, Miami Springs, Florida (1973).

UNIT REPRESENTATIVES TO THE BOARD

(Unit Presidents are listed first; others follow in alphabetical order.)

Alabama: Sara Davis, University; Mildred Ellisor, Auburn University, Auburn; Gerald R. Firth, University of Alabama, Tuscaloosa.

Arizona: Evelyn Johnson, John W. Powell School, Phoenix; James J. Jelinek, Arizona State University, Tempe; Dorothy G. Talbert, Tucson.

Arkansas: John H. Barker, Osceola Public Schools, Osceola; Calvin G. Patterson, Fort Smith Public Schools, Fort Smith.

California: Helen James, Carmichael; Ray Arveson, Hayward Unified School District, Hayward; Arthur L. Costa, Sacramento; Don M. Russell, Mt. Diablo Unified School District, Clayton; Burton C. Tiffany, Chula Vista City Elementary Schools, Chula Vista.

Colorado: Dick Telfer, Boulder Valley Schools, Boulder; William Liddle, Colorado Springs Public Schools, Colorado Springs; Doris Molbert, University of Denver, Denver.

Delaware: John Allen, Newark School District, Newark; Melville F. Warren, Dover.

District of Columbia: Bessie D. Etheridge, Spingarn Instructional Unit; Lorraine H. Whitlock, D.C. Public Schools.

Florida: E. J. Bass, Florida State University, Tallahassee; Aquilina C. Howell, Leon County Public Schools, Tallahassee; Harry McComb, Ft. Lauderdale; Patrick Mooney, North Miami; Evelyn Sharp, Bethune-Cookman College, Daytona Beach.

Georgia: Ferris Johnson, Athens; Emmett L. Lee, Clayton County Schools, Jonesboro; John H. Lounsbury, Milledgeville; Susie W. Wheeler, Cartersville.

Hawaii: Kengo Takata, Kaneohe; James R. Brough, The Kamehameha Schools, Honolulu; Sigfried Ramler, Punahou School, Honolulu.

Idaho: Gordon Murri, Pocatello School District No. 25, Pocatello; Parker E. Richards, Pocatello School District, Pocatello.

Illinois: Mary K. Huser, Bloomington; Margaret L. Carroll, Northern Illinois University, DeKalb; Reuben M. Conrad, Township High School District 214, Mt. Prospect; Lillian S. Davies, Illinois State University, Normal; Earl Dieken, Glen Ellyn Public Schools, Glen Ellyn; Raymond E. Hendee, Board of Education, District 41, Glen Ellyn; Mildred Hindman, Herrin.

Indiana: J. Earl Hefner, Portage Public Schools, Portage; Ruth Hochstetler, Ball State University, Muncie; Charles E. Kline, Purdue University, Lafayette.

Iowa: Russell W. Clarke, Mason City Community School District, Mason City; Horace S. Hoover, Community School District, Dubuque; Fay Layne, Blackhawk City Schools, Waterloo.

Kansas: Robert McKenzie, Winfield Public Schools, Winfield; Eunice Bradley, Manhattan; Barbara Keatings, Wichita Public Schools, Wichita.

Kentucky: Sue Jent, Hopkins County Board of Education, Madison; Sister Mildred McGovern, Covington; Pat W. Wear, Berea College, Berea.

Louisiana: Travis Funderburk, Rapides Parish School Board, Alexandria; Edwin H. Friedrich, New Orleans Public Schools, New Orleans; Emelie M. Wilkomm, New Orleans Parish School Board, New Orleans.

Maryland: Franklin Pumphrey, Maryland State Department of Education, Baltimore; L. Morris McClure, University of Maryland, College Park; Elizabeth McMahon, Board of Education, Upper Marlboro; Richard F. Neville, Silver Spring.

Massachusetts: Gilbert W. Berry, Maria Hastings School, Lexington.

Michigan: Jack Wickert, Kalamazoo Public Schools, Kalamazoo; Morrel J. Clute, Wayne State University, Detroit; James E. House, Jr., Wayne County Intermediate Schools, Detroit; Ruby King, Grand Rapids; James L. Leary, Clarenceville School District, Farmington; Stuart C. Rankin, Detroit Public Schools, Detroit.

Minnesota: Stanley Gilbertson, Bloomington; Floyd Keller, Independent School District No. 834, Stillwater.

Mississippi: O. E. Jordan, State Department of Education, Jackson; R. B. Layton, Jackson Public Schools, Jackson.

Missouri: Kenneth Lewis, Consolidated School District No. 2, Raytown; Edward R. Edmunds, Parkway School District, Chesterfield; Richard King, State Department of Education, Jefferson City; Harry Lossing, Independence.

Montana: Tom Miller, Jefferson School, Helena; Lloyd B. Ellingsen, Billings.

Nebraska: Jean Buck, Kearney Public Schools, Kearney; Gerald Bryant, Grand Island Public Schools, Grand Island; Dale D. Rathe, Lincoln Public Schools, Lincoln.

Nevada: Robert Dunsheath, Las Vegas Public Schools, Las Vegas.

New England: Joan D. Kerelejza, Whitman School, West Hartford, Connecticut; Annabelle Allen, New Canaan Public Schools, New Canaan, Connecticut; Edward G. Hunt, City of Warwick Public Schools, Warwick, Rhode Island; Lyman C. Hunt, Jr., University of Vermont, Burlington; Villa H. Quinn, State Department of Education, Augusta, Maine.

New Jersey: Gabriel A. Massaro, Paramus; Robert Chasnoff, Newark State College, Union; Kathryn N. Cooper, Midland Park; Mary Jane Diehl, Pennington; Nicholas J. Sferrazza, Chas. W. Lewis School, Blackwood.

New Mexico: Juanita M. Gomez, Alamogordo; Wendell Henry, Alamogordo Public Schools, Alamogordo; Chon La Brier, Dulce Elementary Schools, Dulce.

New York: Helen F. Rice, Rochester; Arthur Haas, Latham; George C. Jeffers, State University College, Potsdam; Robert G. Pierleoni, University of Rochester, Rochester; Thomas A. Schottman, Lincoln School, Scotia; Robert E. Sudlow, Williamsville Public Schools, Williamsville; Walter R. Suess, Wantaugh Public Schools, Wantaugh.

North Carolina: Marcus C. Smith, Salisbury City Schools, Salisbury; Robert C. Hanes, Chapel Hill–Carrboro City Schools, Chapel Hill; Doris Hutchinson, Greensboro Public Schools, Greensboro.

Ohio: Robert Alfonso, Kent State University, Kent; Gary H. Deutschlander, Berea High School, Berea; Lloyd W. Dull, Akron City Schools, Akron; Anna Freeman, Franklin County Schools, Columbus; Alice W. Holt, Wood County Schools, Bowling Green; Hugh S. Morrison, Miami University, Oxford.

Oklahoma: Otis O. Lawrence, Oklahoma City Public Schools, Oklahoma City; Gene Shepherd, University of Oklahoma, Norman.

Oregon: Charles G. Kingston, Jr., Portland; William B. Brewster, Central Point Public Schools, Central Point; Charles R. Gengler, Independence; Robert E. McKee, Roseburg Public Schools, Roseburg.

Pennsylvania: Hughes Brininger, Millcreek School District, Erie; Norman R. Dixon, University of Pittsburgh, Pittsburgh; Frederick P. Haas, Interboro School System, Lester; Marlin H. Kessler, Upper Darby School District, Upper Darby; Margaret McFeaters, Pittsburgh; Claude P. Swartzbaugh, Jr., Derry Township School District, Hershey.

Puerto Rico: Gladys D. Fuentes, University of Puerto Rico, Rio Piedras.

South Carolina: Keith Parris, Spartanburg School District No. 6, Spartanburg; Olive C. Bennett, Brookland-Cayce Schools, Cayce; Jack H. Boger, Winthrop College, Rock Hill.

South Dakota: Orville J. Pederson, Mitchell Public Schools, Mitchell; Lincoln Henry, Black Hills State College, Spearfish.

Tennessee: Perle C. McNabb, Newport Public Schools, Newport; W. Elzie Danley, Memphis State University, Memphis.

Texas: Rita S. Bryant, East Texas State University, Commerce; Gwyn Brownlee, Dallas; Shelma Carlile, Texas City Public Schools, Texas City; Warren W. Green, Tyler; Donald McDonald, Texas Technological College, Lubbock.

Utah: Joe A. Reidhead, Nebo School District, Spanish Fork; Lynn F. Stoddard, Hill Field Elementary School, Clearfield.

Virginia: Larry Bowen, University of Virginia, Charlottesville; Evelyn L. Berry, Petersburg Public Schools, Petersburg; William J. Hopkins, Sussex County Schools, Sussex; Gennette Nygard, Arlington County Public Schools, Arlington.

Washington: Robert J. Marum, Seattle; Donald Hair, State Office of Public Instruction, Olympia; Clifton Hussey, Inter School District 101, Spokane.

West Virginia: Ernest Page, Jr., Mineral County Schools, Keyser; Lucille Heflebower, Jefferson County Schools, Charles Town; Betty Livengood, Mineral County Schools, Keyser.

Wisconsin: Harold Anderson, Beaver Dam; William Ernst, Madison; Robert D. Krey, Wisconsin State University, Superior; Gordon W. Ness, Portage.

Wyoming: Carol Arnold, Laramie County School District No. 1, Cheyenne; Laurence A. Walker, University of Wyoming, Laramie.

ASCD Review Council
as of November 1, 1972

WILLIAM VAN TIL, *Chairman,* Lotus D. Coffman Distinguished Professor in Education, Indiana State University, Terre Haute

WILLIAM M. ALEXANDER, Professor of Education, University of Florida, Gainesville

KARL OPENSHAW, Dean of Education, University of Colorado, Boulder

JOHN E. OWENS, Superintendent, Roslyn Public Schools, Roslyn, New York

DEBORAH P. WOLFE, Professor of Education, Queens College, Flushing, New York

ASCD Headquarters Staff
as of November 1, 1972

Executive Secretary, Neil P. Atkins

Associate Secretary; Editor, ASCD Publications, Robert R. Leeper

Associate Secretary, Ronald Stodghill

Associate Secretary, Clark Dobson

Administrative Assistant, Virginia O. Berthy

Staff Assistants:

Sarah Arlington
Jacqueline C. Boffa
Elizabeth A. Brooks
Martha M. Broomhall
Barbara Collins
Marie Jamison
Teola T. Jones
Carvangeline B. Miller

Frances Mindel
Nancy Olson
Mary Albert O'Neill
Julita C. Pearce
Lana Pipes
Carolyn M. Shell
Alice H. Sidberry
Barbara J. Sims

ASCD Publications, Spring 1973

Yearbooks

Balance in the Curriculum (610-17274)	$5.00
Education for Peace: Focus on Mankind (17946)	$7.50
Evaluation as Feedback and Guide (610-17700)	$6.50
Fostering Mental Health in Our Schools (610-17256)	$4.00
Freedom, Bureaucracy, & Schooling (610-17508)	$6.50
Guidance in the Curriculum (610-17266)	$5.00
Individualizing Instruction (610-17264)	$4.00
Leadership for Improving Instruction (610-17454)	$4.00
Learning and Mental Health in the School (610-17674)	$5.00
Learning and the Teacher (610-17270)	$4.50
Life Skills in School and Society (610-17786)	$5.50
New Insights and the Curriculum (610-17548)	$6.00
A New Look at Progressive Education (610-17812)	$8.00
Perceiving, Behaving, Becoming: A New Focus for Education (610-17278)	$5.00
Role of Supervisor and Curriculum Director (610-17624)	$5.00
To Nurture Humaneness: Commitment for the '70's (610-17810)	$6.00
Youth Education: Problems, Perspectives, Promises (610-17746)	$5.50

Books and Booklets

Bases for World Understanding and Cooperation: Suggestions for Teaching the Young Child (611-17834)	$1.00
Better Than Rating (611-17298)	$2.00
The Changing Curriculum: Mathematics (611-17724)	$2.00
The Changing Curriculum: Modern Foreign Languages (611-17764)	$2.00
The Changing Curriculum: Science (611-17704)	$1.50
Changing Supervision for Changing Times (611-17802)	$2.00
Children's Social Learning (611-17326)	$1.75
Cooperative International Education (611-17344)	$1.50
Criteria for Theories of Instruction (611-17756)	$2.00
Curricular Concerns in a Revolutionary Era (611-17852)	$6.00
Curriculum Change: Direction and Process (611-17698)	$2.00
Curriculum Decisions ⟷ Social Realities (611-17770)	$2.75
A Curriculum for Children (611-17790)	$3.00
Curriculum Materials 1973 (17922)	$2.00
Dare To Care / Dare To Act: Racism and Education (611-17850)	$2.00
Discipline for Today's Children and Youth (611-17314)	$1.50
Early Childhood Education Today (611-17766)	$2.00
Educating the Children of the Poor (611-17762)	$2.00
Educating the Young People of the World (611-17506)	$2.50
Educational Accountability: Beyond Behavioral Objectives (611-17856)	$2.50
Elementary School Mathematics: A Guide to Current Research (611-17752)	$2.75
Elementary School Science: A Guide to Current Research (611-17726)	$2.25
Elementary School Social Studies: A Guide to Current Research (611-17384)	$2.75
Ethnic Modification of Curriculum (611-17832)	$1.00
Freeing Capacity To Learn (611-17322)	$2.00
Guidelines for Elementary Social Studies (611-17738)	$1.50
Human Variability and Learning (611-17332)	$2.00
The Humanities and the Curriculum (611-17708)	$2.00
Humanizing Education: The Person in the Process (611-17722)	$2.75
Humanizing the Secondary School (611-17780)	$2.75
Hunters Point Redeveloped—A Sixth-Grade Venture (611-17348)	$2.00
Improving Educational Assessment & An Inventory of Measures of Affective Behavior (611-17804)	$3.00
Influences in Curriculum Change (611-17730)	$2.25
Intellectual Development: Another Look (611-17618)	$1.75
International Dimension of Education (611-17816)	$2.25
Interpreting Language Arts Research for the Teacher (611-17846)	$4.00
The Junior High School We Saw (611-17604)	$2.00
Language and Meaning (611-17696)	$2.75
Learning More About Learning (611-17310)	$2.00
Linguistics and the Classroom Teacher (611-17720)	$2.75
A Man for Tomorrow's World (611-17838)	$2.25
New Dimensions in Learning (611-17336)	$2.00
Nurturing Individual Potential (611-17606)	$2.00
On Early Learning: The Modifiability of Human Potential (611-17842)	$2.00
Open Schools for Children (17916)	$3.75
Personalized Supervision (611-17680)	$1.75
Removing Barriers to Humaneness in the High School (611-17848)	$2.50
The School of the Future—NOW (17920)	$3.75
Selecting New Aids to Teaching (611-17840)	$1.00
Social Studies Education Projects: An ASCD Index (611-17844)	$2.00
Strategy for Curriculum Change (611-17666)	$2.00
Student Unrest: Threat or Promise? (611-17818)	$2.75
Supervision: Emerging Profession (611-17796)	$5.00
Supervision in Action (611-17346)	$1.50
Supervision: Perspectives and Propositions (611-17732)	$2.00
The Supervisor: Agent for Change in Teaching (611-17702)	$3.25
The Supervisor: New Demands, New Dimensions (611-17782)	$2.50
The Supervisor's Role in Negotiation (611-17798)	$1.00
Toward Professional Maturity (611-17740)	$1.50
The Unstudied Curriculum: Its Impact on Children (611-17820)	$2.75
What Are the Sources of the Curriculum? (611-17522)	$1.50
Child Growth Chart (618-17442) min. order 10 for	$2.00

Discounts on quantity orders of same title to single address: 10-49 copies, 10%; 50 or more copies, 15%. Make checks or money orders payable to ASCD. All orders must be prepaid except those on official purchase order forms. Shipping and handling charges will be added to billed purchase orders. **Please be sure to list the stock number of each publication, shown above in parentheses.**

Subscription to **Educational Leadership**—$8.00 a year. ASCD Membership dues: Regular (subscription and yearbook)—$20.00 a year; Comprehensive (includes subscription and yearbook plus other publications issued during period of the membership)—$30.00 a year.

Order from: **Association for Supervision and Curriculum Development
1201 Sixteenth Street, N.W.   Washington, D.C. 20036**